Dining Room
and
Banquet Management

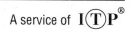

Dining Room and Banquet Management

SECOND EDITION

ANTHONY J. STRIANESE

Delmar Publishers

 an International Thomson Publishing company

Albany • Bonn • Boston • Cincinnati • Detroit • London • Madrid
Melbourne • Mexico City • New York • Pacific Grove • Paris • San Francisco
Singapore • Tokyo • Toronto • Washington

NOTICE TO THE READER

Cover Photos by: Randall Perry

Delmar Staff
Acquisitions Editor: Christopher Anzalone
Editorial Assistant: Judy A. Roberts
Developmental Editor: Jeffrey D. Litton
Project Editor: Eugenia L. Orlandi
Art and Design Coordinator: Douglas J. Hyldelund

COPYRIGHT © 1997
Delmar is a division of Thomson Learning. The Thomson Learning logo is a registered trademark used herein under license.

Printed in the United States of America
5 6 7 8 9 10 XXX 02 01 00

For more information, contact Delmar, 3 Columbia Circle, PO Box 15015, Albany, NY 12212-0515; or find us on the World Wide Web at http://www.delmar.com

International Division List

Japan:
Thomson Learning
Palaceside Building 5F
1-1-1 Hitotsubashi, Chiyoda-ku
Tokyo 100 0003 Japan
Tel: 813 5218 6544
Fax: 813 5218 6551

Australia/New Zealand
Nelson/Thomson Learning
102 Dodds Street
South Melbourne, Victoria 3205
Australia
Tel: 61 39 685 4111
Fax: 61 39 685 4199

UK/Europe/Middle East:
Thomson Learning
Berkshire House
168-173 High Holborn
London
WC1V 7AA United Kingdom
Tel: 44 171 497 1422
Fax: 44 171 497 1426

Latin America:
Thomson Learning
Seneca, 53
Colonia Polanco
11560 Mexico D.F. Mexico
Tel: 525-281-2906
Fax: 525-281-2656

Canada:
Nelson/Thomson Learning
1120 Birchmount Road
Scarborough, Ontario
Canada M1K 5G4
Tel: 416-752-9100
Fax: 416-752-8102

Asia:
Thomson Learning
60 Albert Street, #15-01
Albert Complex
Singapore 189969
Tel: 65 336 6411
Fax: 65 336 7411

Library of Congress Cataloging-in-Publication Data:
Strianese, Anthony J.
    Dining room and banquet management / Anthony J. Strianese. – 2nd ed.
        p. cm.
    Includes bibliographical references and index.
    ISBN 0-8273-7566-2
    1. Food service management. I. Title.
TX911.3.M27S76 1997
647.95'068—dc20

96-23883
CIP
AC

Contents

Preface

Dining out has been a passion of mine throughout my life. Each dining experience brings a new challenge. That challenge is to find a restaurant that offers excellent service to the guest. Whether I am dining at a restaurant in my own region, on vacation, taking one of many soccer trips, or participating in a professional site inspection visit, I am constantly searching to discover the perfect restaurant that has outstanding service. Each wedding, bar mitzvah, or banquet attended is also a research trip. To find perfect service at both a restaurant and a banquet facility is my goal.

My research has taken place in restaurants as diverse as large chain restaurants like TGIFridays, mom and pop operations such as The Bears, and haute cuisine restaurants like Union Square Cafe in New York City and the Inn at Shelburne Farms in Shelburne, Vermont. Banquets have been attended at Elks Clubs, VFW posts, church halls, four-star resorts and elegant country clubs. The service has ranged from awful to outstanding.

My first job as a banquet manager was at a hotel in the middle of a decaying inner city. I quickly learned the secret of success in the banquet business. The secret—service. Service was of utmost importance to all guests regardless of their socioeconomic status or any other classification with which society labels individuals. Day after day this fact was confirmed by letters and thank-you notes; but most convincing was the fact that the banquet business increased, when by all other indicators it should have been declining or nonexistent.

My next job was as a food and beverage manager at a brand new hotel. Again the importance of service was taught to the staff. The restaurant and banquet rooms were filled to capacity nightly. Unfortunately, the food was not consistently excellent; in fact, at times it was embarrassingly bad. The conclusion: excellent service will make up for mediocre food.

In 1974, I became a hospitality educator at Schenectady County Community College, assigned to teach courses in dining room and banquet management. In researching material for the courses, I soon discovered the reason for the poor service in America. First, the service person's job was (and still is) not considered a profession as it is in Europe. It seems that most individuals treat it as temporary until they can obtain their "real job." In many instances the job of service person was looked down upon by the American public. Therefore, very few companies took the time to train American workers in the proper methods of service. Additionally, because America is such a melting pot of cultures, the methods of serving have evolved and resulted in a hodgepodge of French, Russian, and a made-up type of service, called American.

Like so many of my peers in the hospitality education field, I soon discovered that there were very few textbooks addressing this subject. I could find no easy-to-read, easily understood book that explained the importance of service and the proper method of service. I did discover books and articles on the subject, but most of them explain how to serve as it applies to their own particular area of the country. These books are too simple in explaining the importance of service. Other books that tried to take a more professional approach contradicted the proper guidelines of service and were too complex. None of them gave substance to the logical reason for service.

I could not find any book that would be a comprehensive guide to fit the needs of students, as well as dining room and banquet managers. In addition, the few books that were found on the subject either specialized in banquet or a la carte dining. There was no one comprehensive book that addressed the importance of service in both the restaurant and the banquet field.

Since 1974, my staff and I have used the techniques written in this book to provide excellent service at Schenectady County Community College in serving both banquets and a la carte patrons. Both our banquets and our a la carte restaurant, The Casola Dining Room, are filled to capacity each semester by patrons wanting to experience our great food and great service. Service has made our restaurant and banquets stand out. We have created such a demand for our evening meals that we can book up completely for the night in as little as four minutes!

The target market for this book is the student in two- or four-year college courses in restaurant and banquet management. It is written with the student in mind, and developed after years of research. I related many true stories about the type of service I have received in my travels. There are also unique review features that are included to increase the student's learning and interest.

My goal and vision is for the service profession to become as respected as the culinary profession in the United States.

SYSTEMATIC SEQUENCE OF BOOK

One of the major strengths of *Dining Room and Banquet Management* is an easy-to-read format and the smooth flow of ideas. In addition to presenting these ideas, it explains to the reader the practical application of these ideas to achieve excellent service. This book introduces new theories in the evolution of service.

The book is divided into three parts. Part One consists of information that every person must know, regardless of what area of the hospitality industry becomes his specialty. Part Two consists of the important information that is needed to provide excellent service in an a la carte restaurant. Part Three consists of information needed to provide excellent service in a banquet facility. Therefore, after completing Part One, you may proceed to Part Three if your interest lies in banquets. Parts Two and Three are independent of each other. The book follows a logical pattern; one that I know you will enjoy.

LEARNING OBJECTIVES AND PROBLEM QUESTIONS

At the beginning of each chapter, there is a comprehensive set of learning objectives addressing the main concepts covered in the chapter. In all chapters there are problem questions that allow for an open-ended discussion of the situation. These open-ended questions were designed to make you think. Many of these questions have several solutions—just like the situations you will encounter in the dining room or banquet business. A test bank has been supplied to adopting teachers. This bank of questions will test the reader's knowledge of the objectives presented at the beginning of the chapter.

PROBLEM CASES

All chapters include real life situations describing the problems I have experienced as a banquet and restaurant manager or as a guest at a restaurant. These problem cases are often used to illustrate how not to do some task; but many times you will be asked to explain what is wrong with the situation. These situations are interesting, and also may generate much controversy.

PICTURES

One of the unique features of this book is that there is a series of pictures that illustrates both correct and incorrect types of service.

TIPS

In every chapter, the reader will discover many TIPS (To Insure Proper Service) for a better understanding of the goal of this book. The TIPS provide readers with short, interesting facts that should be used in their careers to provide quality service.

Acknowledgments

There are many individuals who have made this second edition possible. Without them it never would have been written. I would like to offer special thanks to the following individuals:

My wife, Pam, who continues to be my guiding light and inspiration to share my knowledge with others.

Jeff Litton, my editor at Delmar Publishers, who used his experience from the hospitality business to guide this second edition.

Douglas Hyldelund, the Art & Design Coordinator of Delmar Publishers, who shared his special talents to make certain the pictures were appropriate for the book.

Christopher Anzalone, the Administrative Editor at Delmar Publishers, who got the text approved by Delmar.

Michael Hurst, the owner of the 15th Street Fisheries in Fort Lauderdale, Florida, and former National Restaurant Association President, who shared his vision on our ride to the airport and over lunch.

Thanks to all my staff at Schenectady County Community College who have given and continue to give me feedback on the service in the hospitality industry. A special thank you to the Dining Room and Banquet Management faculty who have used the first edition of the book:

Lisa Cohn who reports on the service she receives at all the restaurants in which she dines throughout the world;

Laurie Brenensthul, who shares my passion for great service;

Gary Brenensthul, my former office mate, who continues to contribute many insightful suggestions and information needed in this text;

Bob Payne, of The Bears family, who shares his family's passion for excellent service.

I thank all of my former and current students who granted me interviews and obtained pictures for me.

Thanks also to Kim Williams, who provided me with much of the information for the first edition when she worked at the Astrodome in Houston, Texas, and continues to share information on service that she obtains from serving the "rich and famous" at the Kentucky Derby each year.

A special thanks goes out to these individuals for posing for pictures: Thomas Anderson, Brandi Curtis, and Lynne Locy.

Thanks to Randall Perry for his superb photographs and to Tony Farone of Quality Food Management, who provided the props for the picture shoot at Schenectady.

I would also like to thank the following reviewers, who gave me many valuable comments and suggestions:

David Cohen
Bergen Community College
Paramus, NJ

Robert O'Connor III
Bay State College
Boston, MA

William Dunham
Cuyahoga Community College
Cleveland, OH

Robert Ard
Del Mar College
Corpus Christi, TX

G. Michael Harris
Bethune Cookman College
Sanford, FL

Tannis Reinhertz
San Francisco City College
San Francisco, CA

Duncan Howden
Northampton Community College
Bethlehem, PA

About the Author

Anthony J. "Toby" Strianese, Chairperson and Professor of the Hotel, Culinary Arts, and Tourism Department has been a member of Schenectady County Community College's (SCCC) faculty since 1974. He holds a Bachelor's degree in Business Administration from Bryant College, Smithfield, Rhode Island, and obtained his Master's degree in Educational Psychology from the College of St. Rose in Albany, New York. He was awarded an honorary Ducktorate in Resort Studies from the Disney University. Mr. Strianese was instrumental in having Schenectady accepted into the Walt Disney World College Program and serves as the Walt Disney World Coordinator for SCCC. Under his leadership, the Culinary Arts program has been accredited by the American Culinary Federation Educational Institute Accrediting Commission (ACFEI). He has served as on-site team evaluator for the ACFEI at education institutions applying for accreditation. Professor Strianese is the author of *The Wine Steward*, a computer software program and an additional Delmar product, *The Food Service Industry Video Series*. He serves as a consultant to many excellent restaurants and companies. Before coming to SCCC he was banquet manager at the DeWitt Clinton Hotel in Albany and food and beverage manager at the Roundtowner Motor Inn in Colonie. In addition, he has been published in the *Journal of Hospitality Education* and regularly presents lectures on wine, banquet, and dining room service. His speeches and training sessions have been given to community groups, restaurant and country club employees, local American Culinary Federation branches, local Restaurant Association Chapters, and the National Convention of the American Culinary Federation.

Part One

The Food Service Industry

The Importance of Service

OBJECTIVES

At the completion of this chapter, the student will be able to:

1. Verbally define service as it relates to the hospitality industry
2. Give examples of excellent service
3. List Maslow's Hierarchy and explain its importance in the hospitality industry
4. Distinguish the different types of service the dining room manager and banquet manager must provide
5. Write a definition for the word *ubiquitous* and give an example of it as it relates to the hospitality industry
6. List and explain the qualifications that managers must possess to provide excellent service

Service for the Present and Future

The end of the twentieth century has brought with it a lifestyle change that has affected Western society and has also had an impact on the restaurant business. This change is most apparent in our guests' lifestyle (changing from formal to relaxed) and in the dressing down of their clothing. Today, guests have more choices and styles of restaurants to patronize than ever before!

The formal white tablecloth restaurants that were almost exclusive in the 1950s and 1960s are being joined by the casual, less formal restaurants of today. Fortunately, there is a demand for all types of restaurants. The white tablecloth restaurant will never become obsolete. It will always be the place where a guest will bring a date, celebrate a relative's birthday or anniversary, or entertain business clients. More and more of our guests, who have the income to patronize restaurants, do not have the time to cook because of the demands of their job or family activities. For instance, after watching their child's sporting or school event, many people patronize a restaurant they can go to directly from their children's activities.

TIP$

To Insure Proper Service
When greeting a guest always make eye contact and smile.

Guests in the twenty-first century will be no different from guests throughout the ages. All guests want to be and appreciate being pampered. When leaving their homes for an evening out to spend their hard-earned money, they want an enjoyable, entertaining evening. More and more individuals are choosing a restaurant not only for their special evening out, but also for regular family meals. After a hard day's work, the choice for many two-income families is to dine at a restaurant rather than cook a meal. As competition becomes more intense between restaurants, the one difference that will make a restaurant stand out is the **service** it offers to its guests. Many business people choose a banquet facility or restaurant in which to conduct important business meetings. It is up to you, the restaurant and banquet manager, to make their experience enjoyable.

Reasons to Provide Good Service

Guests enjoy talking about their experiences at a restaurant. They *like* to talk to their friends about good service, and they *love* to tell their friends about poor service. Every restaurant manager or potential restaurant manager should know the following facts about service and customers. Michael Hurst, owner of the 15th St. Fisheries in Fort Lauderdale, Florida, states that managers should "think customers, not dollars!" In a June 1995 speech, Michael Hurst illustrated the positive value of word of mouth. He said he has one guest who spends $150 a year in his restaurant. This guest is pleased and tells two friends, who also spend $150 each. If this pattern is repeated for ten years, this will result in sales of over $600,000 for the next ten years! Since many guests dine with other people, think of how effective word of mouth can be. Word of mouth can be so effective that the value of a party of four guests spending $150 can result in sales of over $2,000,000 dollars!

TIP$

....

To Insure Proper Service

"A good server can save a bad meal, but a good meal can't save a bad server," says Doug Roth, Bistro 100 proprietor.[1]

....

On the other hand, negative word of mouth is devastating to a business. Writing in *Nation's Restaurant News* (NRN), Robert L. Desatnick, President of Creative Human Resources Consultants, states: "Ninety-six percent of unhappy customers never complained about rude or discourteous treatment. Ninety percent or more of those dissatisfied with the service will not buy again or come back. All of those displeased customers will tell their stories individually to at least nine other people. Thirteen percent of those former customers will tell more than 20 other people."[2] With a little simple math, you can see that a negative experience can affect that restaurant's business substantially. This is called word of mouth. It is the best and worst type of promotion for a business. Word of mouth has more effect on business at a restaurant or banquet house than any other factor. Why? Because people like to ask other people where to find a great place for dining or holding banquets. They trust recommendations from a friend rather than advertising. The following story illustrates the point.

Word of Mouth

A woman entered a restaurant with her fiancé. Being a vegetarian, she asked for a tuna sandwich on a hard roll. The service person said they were out of that item. The guest patiently explained that she was a vegetarian and asked about the availability of nonmeat items. The service person, by means of body language and nonverbal communication, gave the distinct impression of being annoyed. After visiting the kitchen again, the service person reported that the manicotti was meatless. The woman asked if the sauce was also meatless. The service person made a third trip to the kitchen to inquire, returning with the news that the cook could make a meatless tomato sauce. The guest agreed and placed the order. However, she and her fiancé discussed the attitude of the service person and wondered if the sauce would really be meatless. They decided to leave the restaurant, but knew they should first try to find their service person to tell their service person to cancel the order. Standing near the opened kitchen door, the couple heard and saw their service person say, "Cancel that manicotti. That witch has changed her order three times!" Furious, the guests sought out the manager and complained.

The woman could not wait to volunteer this story to her friends and her classmates. All of the students in the class wanted to know the name of the restaurant. She gladly told them the name of the restaurant and where it was located.

Guests that patronize restaurants and banquet houses love to tell their friends about the service they received from the establishments. Therefore, it is imperative that restaurant and banquet managers strive to provide excellent service and make word of mouth work positively for them in order to make their business successful.

WHAT GUESTS THINK OF SERVICE

Historically, poor service has been the biggest complaint about restaurants. The results of a MasterCard Dining Out Study highlighted rude and slow table service as the two biggest problems identified by a study group of four hundred national consumers, fifty restauranteurs,

FIGURE 1-1

This is what occurs when a restaurant has ninety unhappy guests. By the power of word of mouth, 1,070 people will believe that your restaurant is poor. This is the impact of negative word-of-mouth publicity.

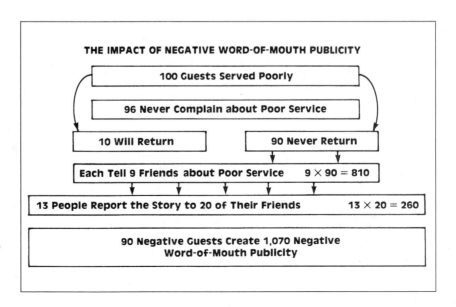

THE IMPACT OF NEGATIVE WORD-OF-MOUTH PUBLICITY

100 Guests Served Poorly

96 Never Complain about Poor Service

10 Will Return   90 Never Return

Each Tell 9 Friends about Poor Service   9 × 90 = 810

13 People Report the Story to 20 of Their Friends   13 × 20 = 260

90 Negative Guests Create 1,070 Negative Word-of-Mouth Publicity

and fifty restaurant critics.[3] Conversely, they stated that friendly service is the number one reason why families will eat away from home. Parents stated that the key criteria for choosing a restaurant are service, value, and family atmosphere.

T I P $

TO INSURE PROPER SERVICE

When will the waitstaff figure out that there is a direct correlation between giving guests poor service and receiving a poor tip?

The restaurant industry was and is built upon excellent food and service. The dictionary definition for service is "the act or manner of serving food and drink."[4] There are many ways to serve food and beverages. Unfortunately many of these ways are poor. Year after year, survey after survey, the number one reason why guests would not return to a restaurant is always poor service!

Tim Zagat, cocreator of the Zagat Survey Dining Guides, after reviewing 75,000 responses, told restaurant operators attending a four-day Food & Wine Magazine Classic in 1995 that, "Service has improved and is improving, but service is still the major deficiency in the restaurant industry." Nearly one-half of all complaints from his contributors relate to service while only 15 percent concern food. "There is no question about it; service is the weak link."

WHAT THE HOSPITALITY INDUSTRY THINKS ABOUT SERVICE

At a NRN-sponsored meeting of restaurant operators, the keynote speaker was Marvin Cetron, a prominent futurist, author, and consultant to business and government. The overriding priority in food service, "used to be location, location, location," said Cetron. However, "Now, it's going to be service, service, service; people want to be treated properly," he added. Reporting in NRN, Milford Prewitt writes that Westin Hotels feels that service will be the most strategic marketing trend in the future.[5]

T I P $

TO INSURE PROPER SERVICE

Michael Hurst says, "Good service is what differentiates restaurants in today's saturated marketplace. We are not selling food in my restaurants; we are selling a pleasant experience."[6]

At a National Restaurant Association Show in Chicago, speakers stated that service is more of an assumption for customers. It is no longer a luxury.

At another NRN-sponsored meeting of restaurant operators held in Atlanta, Georgia, a panel of industry leaders stated that "customer service has become the No. 1 issue in the food service industry today, and finding first-rate employees to fill this need is the No. 1 challenge."[7] In today's society, which continues to move toward more computers and impersonal service, the customer wants smiles and human interaction in place of cold, nonthinking, unemotional computers. It becomes essential that the restaurant and banquet managers of the twenty-first century know how to give and train their employees to provide excellent service to their guests.

WHO IS RESPONSIBLE FOR GREAT SERVICE?

Too many times, the service person is blamed for good or poor service. It appears to the guest that the service person should take the credit or blame. However, the blame or credit falls on the manager. It is up to the manager to set the tone of the business. If the manager cares about his guests, then the message will be loud and clear to the service staff. If the manager gives the impression that he is only there because he has to be and that the guests are an imposition on his time, the service staff will get that message also. Over and over again, the one common thread in all restaurants that are judged to be outstanding is the care and concern of the owner or manager toward the guests and staff.

Three successful restaurant operators are Nick Nickolas, Kevin O'Donnell, and Erik Blauberg. Nick Nickolas believes the reason that Nick's Fishmarket is prospering is because his staff make his guests feel, "important, sexy, romantic, like a million bucks." He states, "You cannot compromise for a minute on food or service if you expect to stay in this business. Service should be the foundation on which restaurants are built. Service is not allowing one customer to light his own cigarette, service is water glasses full, service is treating your customers as they should be, like honored guests. And it's not second nature. It must be taught."

Kevin O'Donnell, the Inn Manager at the Inn at Shelburne Farms in Shelburne, Vermont, states that guests are experts concerning the cost of food. He asks his staff, "Why should someone pay ten times more in a restaurant for a Chicken Kiev than buying it already prepared at a gourmet section in a supermarket and eating it at their kitchen table?" The answer is the service that is provided to our guests.

FIGURE 1-2

A restaurant manager making the guests feel important. Photograph by Randall Perry.

Owner Erik Blauberg of the American Renaissance restaurant in New York's TriBeCa district believes that if customer service is outstanding and the food quality unmatched, location will hardly factor in a restaurant's fortunes.[8] Who makes the best type of manager? The authors of *A Passion for Excellence* state that "the best bosses are neither exclusively tough nor exclusively tender. They are both: tough on the values, tender in support of people who would dare to take a risk and try something new in support of those values.[9] One of the authors' most valuable points is that successful managers "pay an obsessive attention to detail."[10] In the highly demanding restaurant business, the restaurants that succeed and prosper are the ones whose owners take the time to pay attention to details and make their guests feel welcome in their restaurant.

MBWA

The authors of *A Passion for Excellence* state that there are only two ways to create superior performance. The first is to take exceptional care of your customers via superior service. One of their techniques is called **MBWA**, or "management by wandering around." They claim that an effective manager must be where the action is. In a restaurant, the manager should be walking around talking to the guests. In a banquet, the banquet manager should make certain that the guests are happy. By wandering around, the manager can observe all situations and solve problems before they occur.

Service Defined

In the restaurant industry, service is defined by two words—competence and friendliness. Competence can be defined as serving food and drinks in the correct manner to the guest: The service person knows who gets the shrimp scampi and who gets the prime rib without asking the guests; the service person serves all food to women first; the service person removes one course before serving the next. Competent service often is not noticed, but it results in a good feeling about the restaurant by the guests. After the meal is complete, the guests know that they had a pleasant experience, but they do not necessarily realize why. The service person paid attention to the details. However, competence alone does not make a good service person.

A service person must also have the other attribute—friendliness. It is much more important than competence. The service person should make the guests feel that they are guests in a private home. When someone comes to your house, you ask them if they want a drink. You pay attention to them. You are nice to them. However, the service person must be realistic and not overly friendly to the guest. If possible, a service person should address the guest by name (not first name, of course) and be able to make the guest feel welcome in the restaurant. But—a word of caution—do not be a phony. Too many of the 1980s fern bars had the waiters and waitresses running up to the table with a canned speech: "Hi, I'm Gary (or Sue) and I'll be your waiter (or waitress) tonight. Our specials for the evening are…"—and then they went on with what seemed like a five-minute speech outlining specials, pushing drinks and food, and in general boring the customer. A service person should be a professional combining competency with friendliness.

What is Excellent Service?

Excellent service occurs when guests in a restaurant never have to ask for anything. Many times guests do not realize they have received excellent service until they have left the establishment. The service person does everything correctly without the guests' knowing it. When guests reach for the coffee cup, the handle is right where their thumbs and fingers naturally go. The water and wine glasses are always filled. It is never necessary to ask for the ketchup or butter or more bread. A second cup of tea or coffee is poured before the guests request it. The correctly added check is even presented to the guests without having to be requested; and the service person and host thank the guest for patronizing the restaurant. It bears repeating: Excellent service is friendliness combined with competency.

The Best Service in the World

Walt Disney World near Orlando, Florida, has a multifaceted philosophy of food service. One of the points is to have "fast and efficient service." The most important ingredient in successful service is the human element, that is, concern for the guest. Walt Disney World has been praised for its excellent service, and it has been featured in the book and the television show, *In Search of Excellence*. Managing an operation that employs over 32,000 people requires excellent training and attention to detail. How do they accomplish it? That was the question that was put to Tony Jenkins, Manager of Diversity Programs for Walt Disney World Company.

DISNEY TRAINING

According to Tony Jenkins, all new employees have to attend orientation classes, where they learn about the history, philosophy, and style of Disney.

All service staff employees receive an initial three-day training period with approved trainers. These trainers are employees who have worked at the restaurant for a period of time and who are themselves products of the Disney training classes.

On the first day at the job, the new employees follow and observe their trainers for half a day. This procedure is called **shadowing**. During this time, the trainers explain how to present the menu and how to serve the food. All of the methods are standard for all service staff at Disney.

In the second half of the day, the new employees carry out the trays for the trainers. The trainers, since they are regular service persons, have their own stations in the restaurant. All the training in this phase is accomplished on the job, and the new employees have to meet and follow all the standards set down by Disney. For example, every item that comes from the kitchen to the dining room must be carried on a tray.

Disney insists on the same standards for all its restaurants, the same service to all its guests at all locations.

On the second day of training, the new employees have contact with the guests. They approach the guests, present the menu, and take the order. The trainers are now shadowing the new employees. Throughout the day, the new employees are encouraged, reminded, and taught the correct ways to serve Disney guests.

On the third day, each new employee begins the day by being assigned two or three of the trainer's tables. By the end of the day, the new employee is waiting on and serving all five tables in the station.

"The key to the Disney training is follow-up," says Tony Jenkins. "Each restaurant has periodic service meetings. Perhaps one or two a month to go over new procedures, price changes, and new menu items."

Another key is the use of mystery shoppers at Disney. These shoppers patronize the restaurants for the sole purpose of observing their operation. Included in their observations is a report on the service by the service person. Therefore, the management of the restaurant has an unbiased report on its operation and can take steps to clear up any problems.

All of the above sounds great. But can it really work? The question was posed to Colleen Sherman, who worked as a food and beverage hostess at Disney on the Walt Disney World College Program. She feels, as Tony Jenkins does, that the follow-up is the key to making the system work. She said, "When I made a mistake the supervisor would take me aside as soon as possible and tell me what my mistake had been. Then I was able to correct it and the Disney service concepts were reinforced."

What is Poor Service?

Poor service is easy to recognize. Ineffective service can be frustrating and embarrassing for a restaurant. For instance, you, as a guest, are served your meal, and a few minutes later your dining companion is served. Or, how many times have you had to wait for a check before you could get to that show on time? And how many times have you been met and upset by rude servers with an "I-don't-care" attitude?

Charles Bernstein, writing in NRN, reports on a survey by *U.S. News & World Report*. The survey reported on why guests stop patronizing a particular restaurant or store or cease to buy certain products. "Sixty-eight percent quit because of an attitude of indifference toward customers by a dealer or some employee." Bernstein went on to say that, "One unfriendly or nonsmiling reaction to a customer is enough to turn off that person and send him or her scurrying to the nearest competitor next time." Guests tend to remember their last experience in a restaurant. He further states that a lack of friendly service rates as a leading cause for poor sales. Guests often try five different restaurants before encountering some sort of satisfactory experience.[11]

Leonard Roberts, Arby's former president, has said that customer comment cards are almost always focused on how they are treated as people and as customers. Jane Wallace, writing about the explosion in takeout sales in *Restaurants & Institutions* says: "Eating out has become such a hassle. What the industry seems to have forgotten is that enjoyable eating out is a combination of food and service. Most operators have done a good job tempting the public with food and menu concepts. But when service becomes such a hassle that customers prefer to take food home, things have reached a sorry state indeed."[12]

THE REASON FOR POOR SERVICE

Statistics indicate that 93 percent of restaurant failures stem from poor management. People who manage restaurants very often have no concept of how to please their guests. Many managers prefer operational tasks to the actual running of a restaurant.

Employees, during the first thirty days after being hired, will establish their work pattern, often based on their manager's style. If a manager fails to conduct formal training sessions and fails to express the restaurant's philosophy on guest service, the results will be poor service from the employees. After all, the manager does not seem to care about the guests.

On the other hand, if you have a manager who cares and trains the staff properly, the business will prosper. The Union Square Café and Gramercy Tavern have tackled the tough New York City market, and both restaurants are a success. Owner Danny Meyer has done it by providing good value, friendliness, and warm comfort—to please people and really make people happy. The intention was and is to develop a great **front of the house** so that people will feel good while they are eating in the restaurant. In a sense, the core is honesty in hosting, while providing really great, high quality, interesting food and wine in a nonthreatening atmosphere.

TIP$

TO INSURE PROPER SERVICE

Never let your guests' water or wine glasses become less than one-quarter full.

For example, a bottle of wine ordered at Gramercy Tavern is never placed near the guests, however, their glasses are never empty.

The hiring process is highly structured at Gramercy Tavern. References are checked, and a final interview is held with the general manager. After passing the general manager's interview, the prospective service person has as many as four nights of trial performances. The waitstaff then report on the applicant. (Michael Hurst also uses this strategy at 15th St. Fisheries.) The applicant then has to pass a six-page test based on a twenty-five-page manual that covers food, wine, and service. Training, attention to detail, and a follow-up system pay dividends for the restaurant.

The Psychology of Service

Every person who considers a career in the restaurant field must realize that most guests do not come to a restaurant or banquet facility merely to eat. In the field of psychology there is a well-known theory formulated by A. H. Maslow called **Maslow's Hierarchy**. This hierarchy deals with human needs. Maslow cites five basic needs that an average person possesses. These are the **physiological** need and the needs for **safety**, **love** and **belonging**, **esteem**, and **self-actualization**. The first four are referred to as **dependent needs** because they are obtained from other people. Self-actualization comes from oneself. Restaurant managers should know and understand how these needs affect their guests.

The theory states that a person must significantly satisfy one need before moving on to the next need. However, it has been demonstrated that it is possible to satisfy portions of two needs simultaneously. Let us relate Maslow's Hierarchy to the restaurant business and understand why this theory is important to a restaurant and banquet manager.

A restaurant and/or banquet manager should realize that two of the needs, the physiological and the need for love, most often will have been met before the guest enters the hospitality establishment. The final need, self-actualization, is an internal need that the manager deals with indirectly. The major needs that the manager and the employees must deal with are those for safety and esteem.

The physiological need means that if we do not have enough money to provide food for ourselves or our family, we will spend the greatest portion of our time trying to earn enough money or to obtain food to satisfy this need. All restaurant guests have satisfied this need because they are not starving.

Once the physiological need is satisfied, the person moves on to the next need—the safety need. The safety need can play an important part in the success or failure of a restaurant or banquet facility.

FIGURE 1-3

Maslow's Hierarchy of Human Needs. Every individual has to satisfy the lower need before moving on to the higher need. The physiological, safety, love and belonging, and esteem needs are dependent needs—they occur with the help of the restaurant employees or outside factors. Self-actualization occurs internally when the dependent (external) needs have been met.

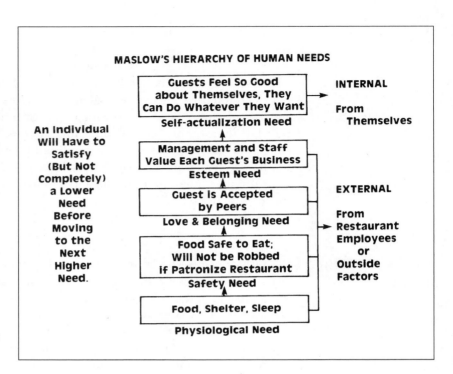

Restaurant guests generally have satisfied the safety need, because they probably live in a community that makes them feel comfortable and fearless. However, some restaurants may have a problem in satisfying the safety need. Problems will arise with an establishment located in a dangerous section of town or one that disruptive customers are allowed to patronize. Guests in these establishments will not be able to enjoy their meals because they will be concerned about their safety after they leave the restaurant. Thus, even though their safety need was satisfied in their own neighborhood, it is not satisfied at the restaurant. Because of this, they will not patronize the restaurant. Therefore, the restaurant must make certain that its guests' safety need will be satisfied. Another part of the safety need can be thought of with regards to sanitation. If the establishment has been shut down by the health department because of unsanitary conditions at any time in the past, guests will most likely not want to patronize the restaurant.

Once the safety need has been satisfied, the guests now move to the love and belonging need. This need refers to being accepted by other people and groups. Most guests have made friends and formed associations with their peers. At times, this need benefits the restaurant and banquet facility greatly, because the guests belong to groups that patronize restaurants and banquet facilities.

For the most part, guests received into restaurants and banquet facilities have all significantly satisfied the first three needs: physiological, safety, and love and belonging.

The need that all restaurant managers, banquet managers, and service staff can satisfy is the fourth need—the esteem need. This need centers on self-respect and is generally thought of as ego needs. It means that someone (namely, you, the manager or service person) gives the people respect and makes them feel important. For example, addressing the guest by his or her name or inquiring about the guest's family or job are ways to satisfy the ego need. This esteem need is not a new theory. Even back when our country was being founded, Ben Franklin is reported to have said "The taste of the roast is determined by the handshake of the host." This esteem need should almost always be positive, but sometimes it can appear to be negative and still result in ego gratification.

Ego Gratification

There was a local diner in a small community. Since the diner was open twenty-four hours, townspeople congregated there at all hours, and some came in three or four times a day. One guest, who came in more than others, was greeted by the words: "You again Frank. We'll put a bed in the back so you can sleep here." Frank enjoyed this attention so much that he increased his trips to the restaurant. He felt important and his need for esteem was being recognized.

The fifth need is the need of self-actualization, which comes from within the person. This is when the person develops his or her maximum potential. Restaurant managers indirectly contribute to the development of this need because they have helped to satisfy the fourth need—the esteem need.

All restaurant and banquet managers should know how and when to use Maslow's Hierarchy to understand their guests. Of course, many restaurant owners have no idea why they should know or even use this theory. The following story illustrates how *not* to treat guests.

Mistaken Identity

A recent college graduate invited two fraternity brothers up for a day of watching thoroughbred racing. After a very successful day of playing the horses, his friends asked him where they should go for dinner. Because his father went to a particular restaurant all the time and was a friend of the owner, he suggested they go there.

As they walked into the restaurant, he could see the line of people waiting for tables. This did not bother any of them. They would go in, ask for a table, and go to the bar and have a few drinks.

Proud of himself for recommending an obviously fine restaurant, he marched up to the hostess desk and, to his delight, saw the owner.

The owner looked up, not recognizing the young man, and said "Yes?"

"Hi, I'd like a table for three," he said. And then he added, "I'm Spenser Marchetta, Art's son."

In a loud voice the owner replied, "I don't care who you are, you will have to wait your turn just like anyone else!"

As Spenser walked back to the end of the line, his face was flushed with embarrassment. His friends could not wait to tell him what great influence he had.

A few years later the restaurant closed its doors. However, every time Spenser sees his fraternity brothers, they still remind him about that restaurant.

Being Ubiquitous

All individuals who work in a restaurant must be **ubiquitous.** It is one of the most important qualities for restaurant business employees. Ubiquitous means being everywhere at the same time. The restaurant manager must know what is going on at all times. A ubiquitous manager will appear to have eyes in the back of his or her head. If the manager, host, or hostess is talking to a guest at the guest's table, he or she must also be aware of what is occurring in the entire dining room. If a new party enters the restaurant, the host must excuse himself or herself and greet the new guests.

The same is true of the service staff. An example of a ubiquitous service person is one who fills your water glass without your having to ask. The service person knows what you want without your having to request it.

The banquet manager must be ubiquitous also. The main job of the banquet manager is not to serve or cook food, but to take responsibility of the party off the host's shoulders and put it on his or her own shoulders. People hosting parties want to be able to spend time with their guests. Therefore, a banquet manager must take care of all the minute details to make the banquet a success. He or she must be able to handle all problems for the host of the party.

If the flowers are wrong at a wedding, the banquet manager soothes the bride and her parents and corrects the problems. The banquet manager is ubiquitous and ensures that the party runs smoothly. The

FIGURE 1-4

The banquet manager must take care of all the minute details to ensure that the banquet is a success.

job of a banquet or catering manager is one of the most exciting and rewarding but stressful positions in the hospitality industry.

Successful Management

The successful manager, whether of banquets or of a la carte dining, must have the following qualifications:

1. He or she must know the different types of service, when to use them, and how to serve properly. There are two main types of banquet service: Russian and American. A la carte service is American, French, Russian, or a combination of all three.
2. The manager must know the proper methods of beverage service, as well as how to organize, plan, and implement beverage service for banquets and a la carte dining. Included are open and cash bars, and proper wine service. The manager must have a knowledge of wines and the proper pairing of food with wine.
3. The manager must be personable and have a genuine fondness for people. Managers must realize the importance of talking to guests

QUALIFICATIONS FOR SUCCESSFUL MANAGEMENT

1. Knowledge of food service
2. Knowledge of beverage service
3. Friendly, outgoing personality
4. Organizational skills
5. Ability to stay calm under pressure
6. Good physical condition
7. Ability to resist temptation
8. Diplomacy
9. Knowledge of training employees
10. Ability to handle complaints

FIGURE 1-5

A condensed list of the most important managerial qualifications.

and making them feel important. Knowledge of Maslow's Hierarchy must be used in recognizing guests. There is nothing as powerful as addressing a guest by his or her name. Both the dining room manager and the banquet manager must be visible in the dining room so they can talk to their guests.

4. Organization is the key for a successful dining room or banquet manager.

5. The manager must possess the ability to stay calm under pressure. This is especially necessary for catering and banquet managers. One factor can be guaranteed at a banquet: No matter how rich or poor, how influential, or how educated the hosts of the party may be, they are always under a tremendous strain. They want the party to be a success. The banquet manager is the person who must keep them calm.

6. The manager must be in good physical condition to withstand the long, unusual hours and stressful conditions. The job involves much physical labor, since the manager often helps move tables, transport food to catering events, and lift heavy items that are needed either in the restaurant or at the banquet.

7. The manager must be able to resist temptation. Since there is so much food and liquor available, managers find it easy to drink and eat too much.

8. The manager must be able to deal effectively with both employees and guests. Any person considering the restaurant business as a career is advised to take as many psychology courses as possible so he can manage all the idiosyncrasies of his guests and employees.

9. The manager must know how to train employees. In this industry, most of the training is done on the job. The successful manager will have a training plan, implement it, and have a follow-through system like that of Walt Disney World Company.

Successful managers have many other qualifications; this is not a complete list. However, there is one more important qualification a manager must have. It is the ability to deal with and handle complaints.

T I P $ **TO INSURE PROPER SERVICE**
Your bottom line will hit bottom if you reduce service.

How would you handle the following letter of complaint?

May 28, 1996

Ms. Lori Smith, Manager
The Restaurant
Anywhere, USA

Dear Ms. Smith:

At approximately 6:30 P.M., on Sunday, May 20, my family and another family of four had dinner at your restaurant. This letter is to inform you about our dining experience.

Our first impression of the restaurant was excellent. The hostess greeted and seated us at the round 8-top on station or table 35, on the second level. Anne (I believe that is the name she wrote on the check) was asked for two separate checks for the two families. She did not appear to be too pleased about the request, but reluctantly complied (check number 614176). Three glasses of Parducci Chardonnay were ordered along with other beverages. Upon receiving and smelling the wine, the three of us knew it was not Chardonnay. I went to the main bar and asked the bartender to smell the wine and tell me its variety. He informed me that he could not and if I had a problem, I should tell my waitress. Doing this, my waitress said she ordered Chardonnay. We stated it was not, so she took the glass back to the service bar to check. She returned and said, "We are out of the Chardonnay, so the bartender gave you Chenin Blanc." I asked if this was the house white wine and she repled "yes." We told her we would drink the wine.

Why would a bartender and a waitress substitute Chenin Blanc for Chardonnay? It would be like a cook substituting a hamburger for the Philly steak sandwich because they are both beef, which I doubt has ever happened. The waitress would have been informed by the cook that they were out of the menu item and she would inform the customer.

If this was the only problem, I could have overlooked it. Another problem was Anne's attitude. If she said she made a mistake that would have been OK. But she made us feel like the wine mix-up was our fault. The final straw that prompted me to write occurred when we got our bill. The Chardonnay read $2.45 per glass. When we pointed out the mistake on the bill, she said she charged us the right price for the Chenin Blanc, even though the check read Chardonnay. Since we thought we drank the house white wine (as she said before) @ 1.75 per glass, we felt overcharged. Then to insult us more, she brought the menu to prove she was right and we were wrong. On the check, I wrote "very poor service, letter will follow." In addition to the above, she never checked back with us to see if everything was OK nor did she follow any proper guidelines of service. She served the drinks from one spot, just placing them on the table, not asking anyone to pass the drinks, not a friendly word. She avoided the table as much as she could.

On our way out the hostess did an excellent job. She asked if everything was all right. When I told her it was not, she asked what happened. I stated "a lot!" and kept walking. The hostess continued to ask all members of my party what the problem was. Finally, my wife (the last person out) explained the problem. The hostess tried to get my wife to talk to the manager on duty, but since we were on our way home, we did not want to take the time. The hostess is to be commended for reacting to the situation the way she did.

In summary, the food and hostess were great, but the waitress and bar people should be trained properly and change their attitude. Remember the customer is not always right, but is never wrong!

Very truly yours,

Wayne Bruno

cc: Mr. John Jones
President of the Restaurant Corporation

SUMMARY

1. Excellent service is defined as competence plus friendliness.
2. Bad service is easy to recognize. One example occurs when the guest has to wait over five minutes to receive the check.
3. Maslow's Hierarchy plays an important part in the restaurant and banquet business. A manager who understands the hierarchy and how to use it will make the guests feel important.
4. The restaurant manager has the choice of giving guests either American, French, or Russian service. The banquet manager can offer the guests American or Russian banquet service.

5. Managers must know, and give the appearance that they know, everything that is occurring in the restaurant or banquet at all times. This is called being ubiquitous.

6. To qualify as a manager of a restaurant or banquet, an individual must possess the ten qualifications listed in Figure 1-5.

REVIEW QUESTIONS

1. Define service as it relates to both restaurants and banquets.
2. Give five examples of excellent service you have experienced at a hospitality establishment.
3. List the five stages of Maslow's Hierarchy and explain its importance in the hospitality industry.
4. List and explain the different types of service that the dining room and banquet manager must provide to the guests.
5. Write a definition for the word **ubiquitous** and give an example of it as it relates to the hospitality industry.
6. List and explain the qualifications that managers must possess to provide excellent service in the hospitality industry.
7. List the three types of a la carte service a restaurant manager can offer to guests and the two types of banquet service that are available to guests.
8. Give five examples of bad service you have experienced in a restaurant and explain why the service was poor.
9. Explain word-of-mouth publicity. Why is it the most potent form of publicity?
10. What is the key to making the Walt Disney World Company training successful? Explain your answer.

REFERENCES

1. "Ivy Operators Share Tips for Cultivating Staff," *Restaurants and Institutions,* 30 May 1996, 115.
2. Robert L. Desatnick, "Seizing The Competitive Advantage," *Nation's Restaurant News,* 28 September 1987, F68.
3. "Survey Points to Restaurants as Growing Magnet for Family Time," *Nation's Restaurant News* 30, no. 10 (11 March 1996): 72.
4. *The Random House Dictionary,* S.V. "service."
5. Milford Prewitt, "Westin's Magnan Tag Service as the Edge for Success in the 90's," *Nation's Restaurant News,* 22 October 1990, 42.

6. Michael Hurst, "Wise Words for the Operator: Share Secrets, Generate Talk," *Nation's Restaurant News*, 17 April, 1989, F6.

7. "Customer Service As Primary Challenge," *Nation's Restaurant News.*, May 1987, 25.

8. "Service: Harder to Create Competitive Edge," *Nation's Restaurant News* 29, no. 25 (19 June 1995): 57.

9. T. Peters and Nancy Austin, *A Passion for Excellence*, The Leadership Difference (New York: Warner Books, 1985), xviii.

10. Ibid.

11. Charles Bernstein, "The Two Restaurant Kings: Customers, Managers," *Nation's Restaurant News*, 7 May 1990, 41.

12 Jane Wallace, "Eating Out: A Pleasure or a Hassle?" *Restaurants & Institutions*, 4 March 1987, 16.

The Importance of Sanitation and Appearance

OBJECTIVES

At the completion of this chapter, the student will be able to:

1. Define sanitation and explain its importance to management in a dining room facility
2. Find the health regulations for the particular locality (state, county, city) in which the business is located
3. Describe acceptable cleanliness and appearance standards for employees
4. List reasons for handling utensils, glasses, and plates by their bases or rims
5. Identify the "freedoms from soil"
6. Explain why tables cannot be set with silverware in advance
7. Know the importance of a clean-looking establishment as it relates to the hospitality industry

Sanitation

Sanitation is "the development and application of sanitary measures for public health."[1] This simply means that when customers enter a restaurant to eat, the food and the conditions of the restaurant are clean enough so they will not get sick from patronizing the restaurant. The National Institute for the Food Service Industry (NIFI) defines sanitation this way: "In the food service situation, sanitation means wholesome food, handled in a hygienic environment by healthy food handlers in such a way that the food is not contaminated with disease-causing or otherwise harmful agents."[2] Sanitation refers to visual as well as physical. Guests will perceive a restaurant to be dirty if the restrooms are dirty. Any positive impression a customer might have about a restaurant can be ruined by a trip to a dirty or a bad smelling restroom. Countertops and other restroom surfaces breed germs which can be transferred to food or utensils by restaurant personnel. It is the responsibility of the manager to keep the restrooms spotlessly clean.

T I P \$

To Insure Proper Service
Make sanitation proactive, not reactive!

If your guests are waited on by a person with dirty, scuffed shoes, they may think that the cook is not clean. To the guests, the service person is the restaurant. The guests may be right, or they may be wrong, but their perception determines if the restaurant is clean. They are the customers and the customers are always right. Often, if the **front of the house** (the physical area in which the employees serve the guests) appears to be dirty, customers believe the kitchen is dirty even though it is not. They are scared to eat at the restaurant because they may get sick as the result of a dirty kitchen.

Some of the illnesses that guests pick up at restaurants are not worse than getting the flu, but others can be fatal.

WHO MONITORS THE CLEANLINESS OF THE RESTAURANT?

In each community in the United States there are stringent health rules to protect the public. They have been established because, for many years, businesses lacked concern for both the cleanliness of their establishment and the safety of the food that they served to their guests. Because of this, each state has health laws that restaurant managers must abide by if they are serving the public. In many communities, the restaurant must have a permit to operate, which is issued by the local **health department**. Once the restaurant is awarded a permit to operate, management has the obligation and responsibility to know correct sanitation practices—and to make sure all employees know and use them. In addition, the health department of the community in which a restaurant is located will conduct surprise inspections of the establishment. If the health department, when inspecting a restaurant, discovered health code violations, the restaurant could be fined and shut down.

TIP$

TO INSURE PROPER SERVICE
Ask the health department for information about sanitation.

Poor sanitation practices continue to be highlighted by the media. Television shows, newspapers, and magazine articles marketed to the consuming public use their sensational reporting style to drive home the point that restaurants are not safe. The negative publicity will seriously harm the business.

How Improper Sanitation Practice Can Devastate Your Business

For a special party, the host ordered pastries from a specialty restaurant. The pastries were cream-filled. When the host got home, the pastries were placed out in direct contact with the sun, instead of being refrigerated. Sixty-three people became ill from eating the pastries. Negative word-of-mouth publicity spread through the community about the products from the specialty store. The belief among the general public was that it was the store's fault for serving the tainted cream pastries. That facility is but a memory today!

Who is responsible for the sanitation of the establishment? Ultimately the banquet and restaurant managers are responsible, and they must have a plan to clean the restaurant and enforce the highest standards of sanitation. Many food service companies (ARAMARK, for instance) have a specific person to monitor and be responsible for the sanitation practices of the food service establishment.

FIRST APPEARANCE

The first impression is a lasting one. This has been stressed throughout our lives. Little things mean a lot to guests. The way the restaurant appears to the guests will influence them in determining if the restaurant is clean. If it is, they will feel safe, have their meals and banquets, and spend their money at your establishment.

Good sanitation begins with the appearance of a building. Guests perceive the whole restaurant based on the appearance of the building, parking lot, and signage. Hotels have to be concerned with the way their lobbies and public areas appear.

T I P $

TO INSURE PROPER SERVICE

Check bathrooms for cleanliness before, during, and after meal periods.

A Little Assignment (to be done on a regular schedule)

Make this an everyday habit. Approach your restaurant as a guest would approach it. Vary your approach daily, so you will view your building from different angles (not all guests enter your establishment from the same direction). Notice the condition of the parking lot; are there any potholes? Look to see if there are any papers on the ground. How does the landscaping and the condition of the building appear? Is the front door dirty? Are there cigarette butts outside the entranceway? Do this assignment during the daylight and evening hours. You are viewing your business from the guests' perspective. This is called **consumer orientation**. Make notes about what is good and bad, compliment those responsible or devise a plan to correct the problems, and most important, follow through on the implementation of the plan.

The Influence of the Manager

Attention to detail is the key to running a great business. Two of the most influential people in the hospitality industry, Ray Kroc of McDonald's and Walt Disney of the Walt Disney Company, were sticklers on cleanliness. (A little trivia: both of them were in the same ambulance company in World War I, serving as drivers, both underage). People in the hospitality industry should take their lead from the companies these two men founded when it comes to cleanliness and sanitation. In his book, *McDonald's Behind the Arches*, author John Love states that "the characteristic that was possibly most responsible for creating the family image Kroc was looking for was the cleanliness that McDonald's built into its operating system."[3] He further states that "even competitors concede that McDonald's uncommon dedication to running a clean restaurant set a standard in the industry that others aimed for but seldom hit."[4] Ray Kroc used to say, "If you've got time to lean, you've got time to clean."[5] He wanted his stores to be spotless. Any person with a free moment was taught to clean. Whenever Kroc would visit one of his units, he would pick up any papers on the ground before entering the store. This demonstrated to the managers and employees that if the owner of the company can pick up papers, then everyone can pick them up. This is how managers set examples. If your employees observe you stooping over to pick up papers, then they will too. This is also done by the managers at Walt Disney World. The effect is lasting. One alumni of the Walt Disney World College Program remarked that she cannot walk by a piece of paper without picking it up.

Kroc's Zeal for Cleanliness

The difference between a good place and a great place is attention to details. One of the reasons that McDonald's is the most successful food service company is illustrated by the following story. One Saturday morning at the original Des Plains, Illinois, McDonald's, employee Fred Turner (who eventually became president of the company) saw Ray cleaning out the holes in the mop ringer with a toothbrush. No one else had really paid any attention to the mop ringer. But when Ray Kroc looked at the mop ringer he saw built-up crud in the holes. He wanted to clean the holes so the wringer would work better. Ray Kroc built McDonald's on the letters **QSC**, which stands for Quality, Service and Cleanliness. Cleanliness was made a key part of the strategy to make and keep McDonald's number one in the restaurant business. Half of the 1958 operator's manual was devoted to describing recommended procedures on cleaning. Today, McDonald's has the reputation of being the cleanest operation in the hospitality business.

Detail is the Key

Ask parents what factors influence them in choosing a restaurant for their families. Every one of them will rate cleanliness a high priority item—especially the cleanliness of the high chairs. Parents know what a mess little kids can make. Restaurants that have clean high chairs can make quite a positive impression on young parents. Employees should be instructed to clean all high chairs thoroughly after each use. Make certain they are instructed to clean all those little nooks and cracks where the young toddler throws food. After the high chair has been cleaned thoroughly, the tray should be wrapped in a clear plastic wrap. Training employees to do this will increase business, not only when the children are young, but as they grow up.

APPEARANCE OF THE EMPLOYEES

Ray Kroc was not the only one who knew that cleanliness would create the atmosphere that families were looking for; Walt Disney did too. Disneyland was founded because there was no amusement park where Walt could take his family to have a good time together. The generally recognized concept of an amusement park was unacceptable to Walt Disney's way of doing things. Almost all had dirty looking employees, too many people pressuring the guests to buy things, and too many barkers (salespeople). When Walt founded Disneyland, he knew that the presentation of the park and its employees had to achieve standards that would earn the respect of the guests. Walt instituted "The Disney Look." It is a major part of the Disney theme parks. The Disney Company stresses to all its employees (called cast members): "The 'Disney Look' is a tremendously important part of the overall show at both Disneyland and Walt Disney World. This employee excellence has brought more than two decades of compliments and recognition from people the world over."[6]

G. Jack Parisi, Director of Environmental Health for Schenectady County Public Health Services in Schenectady, New York, states that appearance of the waitstaff is important. When he enters a restaurant, he looks at the length and style of a waitperson's hair. No longer does the health department stress that hair nets must be used. Instead, says Parisi, the hair style should be fixed so that if a waitperson is carrying a tray, his or her hair would not be able to fall into the plates on the tray.

THE SERVICE PERSONS' APPEARANCE

In an issue of *Restaurants and Institutions* magazine, the perfect waiter is described. Burt Hixson, owner of the Warehouse Restaurant in Marina del Ray, California, states that good grooming is the most important trait of service persons. Owner Benjamin Bernstein of Mike Fink's in Lexington, Kentucky, says: "Their appearance reflects their regard for themselves. Somebody who doesn't have regard for himself can't make the type of appearance that we want."[7]

Each restaurant should set grooming guidelines for its employees. These grooming guidelines should be explained to the employee when hired. Supervisors have the obligation to refuse to allow people to work if they do not adhere to the standards. For example, all Disney employees when hired know they have to adhere to a strict grooming guideline. Male employees cannot have any facial hair, nor can their hair length be touching their costume collar. Females cannot wear long, dangling earrings. The acceptable size of earrings is stated. Nail polish is limited to a clear color. All new employees have the policy explained to them before they accept the job. It is up to the manager to set the standards, explain, and enforce them.

Dining Out, a Pleasant Experience?

A couple had invited their neighbors to dinner at a nice, upscale restaurant. The couple had been telling their neighbors for weeks about the good food at this restaurant, the reasonable prices, and the enjoyable evening they would have. Once the four people were seated, their waiter approached the table. He had on a white shirt with the sleeves rolled up. He had hair almost to his shoulders that looked as if he hadn't washed it in a week. The neighbor's wife said, "He should have a hairnet." How was the meal? For the four of them it was disappointing, mainly because of the dirty-looking appearance of the waiter. That was the first turn-off. From that point on, all of the guests felt his service was as poor as his appearance. Whether it was or not, in the minds of the four his appearance had ruined their evening out. Do you think the guests will ever return to this restaurant?

Managers should learn from history. Not long ago, it was common practice for a waiter to be clean and well-groomed when he reported for work. In the late 1800s and early 1900s, at places like the fashionable Belmont Hotel in New York, the waiters had to pass an inspection every morning by the headwaiter. If they were not dressed properly, they were not allowed to work. Later on, in the Great Depression, if they could not pass inspection by the headwaiter, they were fired immediately. During the Depression, unemployment was so high that people waited outside the back doors of restaurants every morning at lineup time. They knew that if they could get a job in a restaurant they could at least get a good meal. Waiters were clean, well-groomed, and had an immaculate uniform.

Since the 1950s, we in America let people do "their own thing." Restaurant owners allowed employees to dress any way they wanted. Standards were dropped and the appearance of the service person suffered. However, a business that continued to set and enforce standards was the Walt Disney Company. Today, as always, there is a lineup daily. If a male employee has a one-day growth of hair on his face, he is not allowed to work until he shaves—and is issued a warning. One day a cast member appeared at the daily lineup with a new hairstyle. It was too extreme for the rules. The employee was not allowed to work until wearing an acceptable hairstyle. Disney employees are given written notification that violation of the appearance policy may result in dismissal from employment.

T I P $

TO INSURE PROPER SERVICE

Before your staff enter the dining room, insist that they have on clean uniforms.

Each business and manager has to set guidelines appropriate for the particular staff and establishment. The uniform and appearance of the staff have to fit the restaurant. A place like TGIFridays or an independent local mom & pop pizza place has a different concept from Disney. Their uniforms are different from one another's. They are less structured than places like McDonald's or Disney, which is fine, as long as they are clean and comply with the standards set by management. Managers must set guidelines for appearance and cleanliness. A checklist (either mental or written) must be developed. Managers must follow this checklist and not let anyone work who deviates from the standards of the checklist.

To reemphasize, the manager must set the standards of grooming, inform the employees, and enforce the policy.

In his book, *The Best of Gottlieb's Bottom Line*, Leon Gottlieb writes about the problems with dress codes. "Most importantly, do you enforce your dress code? We suggest you do not—not entirely or consistently. Too many houses have allowed their crews to become sloppy, to everyone's disadvantage. You are not a good boss if you allow your personnel to be out of uniform."[8] For example, Gottlieb states, "Grooming: Clean shaven, mustaches trimmed above the lip line, clean fingernails, haircut above the collar or worn in a net, should be the type of professional appearance required in your house."[9]

Cleanliness During the Shift

Being a service person is a demanding job. It requires much physical labor. In addition, the service person can get sweaty and dirty and look disheveled during the shift. As a manager, be aware of this. If an employee looks messy, the supervisor should have that person immediately change into a clean uniform.

In many restaurants, both employees and guests use the same restrooms. After working a few hours on a shift, a kitchen worker may not make a good appearance. The kitchen whites have turned brown, covered with grease and gravy. The manager should insist that when employees leave the kitchen, they are dressed cleanly and neatly. It is recommend that cooks and chefs have an extra uniform jacket available so they may change into a clean uniform when they have to appear in the front of the house.

How Do My Employees Smell?

Employees should smell clean. However, some employees have a strong aroma that will turn off your guests for their dining experience. Do not allow service persons to work who are wearing perfume or cologne. Guests become annoyed if all they smell is perfume or cologne. The chef will not be too pleased with the service person ruining the aroma of the food. At one restaurant, the service person's first customer ordered a glass of wine. When the guest lifted the glass of wine to smell the aroma, all that she smelled was the perfume of the service person, who had just doused herself with perfume, liberally putting it on with her right hand. When she served the guest the glass of wine, the perfume was transmitted to the glass. Because taste is 85 percent aroma, the guest tasted only the perfume.

As bad, or worse, is the problem of body odor. It is a must that all service staff use deodorant.

All employees should smell clean. Supply the restrooms with extra soap and deodorant, if needed. Make the guests' dining experience pleasant because they enjoy the aroma of the food. Do not let other aromas mask the flavor of the food.

The Handling and Storing of Utensils, Glasses, and Plates

Sanitation is extremely important in handling and storing utensils, glasses, and plates. The service staff must be trained to pick up the silverware by the handle, not by the part of the utensil that goes into the guest's mouth, which is illustrated in Figure 2-2. The same is true of plates and glasses. Train service staff not to touch the part of the glass or plate that the guest will drink or eat from.

FIGURE 2-1

The incorrect way to hold a glass. Service staff should never handle the glass on the part that will go into the guest's mouth. Photograph by Randall Perry.

FIGURE 2-2

The correct way to hold silverware. Service staff should be trained to pick up the silverware by the handle, not by the part of the utensil that goes into the guest's mouth.

TIP$

TO INSURE PROPER SERVICE
Both clean and dirty silverware should be held by the handle, not the food area.

There is an important reason for this. Disease can be transmitted from one person to another by improper handling of serving items. Not only can a disease be transmitted, but guests get upset when they see this type of carelessness on the part of the service staff.

The following letter is as relevant today as when it was written.

Teach Your Staff How to Handle!

Editor, NRN

Restaurant operators need to start acting responsibly by properly training and supervising their food servers. My husband and I eat out quite often and it is sickening to observe the way some food servers handle cups, glasses, and eating utensils.

One would not think anybody needs to be trained to handle a glass or a cup that will be used by someone else. Nobody wants to drink out of a container whose rim has been handled by the server.

I have seen this practice in upscale dining establishments as well as in budget restaurants and airplanes. Flight attendants are the worst!

As a food microbiology professional, I am deeply saddened by this apparent lack of regard for the public's health. Sanitation should be our primary concern and especially so during these times of heightened disease awareness.

We need to boost our employee training programs to address these concerns. Health departments are not staffed to police all areas.

Edith A. Wilkin
Denver, Colo.[10]

(Copyright ©1987, *Nation's Restaurant News,* reprinted with permission.)

As has already been noted, the lack of sanitation in a food service establishment has more serious consequences than the negative impression given the public by unclean conditions. Unsanitary conditions and careless handling of utensils can result in the spread of disease, food poisoning, and even death.

The story of Typhoid Mary should be known by all workers in the food service industry. A lot of people know the name but do not know that she became famous because of the havoc she wreaked in New York City, where she was a cook. Wherever she worked, an outbreak of typhoid followed her. Typhoid was an easily transmitted disease. It spread in various ways. One of the surest ways was for the carrier to touch something that could transmit the disease.

Mary probably did not wash her hands with extreme care. Unless extreme care is used in washing the hands, bacteria may remain on the hands and contaminate anything the carrier touches. This is the reason that you see the signs in all restrooms that say "All employees must wash their hands before returning to work."

To stop disease from spreading, many municipalities have passed laws stating that food service employees must use a barrier (gloves, utensils, etc.) if they have to touch any food or solid (ice cubes for drinks) that a guest will consume. These laws refer to finished products. For instance, raw carrots that will be cooked could be handled by bare hands. However, raw carrots served with a dip and not cooked must be prepared using the barrier method.

TIP$

TO INSURE PROPER SERVICE

To emphasize the importance of using a barrier, do what the health department does when they see a person in violation. Take the product from the person preparing the produce and throw it into the garbage! Word of mouth among your workers will be more effective than many memos.

The less frequently dishes and silverware are handled, the less chance of contamination. Train employees to keep their fingers out of cups, bowls, and glassware. The eating end of silverware should never be touched after the silver comes out of the machine. Sterile dishes and utensils can be recontaminated by the mere touch of a careless hand.

Setting Up Tables in Advance

Health departments have various rules for presetting tables with utensils. Each manager is advised to check the local health agency to determine how many hours or minutes a table can be set up in advance of your guests' arrival. In some localities, silverware must not be preset. It is given to the guests wrapped in a paper or linen napkin when they sit at the table. This is to prevent any germs from contaminating the silverware or cups or saucers. It is possible that germs can be transmitted from people walking through the restaurant if they cough or sneeze.

For a banquet, most health agencies allow the banquet facility to set up from one to two hours before the banquet is to take place. However, all health agencies agree that tables cannot be preset with silverware or dishes overnight. The reason is that a lot of disease-carrying rodents and insects are nocturnal. It is possible that cockroaches and mice could contaminate the silverware at night.

In addition, it is of utmost importance that the manager sees to it that utensils, plates, and glasses are stored properly when not in use. This means a place that is free from insects and areas where they could become contaminated.

T I P $

TO INSURE PROPER SERVICE
Turn plates over and check the undersides for cleanliness.

Cleanliness of Eating Items (Freedom from Soil)

It is generally accepted that unclean utensils do constitute potential health hazards. Each service person must inspect all utensils before using them to make sure they are clean. Food cannot be considered safe if permitted to come in contact with dishes, glasses, and utensils that have not been properly washed.

Guests are concerned with the appearance of the utensils. If they see any food left over on the plate or knife from a previous meal, they will become upset. Before service persons serve an item or set a table, they should look for certain items. If they find any of the following examples of visible soil, the utensils should not be used.

1. *Adhering foodstuffs*, such as dried on eggs remaining from the previous meal. Employees should check both the bottom and the top of plates. Sometimes, when dirty plates sit on top of each other, foodstuffs remain dried on the bottom of the plate.
2. *Stains.* No coffee, tea, or vegetable stains that classify the utensils as rejects.
3 *Physical damage*, such as cracks, or chips. A chipped or cracked dish is one that can never be completely cleaned because soils penetrate these areas. The crack or chip harbors bacteria and renders the dish unfit for use. The dish should be discarded.

If guests see any of the above problems, they will interpret the restaurant to be dirty. Visible soil indicates a lack of cleanliness.

TIP$

TO INSURE PROPER SERVICE

The proper way to wipe water spots off silverware is with paper coffee filters, not with cloth napkins, which can carry disease.

Cleanliness of Banquet Rooms

Management must make certain that the banquet rooms are attractive and beautiful. There should be a maintenance program of regular cleaning, just as in the dining room. In addition, there are certain peculiarities regarding banquet rooms that the banquet manager must attend to in order to give the appearance of a clean and spotless establishment.

Details are extremely important in a banquet room. The banquet room guests sometimes have to circulate around the room, setting their

FIGURE 2-3

Making sure the banquet room is clean and beautiful makes a favorable impression on guests. Photograph by Randall Perry.

drinks on window ledges and running their hands over these ledges. Before every banquet, an employee should be assigned to wipe down the ledges with a damp cloth to remove the dust. Another place that dust is always found is on the lectern. Guest speakers place their hands on the lectern. If it is dusty or feels dirty, they will perceive that the banquet facility is dirty. That cleaning job should also be assigned to the employee. To check on the cleanliness of the banquet room, do what Ellsworth M. Statler used to do whenever he visited one of his hotels. He would enter one of the guest rooms, walk into the bathroom, and lie down in the bathtub. The reason? He wanted to see exactly what a guest would see when the guest took a bath. Was the ceiling paint peeling? Were there any cobwebs on the ceiling? Do the same with the banquet room. Sit in a seat. Look around the room for cobwebs on the light fixtures or for any lights that are burnt out. Taking care of details makes a favorable impression on the guests.

EXTRA TABLES AND CHAIRS

In the regular a la carte dining room, extra tables and chairs are not a problem. They should always be set with the type of cover and place setting that the establishment uses for its business. However, the banquet rooms are different. Extra chairs and tables in view while parties are in progress are not appealing to the eye. In fact, they detract from the appearance of the room. Some banquet houses stack the chairs and put them in the corner of the room with the unused tables. Put yourself in your guests' shoes. You probably would not like to see extra tables and chairs in the room if you were paying for a banquet. Any extra tables and chairs should be stored in another room, or, if there is no other room available, a partition should be purchased to put in front of them.

Keys to Sanitation

RESPONSIBILITIES OF MANAGEMENT

The key to having a sanitary food service operation is education. All employees have to become knowledgeable about sanitation. For instance, did you know that 90 percent of an insect problem is caused by poor sanitation practices? The training of new and current employees has to include proper sanitation techniques. Just like all other forms of training, in order for sanitation techniques to be effective, the training must be ongoing, monitored, and enforced. The rules, the reasons for the rules, and regulations of the local health department must be explained to the staff.

TIP$

TO INSURE PROPER SERVICE

Pouring old catsup from one bottle into a new bottle could contaminate the new bottle. Do not do it!

If Your Restaurant Has a Food-Borne Illness, What Happens?

Schenectady County Director of Environmental Health, G. Jack Parisi, was asked, "If something happens in your business and someone got sick or your restaurant had a serious outbreak, what happens?"

He explained that there is a law in New York state that states if a person calls a food service operator and reports that he or she has gotten sick at your restaurant, you establishment has to report it to the health department. If it is not done, it becomes a violation. Regardless of the law in New York state or any municipality, the manager should inform the health department of the incident so the health department can work with you, not against you.

Many times the individuals who complain are suffering from viruses, since the symptoms of food-borne illnesses are similar to viruses. Mr. Parisi states that many food-related illnesses go undetected or are unreported because of the symptoms. He also states that the health department sees a large increase of complaint calls after the media reports a story concerning poor health practices in the food service industry.

The health department must get more than one complaint for an investigation to take place, except for an outbreak of botulism. If more than one person has reported that they have contracted a food-borne illness, the process is quite involved to determine why the patrons become ill.

The health department builds a history of the case. They investigate the incident. If possible, food samples from the meal, vomit, and stool samples are involved in the collection process. Information about previous meals is collected. Questions about symptoms and how long before the onset of those symptoms are researched.

Once all that information is determined, the health department can determine what kind of organism it is looking for. This is done by sending collected samples to the lab for analysis.

THE VALUE OF USING YOUR LOCAL HEALTH AUTHORITY

The health department can be a valuable partner in the food service industry. Restaurants and banquet facilities should get into the habit of contacting their local health department before a problem develops. Use the health department as an educational tool. It is important that managers do not see them as adversaries. The health department inspectors realize that operators are trying to make money, but Mr. Parisi states, "Money will come if you have a sanitary place and a professionally run operation." He further states that he has a handful of operators who call him constantly to inquire about regulations. When his inspectors visit these establishments, they rarely find a problem because of the proactive stance taken by the operators.

The Importance of Using HACCP

Restaurant, banquet managers, or any person who prepares food for guest consumption should know the purpose of and how to use the Hazard Analysis Critical Control Point (HACCP). The HACCP system enables an operation to identify the foods and procedures most likely to cause illness. It also establishes procedures to reduce the risk of food-borne illness outbreaks and allows management to monitor and ensure food safety. To be successful, a HACCP system needs involvement and commitment from all staff members. Effective day-by-day implementation involves all employees who receive, store, cook, and serve food.

The key to using HACCP effectively is to train the staff to use a Hazard Analysis Critical Control Point Monitoring Procedure Report. Figure 2-4 is a form that the New York State Department of Health uses for monitoring. CCP abbreviated in the left-hand column refer to Critical Control Points. For example, the staff cooks a top round of beef for a banquet. The title *cooking* would be circled. The key person would write that the beef must be cooked at 350 degrees Fahrenheit for 2½ to 3 hours. The temperature of 130 degrees would be filled in "Food temperature at thickest part more than or equal to _____ in the blank where it states "temperature to kill pathogens." At each step in the HACCP process, CCPs are circled and identified. Having the staff use these forms and methods will alleviate many food-borne illness outbreaks and other food safety problems.

Hazard AnalysisCritical Control Point Monitoring Procedure Report

NEW YORK STATE DEPARTMENT OF HEALTH
Bureau of Community Sanitation and Food Protection

HACCP Page 1

COUNTY	DIST.	EST. NO.	MONTH	DAY	YEAR

THIS FORM CONSISTS OF TWO PAGES AND BOTH MUST BE COMPLETED.

Establishment Name_____ Operator's Name_____

Address_____

(T)(C)(V)_____County_____

Food_____

PROCESS (STEP) CIRCLE CCPs	CRITERIA FOR CONTROL	MONITORING PROCEDURE OR WHAT TO LOOK FOR	ACTIONS TO TAKE WHEN CRITERIA NOT MET
RECEIVING/ STORING	☐ Approved source (inspected) ☐ Shellfish tag ☐ Raw/Cooked/Separated in storage ☐ Refrigerate at less than or equal to 45°F	☐ Shellfish tags available ☐ Shellfish tags complete ☐ Measure food temperature ☐ No raw foods stored above cooked or ready to eat foods	☐ Discard food ☐ Return food ☐ Separate raw and cooked food ☐ Discard cooked food contaminated by raw food ☐ Food temperature: More than 45°F more than 2 hours, discard food More than 70°F, discard food
THAWING	☐ Under refrigeration ☐ Under running water less than 70°F ☐ Microwave ☐ Less than 3 lbs., cooked frozen ☐ More than 3 lbs., do not cook until thawed	Observe method Measure food temperature	Food temperature: More than or equal to 70°F, discard More than 45°F more than 2 hours, discard
PROCESSING PRIOR TO COOKING	Food temperature less than or equal to 45°F	Observe quantity of food at room temperature Observe time food held at room temperature	Food temperature: More than 45°F more than 2 hours, discard food More than 70°F, discard food
COOKING	Temperature to kill pathogens Food temperature at thickest part more than or equal to _____°F	Measure food temperature at thickest part	Continue cooking until food temperature at thickest part is more than or equal to _____°F
HOT HOLDING	Food temperature at thickest part more than or equal to _____°F	Measure food temperature at thickest part during hot holding every _____ minutes	Food temperature: 140°F - 120°F: More than or equal to 2 hours, discard; less than 2 hours, reheat to 165°F and hold at 140°F 120°F - 45°F: More than or equal to 2 hours, discard; less than 2 hours, reheat to 165°F and hold at 140°F

FIGURE 2-4

The Hazard Analysis Critical Control Point form used by the New York State Department of Health for monitoring food preparation.

NEW YORK STATE DEPARTMENT OF HEALTH
Bureau of Community Sanitation and Food Protection

HACCP Monitoring Procedure Report (Page 2)

Food _____ Establishment Name _____ Date _____

PROCESS (STEP) CIRCLE CCPs	CRITERIA FOR CONTROL	MONITORING PROCEDURE or What To Look For	ACTIONS TO TAKE WHEN CRITERIA NOT MET
COOLING	Food 120°F to 70°F in 2 hours: 70°F to 45°F in 4 additional hours by the following methods: (check all that apply) ☐ Product depth less than or equal to 4" ☐ Ice water bath and stirring ☐ Solid piece less than or equal to 6 lbs. ☐ Rapid chill refrigeration ☐ No covers until cold	Measure temperature during cooling every _____ minutes ☐ Food depth ☐ Food iced ☐ Food stirred ☐ Food size ☐ Food placed in rapid chill refrigeration unit ☐ Food uncovered	Food temperature: 120°F - 70°F more than 2 hours, discard food 70°F - 45°F more than 4 hours, discard food 45°F or less but cooled too slowly, discard food
PROCESSING SLICING DEBONING MIXING DICING ASSEMBLING SERVING	Prevent contamination by: Ill workers not working Worker hands not touching ready to eat foods Worker hands washed Cold potentially hazardous food at temperature less than or equal to 45°F Hot potentially hazardous food at temperature more than or equal to 140°F Equipment and utensils clean and sanitized	Observe: Workers' health Use of gloves, utensils Handwashing technique Wash & sanitize equipment & utensils Use prechilled ingredients for cold foods Minimize quantity of food at room temperature Measure food temperature	If yes to following, discard: Ill worker is working Direct hand contact with ready to eat food observed Cold potentially hazardous food: More than 45°F more than or equal to 2 hours, discard; More than 70°F, discard Hot potentially hazardous food 140°F - 120°F More than or equal to 2 hours, discard; less than 2 hours, reheat to 165°F and hold at 140°F 120°F - 45°F More than or equal to 2 hours, discard; less than 2 hours, reheat to 165°F and hold at 140°F If yes to following, discard or reheat to 165°F: Raw food contaminated other foods Equipment/utensils are contaminated
REHEATING	Food temperature at thickest part more than or equal to 165°F	Measure food temperature during reheating	Food temperature less than 165°F, continue reheating
HOLDING FOOD, HOT/COLD TRANSPORTING FOOD	Food temperature ☐ More than or equal to 140°F at thickest part ☐ Less than or equal to 45°F at thickest part	Measure food temperature during holding every _____ minutes	☐ Hot holding potentially hazardous food: 140°F - 120°F More than or equal to 2 hours, discard; less than 2 hours, reheat to 165°F and hold at 140°F 120°F - 45°F More than or equal to 2 hours, discard; less than 2 hours, reheat to 165°F and hold at 140°F ☐ Cold holding potentially hazardous food temperature: 45°F - 70°F More than or equal to 2 hours, discard; less than 2 hours, serve or refrigerate More than or equal to 70°F, discard

I have read the above food preparation procedures and agree to follow and monitor the critical control points and to take appropriate corrective action when needed. If I want to make any changes, I will notify the Health Department prior to such a change.

Signature of person in charge_____

Signature of inspector_____

FIGURE 2-4

(continued)

SUMMARY

1. Sanitation means keeping the restaurant free from dirt. A clean establishment is important in order to have a successful business.
2. A manager should know which health department has jurisdiction over the establishment and how to find the health regulations that affect the business.
3. Managers should set acceptable appearance standards for grooming for their own particular operation.
4. Employees should be taught the method and the reason for handling utensils correctly.
5. Employees should know what constitutes "freedom from soil."
6. For health reasons, utensils cannot be set up the day before a party.
7. A clean establishment adds to the comfort and security of the guest.

REVIEW QUESTIONS

1. Define the term *sanitation*. Explain its importance as it relates to you, the manager of the restaurant.
2. How would you discover the correct sanitation procedures for your establishment?
3. What makes the appearance of an employee acceptable? Describe the acceptable standards for your establishment and your reasons for them.
4. Why should utensils, glasses, and plates be handled by their bases or rims?
5. What are the three "freedoms from soil?" What should a manager do when the establishment does not meet the standards?
6. What are the reasons tables cannot be set in advance? Is there any exception to this rule?
7. Why is it important to have a clean-looking establishment in the hospitality business? Include information about extra tables and chairs, light fixtures, and dirty ledges.
8. Where should extra chairs and tables be stored during a banquet? Why should they not be stored in the same room that is having a function? Would there ever be an exception to this rule?
9. Should all restaurants have the same grooming guidelines? Explain your answer, giving examples to support your ideas.
10. What are the minimum standards that all service people must meet in order to serve guests?

REFERENCES

1. *The Random House Dictionary*, S. V. "sanitation."
2. National Institute for the Foodservice Industry, *Applied Food Service Sanitation*, 2nd ed. (Dubuque, Iowa: WCB, 1978), 7.
3. John Love, *McDonald's behind the Arches*, (Toronto: Bantam Books, 1986), 142.
4. Ibid.
5. Ibid, 143.
6. Walt Disney Company, *The Disney Look* (Burbank, California: 1987), 3.
7. "Owners Define Perfect Waiter," *Restaurants and Institutions*, 28 October 1987, 26.
8. Leon Gottlieb, *The Best of Gottlieb's Bottom Line* (New York: Lebhar-Friedman, 1980), 117.
9. Ibid, 123.
10. Edith A. Wilkin, "Cleanliness Training Important," *Nation's Restaurant News*, 12 October 1987, 7.
11. G. Jack Parisi, Director of Environmental Public Health Service, County of Schenectady, Schenectady, NY. Interview with author, 18 November 1995.

3

Styles of Service and Place Settings

OBJECTIVES

At the completion of this chapter, the student will be able to:

1. Explain how service evolved historically
2. Describe the characteristics of French, Russian, and American a la carte services
3. Identify the advantages and disadvantages of the three a la carte services
4. Lay the correct place settings for French, Russian, and American a la carte service
5. Describe American, Russian, and buffet banquet styles
6. Identify the advantages and disadvantages of the three banquet services
7. Lay the place settings for American, Russian, and buffet banquet services
8. Give the definition of cover and the history of eating utensils
9. Explain the uses of tablecloths and how to change the cloths during the busy times

Confusion over Names of Service

Throughout the United States and Canada, there is no definitive type of service. Each restaurant has its own style of service. There are three basic kinds of service used in a la carte restaurants. These are American, French, and Russian. Most restaurants use a combination of all three to serve their guests. Many restaurant personnel have a basic understanding of the three types of service. However, they are not certain about the advantages and disadvantages of each particular service. Likewise, many people are confused concerning the difference between Russian banquet service and French service. Buffet service includes three other types of service, which adds to the confusion. Overall, there is a lot of misinformation about the origins and the exact definition of the different types of service.

Why the Confusion?

For many years service just happened. Only a few textbooks teaching proper service were published before 1950. Service was taught through a "pass it down system." It was learned only by men, who participated in apprentice programs at the great hotels and restaurants of the time. Little was ever written or recorded about proper service methods. The great hotels and restaurants that had excellent maître d'hotels demanded proper service and had strict rules concerning service. Waiters learned how to serve guests properly, and service remained consistent. Once waiters stopped working at the restaurants where they were trained and became transient, styles of service began to blend together.

Everyone took the best parts of a particular service and adapted it to his restaurant. Many ideas about service were passed down correctly, but others were passed down incorrectly.

Only in the past few years have textbooks and articles been written concerning service. Service is now beginning to be as important as cooking.

First Textbook for Waitresses

The first books for waitresses and hostesses were written in the late 1800s and early 1900s. These books were not written for the hostesses and waitresses of today, but for the wife who entertained her husband's guests and the female who worked as a domestic in a private home. The preface of *The Up-to-Date Waitress*, written in 1906 by Janet M. Hill, states: "The manner in which we advocate that the duties of a waitress should

FIGURE 3-1

The different names of service types. A la carte can be French, American, or Russian. Banquets can be either American or Russian. Buffets can be buffet, modified deluxe, or deluxe.

TYPES OF SERVICE COMMONLY USED IN AMERICAN ESTABLISHMENTS		
A la Carte	**Banquet**	**Buffet**
1. American	American	Simple Buffet
2. French	Russian	Modified Deluxe
3. Russian		Deluxe

be carried out has been evolved from a study and comparison of the methods of many housekeepers."[1] The book concentrates on the duties of the waitress serving her employer on a daily basis in his home, as opposed to working in a restaurant. Another book, entitled *The Modern Hostess,* written in 1904, concentrated on the duties of the woman serving at home. However, the beginning of the book does have a description and illustrations of a formal ten-course hotel dinner. Oscar, the great maître d'hôtel of the Waldorf Astoria in New York City, describes how service should occur throughout the ten courses. But Oscar did not explain from what side to serve or clear dirty dishes. The author, R. J. Bodmer, did say that serving the formal dinner would be the hardest part of entertaining, and it would be advised to obtain a professional butler "who understands service" and another waiter to serve the meal.[2]

TIP$

TO INSURE PROPER SERVICE
Remember: Your most important asset is your employees!

The Beginnings of Service

The job of waiting on people evolved from early times, when individuals owned slaves. These slaves, called servants, had to serve their masters food and drink. Unfortunately, many people still perceive the service person of today as a servant rather than as a professional. The first jobs were not as demanding as they are today. Most meals were eaten at home. The only meals a wealthy person ate outside the home were at other wealthy individuals' homes. The servants accompanied their masters to serve them their meals.

The first banquets took place in classical Rome. These banquets were attended by wealthy Romans and were restricted to men. At this time, there were no restaurants or banquet houses, but these wealthy Romans did have banquet halls in their houses. The service given was not the type of service we think of today. The servant did not have to set the table with forks, spoons, or knives because the only utensils put on the table were spoons. There were no napkins to fold and put on the table, since each guest was required to bring his own cloth to wipe his hands.

The servants' job was not without danger. In addition to obtaining food and drink for their masters and peeling their grapes, they tasted the food and drink to make certain that they were not poisoned. If the taster ate the food and lived, then the master ate it.

Early Superstitions and Facts

The Roman people were very superstitious. Guests were seated at a single couch with as few as three or as many as thirty people. The key was to have a multiple of three because that number held divine significance. All guests made certain to enter the banquet hall with their right foot first. This assured them that favorable things would happen to them.

Emperor Augustus, the founder of the Roman Empire, gave women official status in Roman society around 27 B.C. He allowed women to accompany their husbands to banquets. Because there was a great amount of gossip at banquets, anything that was said at the table was not repeated if the host put a rose on the table. This led to the terms **sub rosa**, which means confidentiality.

The First Commercial Establishments

In the years 1000-1500 A.D., travelers would stop for food and lodging at inns and taverns in France and England. Everyone had the same meal served to them. This one choice, a complete meal, was and is still called **table d'hôte.**

In 1533, La Tour d'Argent opened in Paris, France. This was the first restaurant open to the public in the Western world. Guests at La Tour could order their own individual meals from a menu for the first time.

French Service

The first meals served in France were done so with considerable flourish and show. The meal was divided into three separate services. Hors d'oeuvres were served first. Then came the first service. Everything that the guests ate was placed in the dining room on tables and warmers (like today's buffet). Each guest was waited on by a server (called a valet) or two. The valet assisted the guests by obtaining the food for them. Guests, while seated, could serve themselves from the offered dish, but more often the valet would serve them. This sounds very similar to the buffet style of today and was called served buffet service of ancient France. Food and cooking became the rage in France. Any French person who wanted to be considered knowledgeable in the ways of the world learned about cooking. The French palate was becoming sophisticated. Under the reigns of King Louis XIV and Louis XV, it became stylish to employ a famous chef. Families, like Bechamel, were proud to have a new sauce named after them. French people started to entertain more and service became an important element of the meal. Since so many people were becoming knowledgeable about food, service had to become creative to keep up with the new foods. Instead of food being prepared solely in the kitchen, it was prepared in front of the guests with a flourish. As the guests were now civilized, they had **utensils** to eat their food with besides their fingers.

THE BASIC PLACE SETTING

In homes and restaurants, the standard placement of flatware (spoons, forks, knives) generally follows the same pattern. It has not changed substantially from the original **place setting** begun in the homes and restaurants of France. To the left side of the guest is placed the bread and butter dish, and forks. The knives, spoons, glasses, and cups are to the right. A napkin is placed in the center of the place setting. A diagram of the basic place setting is illustrated in Figure 3-2.

TIP$ **TO INSURE PROPER SERVICE**
Use an assembly line to set up guests' place settings.

History of Knives

In the medieval times, knives were used for hunting and protection. Every man carried a knife with him. One of the uses for the knife, discovered by early man, was to spear his food with the pointed end. He could then transport the food to his mouth without using his hands. The inns and taverns in Europe that served food and drink did not provide their guests with any utensils, because they had their own. In addition, medieval times were dangerous; the patron of the inn was in a strange place, never knowing who might attack him. When the patron ate, if he had to lay his knife down on the table, he would put it on his right-hand side. According to Sandy Rose, former Senior Vice President of Harry M. Stevens Corporation, this was in

A Bread and Butter Plate
B Salad Fork
C Main Course Fork
D Main Course Knife
E Coffee Spoon
F Soup Spoon
G Wine Glass
H Water Glass

FIGURE 3-2

The traditional American place setting includes a soup and salad course. Forks are on the left side of the guest; knives and spoons are on the right. Water and wine glasses are placed at the tips of the knife and spoon.

case he was attacked. The knife was in a perfect position, ready to be grabbed for protection. Because most people were right-handed, the knife went on the right side of the guest.

By the 1600s, knives were being placed on the tables at the restaurants. These knives were still pointed at the end. A French statesman, Cardinal Richelieu, a very powerful figure in the time of King Louis XIV, was eating at one of these restaurants. As he was eating his meal, he looked over at another table and saw an individual sitting there picking his teeth with his pointed knife! He immediately ordered all knives be rounded off at the edges instead of pointed.

CORRECT WAY TO SET THE TABLE

Needless to say, both the managers and the staff must know how to set the table. Then the manager must be a stickler for detail by inspecting all tables and correcting mistakes before the banquet begins or the dining room opens. A manager will be able to walk into any room and know immediately what is correct and incorrect about the place settings. In time, setting the table properly will become second nature to the service staff. Figure 3-3 illustrates the proper way to set the table.

Generally, the utensil that will be used to eat the first course is placed the farthest from the guest. If soup were served first, the soup spoon would be the farthest spoon away from the guest's right hand. Next to the spoons are the knives. All blades are pointed toward the forks or center of the place setting. Figure 3-4 illustrates the basic place setting.

Reason for Location of Utensils

Europeans cut their food with their knife held in their right hand. They eat their food holding the fork in their left hand. Americans have the habit of cutting the food the same way and then transferring the fork to their right hand before eating the food. Because of this European tradition, place settings continue to follow this general pattern.

Above the tip of the dinner knife is the water glass. Next to the water glass is the wine glass. Because wine is considered a food in Europe and because it complements the meal, and in some countries water was not fit for human consumption, it is an important part of the meal. Because guests drank more wine than water (if it was served), the placement of the wine glass made it easy for the service person to pour the wine.

On the left side of the place setting are the dinner and salad forks. Immediately above or to the left of the forks is the bread and butter plate.

FIGURE 3-3

A table set up in the proper manner for a banquet. Forks are on the left side of the napkin, a knife and spoon to the right of the napkin. The bread and butter plate is above the forks. Water glass is above the knife.

FIGURE 3-4

The proper diagram for a basic place setting. On the left side of the napkin is the bread and butter plate, the salad fork, and the main course fork. In the center of the place setting is the napkin. To the right of the napkin is the dinner knife (with the edge pointed toward the napkin), coffee spoon, and water glass above the tip of the knife. Notice there is no cup and saucer in this basic setting. However, there is a wine glass that is placed right next to the water glass.

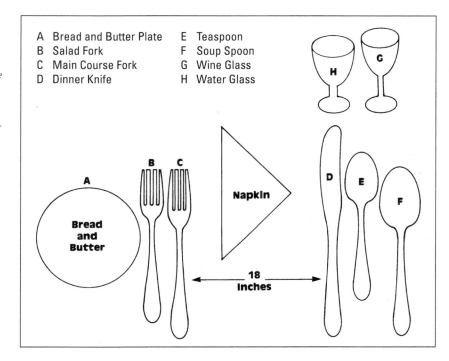

A Bread and Butter Plate
B Salad Fork
C Main Course Fork
D Dinner Knife
E Teaspoon
F Soup Spoon
G Wine Glass
H Water Glass

The distance between the forks and knives should be 12 inches at a banquet, 18 inches at an a la carte establishment. Most service staff, after setting a table for a few days, are able to place the utensils perfectly on the table. There is an easy way for a service person to determine this distance at banquets. The service person should stand facing the table, with a knife in the right hand and a fork in the left hand. These utensils should be placed on the table in direct line with the shoulders. Most adults have shoulders approximately 12 inches wide. The utensils should be placed one inch from the edge of the table. Whether they are put in a straight line or in a staggered up-and-down pattern, as shown in Figure 3-5, is up to the individual management of the restaurant.

Each restaurant can adapt its place settings to its menu, adding or subtracting utensils. For instance, if all guests are served soup with their meal, then a soup spoon is added to the place setting. Notice that there is no coffee cup or saucer at the place setting. These are brought with the dessert course or when the guest orders coffee and placed to the right of the spoons.

The handle on the coffee cup should be located in a position that would be the same as the hour hand on a clock pointing to the number five. This position is called "cup at five o'clock." This is strictly for guest comfort. When the guest reaches for the coffee cup, the handle of the

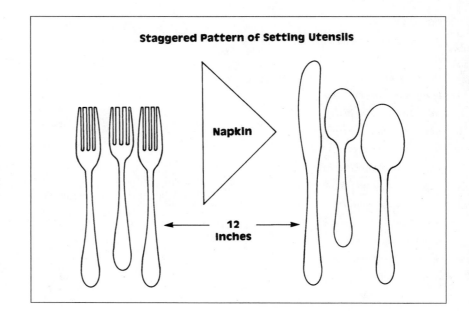

FIGURE 3-5

Flatware placed in a staggered pattern makes for a more attractive place setting.

FIGURE 3-6

The handle on a coffee cup should be placed at a position that corresponds to five o'clock on a watch.

cup will not have to be moved. The guest's fingers will fit perfectly into the handle. This is just another detail that will make a restaurant stand out from its competitors. Everything in the restaurant should be for the benefit and comfort of the guest. Unfortunately, if the guests are left-handed they will be inconvenienced, because the placement of the utensils is a direct result of a right-handed society and European etiquette. When a service person notices (being ubiquitous) that the guest has moved the beverage glass to the left side, the coffee cup should be placed to the guest's left, with the handle at seven o'clock. These are details that make a guest leave a restaurant satisfied, even though nothing exceptional appeared to be done. All that the restaurant did was to take care of the smallest details to make the guest's dining experience complete.

TIP$

To Insure Proper Service

If a guest wears a watch on his or her right arm, he or she is most likely left-handed. Ask if you can place beverage glasses on his or her left side above the forks. Watch your tips increase!

FRENCH SERVICE TODAY

During the period when kings were in power and the wealthy aristocrats were influential in France, all the skilled cooks, chefs, and valets were employed by these individuals. In 1789, a revolution took place; the royalty was overthrown and removed.

As Napoleon gained power, it appeared that France's great culinary development would stop. This was a blessing in disguise for service. Because there was no more royalty, there was very little employment for the great cooks in the homes of wealthy people. The cooks had to find a new place to earn a living. Restaurants gave these cooks an opportunity for employment. Either the cooks worked for someone or opened up their own establishments. From 1765 until 1800, the number of restaurants increased from one to five hundred in Paris. The cooks introduced a new type of service to the French people, using their culinary skills to prepare meals in front of the guest. **French service** as we know it today was born.

Today's French service is characterized by a service person's finishing off (cooking, carving, flaming, and so on) the food in front of the guest. the food is partially prepared in the kitchen and brought to the table on a cart, called a **gueridon**. On the gueridon is a small heating utensil, called a **rechaud**. The food will be prepared on this gueridon, using the rechaud for last-minute cooking in full view of the guests.

Because the people doing the cooking at the table (after the French Revolution) were chefs, the job title of this service person is **chef de rang**. This person might be highly skilled in order to prepare foods in front of the guest. The French look upon food service as a profession; therefore, many talented individuals made a career as a chef de rang. Soon, going out to a restaurant became part of the culture of France. A career in the dining room or front of the house became a proud and acceptable profession. Having the skill to be able to prepare a meal in front of the guests was soon expected by the French public. Even today, food that is not prepared at the table, but served from the kitchen on a plate, is looked down upon. The person who assists the chef de rang is called the **commis de rang**. The main jobs of the commis are to place the food orders in the kitchen, bring the food to the chef de rang, and clear the dirty dishes from the guest's table.

....

TIP$

TO INSURE PROPER SERVICE

To understand French service, dine at a restaurant that serves food using this style of service.

....

French service has some excellent advantages:

1. The main advantage is for the guest, who gets a high degree of personal attention.
2. The service is showy and elegant.
3. Food is prepared with showmanship.
4. It may be possible to decrease the labor cost, because the chef and commis de rang are partially compensated with gratuities. Therefore, fully staffed, highly paid kitchen crew may not be needed.

However, there are more disadvantages than advantages for a restaurant in using French service:

1. The restaurant must employ highly skilled service staff, knowledgeable in cooking as well as service. They must know how to bone fish and poultry, carve meats, dress salads, and prepare **flambé** items. The chef de rang must be knowledgeable about ingredients and must have the personality to perform constantly. These individuals might be impossible to find in some areas of the country. Therefore, a well-planned training program must be instituted and maintained.
2. If a restaurant does not have a good training program, and even if it does, there could be a problem with consistent quality of food prepared by all the chef de rangs at all the tables. It becomes difficult to

ADVANTAGES AND DISADVANTAGES OF FRENCH SERVICE

Advantages
1. Guest obtains high degree of personal attention.
2. Service is showy and elegant.
3. Food is prepared with flourish and showmanship.
4. It may be possible to decrease kitchen labor cost.

Disadvantages
1. Highly skilled waitstaff is required.
2. Quality standards are difficult to enforce
3. Dining room fills with smell of cooked food.
4. Much more physical space is required than in American Service.
5. More and costlier equipment is needed.
6. Residence time is greatly increased, resulting in less turnover.
7. Menu prices are highest in restaurants that use French service.

FIGURE 3-7

enforce standardized recipes and to correct mistakes. Thus, the guests may get different quality food at different visits.
3. Because cooking is done in the dining room, the air may become stale with the odor of cooking unless the dining room has a good ventilation system.
4. Because gueridons must be used, a restaurant using French service will have less space for tables. French service requires 18 square feet per guest, while other services only require 15.
5. It costs more to buy and maintain the gueridons and rechauds. Other equipment must also be purchased which may not have to be purchased using American or Russian service.
6. It takes longer to serve guests using French service. A restaurant cannot serve as many guests in an evening. Generally, restaurants with this type of service have only one sitting a night. Or they have an early and late sitting, if the demand is great.
7. The cost of the meal must be high enough to cover all the above costs. Therefore, restaurants that use French service have to charge considerably more for a meal than those that use any other type of service.

Russian Service

The cuisine of Russia was greatly influenced by the French. Catherine the Great (1762-1796), one of the rulers of Russia, imported French chefs and corresponded regularly with Voltaire. She was a great Francophile. In turn, the service in French restaurants was influenced by the Russians.

Because the Russians did not have many skilled chefs, the food served to wealthy aristocrats was prepared in the kitchen, rather than in front of the guests. To make the food look as appealing as possible, it was served on royalty's best serving pieces: silver trays. As the rulers of the two countries became allies (Peter II, Catherine's son, and Napoleon planned to invade Egypt together), each country influenced the other. When the French returned home from Russia, they brought with them an idea for a new type of service to be used in restaurants. This new style of service in France was referred to as **silver service**.

When this new type of service was introduced to French restaurants, it revolutionized the industry. It became popular in the mid-1800s. No longer did restaurants have to find talented chefs to prepare food at the table—nor did they need gueridons. Now food could be served more quickly to more guests. **Russian service** is characterized by food being cooked and pre-portioned in the kitchen. All the food for a table is presented to the guests on silver trays. The service person then serves the food to the guests' plate from the tray. In the United States and Germany this service is called Russian. A more casual example would be family style service. In France, because it originated in French restaurants, it is called French or silver service.

Russian service has many advantages over French service for a restaurant owner or manager. It is best used for banquets rather than for a la carte service.

1. Food portioned and arranged on a silver platter looks appealing and impressive.

ADVANTAGES AND DISADVANTAGES OF RUSSIAN SERVICE

Advantages

1. Food looks impressive when served.
2. Less floor space is required per table.
3. Guests have more space for comfort.
4. Faster than French service.
5. Waitstaff does not have to be as skilled as French service waitstaff.
6. Quality control of food is maintained.

Disadvantages

1. Service person has to be skilled in serving from platter to plate.
2. Tables must be positioned so they are easy to serve.
3. Different entrees require different silver platters, resulting in cold food for first guest.
4. High initial cost for purchasing equipment. Theft of silver is a possibility.
5. Last guest to be served is presented with an unappetizing platter.

FIGURE 3-8

2. Less space is required than for French service, because gueridons are not needed; therefore, more tables can be placed in the dining room, resulting in more meals served.
3. Guests will be more comfortable at the table, because 30 inches of linear space are needed for Russian service, as opposed to 24 inches for other services.
4. Guests can be served more quickly, which allows for more turnover than does French service.
5. The service staff do not have to be skilled in food preparation.
6. The quality control can be better maintained than with French service, because all food is cooked and put on platters in the kitchen.

Russian service does have some disadvantages:

1. A service person has to be skillful in manipulating a fork and spoon to transfer food from the platter to the guest's plate.
2. All tables must be located so that they can be easily served. If a table is located too close to a wall, it becomes impossible to serve a guest.
3. When guests order different entrees it requires bringing different platters to the table. This is time consuming. The first guest served will end up with cold food to eat if he or she waits for all the guests to be served.
4. There is a high initial cost for purchasing the silver platters. A larger problem is controlling the inventory of silver and preventing theft.
5. If all guests order the same entree, the last person served could find the look of the food picked over and unappealing.

Russian and French Place Settings

Because the two types of service are so similar, the place settings are identical. In both services, the place settings are shown in Figure 3-9.

The difference between this setting and the basic setting is that the dessert fork and spoon are already on the table. One other difference is that the knife is on the bread and butter plate. Notice the placement of the glasses. There should never be more than three glasses at a place setting.

History of Spoons

The spoon is the oldest of all eating utensils. It is also the simplest. The earliest ones were made out of wood. The Egyptian spoons were carved from ivory and wood or various metals. Elaborately shaped handles were designed and were often decorated with lotus blossoms.

The spoon was a mark of class in medieval society. Each person brought his or her own set of utensils to dinner. Children were given their own set when they were old enough to eat with company. The expression "to be born with a silver spoon in your mouth" came about because wealthy families started the practice of giving a set of spoons to their children at birth. This phrase meant that the children came from a well-to-do family.

FIGURE 3-9

Russian and French place settings are identical. The setting is basically the same as American style, except for a dessert spoon and dessert fork placed above the center of the place setting.

A Bread and Butter Plate
B Bread and Butter Knife
C Salad Fork
D Main Course Fork
E Dinner Knife
F Coffee Spoon

K Dessert Fork
J Dessert Spoon
GLASSES
G White Wine Glass
H Red Wine Glass
I Water Glass

Cesar Ritz

French cooking was becoming more popular and common in the 1800s. More restaurants were opening. Russian service, as well as French, was being experienced by more guests. More restaurants were finding that Russian service was more economical to use. Waiters did not get as much respect as the talented chef de rangs of French service. Cesar Ritz is credited with making serving guests a profession.

Cesar lived from 1850 to 1918. His great learning took place when he worked as a commis de rang (assistant waiter) at the most famous restaurant in Paris, the Viosin. He took the job at Voisin so he could learn the best methods in serving techniques. He learned to deal well with people, and was so responsive to their wishes that before long guests were insisting on being served by him. He was a master at details. Soon he was in demand to manage restaurants and hotels all over Europe.

The following incident was typical of his quick-thinking mind and obsession with details. He was working at a mountain-top hotel in Switzerland called the Rigi-Kulm. A group of forty Americans were arriving for lunch. The temperature was eight degrees below zero and the heating system broke down. He had no way to cancel the party.

Ritz changed the setting of the party and the menu to give the guests the impression of warmth. The forty-seat table was moved into a small room and covered with a red tablecloth. Four large copper bowls were filled with methylated spirits; when the guest arrived it was lit. For each guest a hot brick was wrapped in a flannel cloth and placed under his or her feet. The guests began the meal with a hot consommé and ended with crêpes flambées. Because of this obsession with details, the guests had no complaints about the temperature and the luncheon was a success.

Ritz's name and fame soon spread. His treatment of guests and his staff's service was legendary. He and Escoffier (the great French chef) began working together. Ritz would be in charge of the service, Escoffier of the kitchen. Escoffier created new dishes and named them for a favored few of their customers. Ritz chose the customers. Peach Melba, Melba toast, and Sauce Melba were created and named for the great Australian opera singer Dame Nellie Melba. His waiters were taught to give dignified service. They served in silence but were always at hand when needed. The dining room was always planned to be elegant and attractive enough to attract the most elegant of ladies.

In 1887, at age thirty-seven, he married a London hotelkeeper's daughter. While in London, he was asked to take over the management of the Savoy Hotel, where he made the biggest impact on the restaurant industry. He revolutionized dining out and even changed the habits of society. Restaurants were required by law to close at 11:00 P.M. He got

Parliament to change the hour, and soon the Savoy's restaurant was open until 12:30 A.M.

Sunday dining become a feature of the week. The Savoy became known as the place to go and to be seen. He hired orchestras to play dinner music; the first one was led by Johann Strauss. He made evening dress compulsory and banned unaccompanied ladies from the dining room. He was accused of breaking up home life by making dining out fashionable. Because of him men's clubs suffered a loss of business. Men now took their wives out to dine at the Savoy instead of going to dinner at their mens-only clubs. The common people could now go to a fashionable restaurant and dine with the aristocrats. In short, the common people could now "put on the Ritz."

Setting the Cover

As Ritz made it a policy to have elegant surroundings for his restaurants, modern restaurant managers should also have standards for their establishment. Every restaurant and banquet house has a place setting on the table before the guests eat their meal. Our place settings are different from those of Ancient Rome and of medieval times. Some establishments have opulent linens, silver, and crystal, while others have only the bare essentials. The area or space for all utensils (including salt, pepper, and ashtrays) for each guest is called the **cover**. Many people refer to this as the place setting. However, note that the place setting includes *only* the utensils for the guest to eat the meal, while the cover includes all the space for each guest. A restaurant manager should make sure that each cover is set consistently. This is another factor that distinguishes an award-winning restaurant from others. At the Cross Keys Inn in Doylestown, Pennsylvania, owner Walter Conti (a *Nation's Restaurant News* Hall of Fame Winner) is a stickler for details. He inspects everything. At his restaurant each sugar bowl sits on the table facing the customer with its handles to the sides. It is in the same spot on every table to hide the ashtray from view.

With any style of service, enough space must be allowed so that guests are not crowded and service staff can serve them safely. French and American services require 24 linear (straight line) inches of space for guest comfort; Russian service requires 30 inches. All should have an area 15 inches deep. Therefore, in American banquet service, a table that is 8 feet long by 3 feet wide can seat four guests on each side of the table, for a total of eight guests (as is illustrated in figure 3-10). Regardless of the size of the table, the manager must make sure that both the guests and

FIGURE 3-10

Space requirements for American banquet service. Each guest needs 24 linear inches. This table is 8 feet long by 3 feet wide. It can seat four guests on each side of the table.

service staff have enough room so the guest can be comfortable and the service staff can serve properly.

Placemats and Tablecloths

The choice of what to put under the cover is up to the individual establishment. Some restaurants will use a placemat to cover the area for the place setting; others will use a tablecloth; still others use a tablecloth covered by a glass top.

Originally, restaurants that used placemats were usually low-priced coffee shops. Today, more and more restaurants (regardless of the type or the price of the meal) are choosing placemats rather than cloth because they are less expensive. The placemats range in quality from paper to plastic or cloth. The placemat should be set about 2 inches from the edge of the table. The utensils go on the placemat.

Tablecloths are used for most banquets and, generally, in restaurants that have a high check average. Tablecloths should be placed on tables in banquet rooms by two people. The service persons stand on either side of the table while unfolding the tablecloth and laying it on the table. Tablecloths should be hung even with the seat of the chair. In an a la carte restaurant, one person can place the cloth on the table, because the tables are smaller. In an a la carte restaurant, it may become necessary to change the cloth without exposing the bare tabletop to the guests. Changing a cloth should be done discreetly, without a flourish that would distract the guests.

HOW TO CHANGE A TABLECLOTH

1. Remove all dirty plates and napkins from the table and place them on a tray (which is set on the tray stand, not on the table).
2. Move to one side of the dirty tablecloth all salt shakers, pepper shakers, flower vases, sugar bowls, and any other items that are part of the cover and must remain on the table.
3. Fold back one edge of the dirty cloth and place the clean cloth on the bare part of the table.
4. Unfold the clean cloth to the center of the table, so it is almost touching the cloth to be changed.
5. Return all the items that are part of the cover to the clean tablecloth.
6. Complete unfolding the tablecloth.
7. Set the cover in the proper way, as required by management.

When service persons change cloths, they should never expose the bare table or place anything (clean or dirty items) on the chair. All personnel should know how to change a tablecloth and reset the cover. No guests should ever be allowed to sit at a dirty table.

TIP$

TO INSURE PROPER SERVICE

Catch a staff member changing the tablecloth correctly. Reward him or her with a small token of appreciation (like a bottle of wine or a lottery ticket, where legal).

Glass Tops

Some restaurants have discovered a new way to cut costs while still using tablecloths to make the restaurant look nice. The table is covered with a tablecloth, then a glass top (which has been specially made for each table) is placed over the cloth. The cover may be set directly on top of the glass. One disadvantage is that the glass has to be cleaned with a glass cleaner after every meal. The smell of the cleaner might be offensive to some guests. Another disadvantage is that the use of glass tops adds to the noise level in a restaurant.

Completing the Cover

To complete the cover the table is finally set with a napkin, either cloth or paper. The napkin should be the last item placed on the table. Before the service person places the napkin on the table, the cover must be correct. The napkin can go in the center of the place setting, in a water glass, or in the center of the starter plate (for establishments that use a starter plate). The napkins should not go under the forks. Depending on the policies of the restaurant, management may have the napkins folded in an artistic manner. The appendix of this book has a section on how to fold napkins.

Napkins

The use of table linen began when the very rich started to cover their dining room tables with expensive decorated linen or silken drapes. The dining tables of that time were long and narrow. The cloths were generally square. To make the dining room look as attractive as possible, the cloths were set diagonally along the table. A corner of the cloth would hang over the edge of the table in front of each guest.

The eating habits and table manners of the guests were not good. It was common practice for the guests to wipe their greasy hands upon their clothes and spill food and drink on the cloths. It was not long before guests realized that there was no need to wipe their hands on their clothing and get their fine clothes dirty. They quickly figured out that this linen would be a great convenience for wiping their hands. Because of the way the cloth was situated on the table, they began to tuck the corner of the cloth under their chins to prevent the food from falling into their laps. And, or course, they wiped their face with the linen at the end of the meal. Hostesses soon (as early as the fifteenth century) had their servants make square pieces of cloths to match their tablecloths. That is how napkins were discovered.

Attention to details, especially in regard to table settings, is critical for a guest's first impression of your establishment. Tablecloths should be draped evenly at all tables. The proper length is 14 inches. When the drape of the tablecloth is longer or shorter than 14 inches, the dining or banquet room looks unappealing.

Whatever type of tablecloths, placemats, and napkins are used in a restaurant, they should be attractive, clean, and appropriate to the restaurant's style.

The History of American Service

Dining in America was affected by the Puritan influence. There was only one purpose for eating: to refuel the body. To dine or enjoy the meal was thought to be bad.

The restaurant business in America got its start in the 1800s at taverns and roadhouses. Service at the beginning of this century was terrible. American service was and is still characterized by "Food on the plate, no wait." This was the American custom. All food was put on one plate and served to the guest, as opposed to French service, where separate plates for vegetables were used. All guests sat in a common room and ordered from a very limited menu. Large quantities of food were served to the guest. The eating hours were set for the convenience of management.

During the 1830s, a great influx of French immigrants entered America, bringing their way to serve food. At about the same time, many German and Italian waiters and cooks came to the United States, because they had heard that the streets were paved with gold. They also brought with them a better style of service than was available in America. As they found employment in America, they introduced their methods of service in the places where they worked. Eventually, service got better and a style of service began to develop.

Another reason that service got better was that employers went to Europe and got entire kitchen and dining room staffs to come to America. The owners paid for the workers' trip over. This was a way to get to those gold-paved streets. The owners would offer to pay wages to the cooks, but told the service staff they could work only for tips. Restaurant owners did this to cut down on their labor costs. It worked; many people were looking to go to the new world, and they were pleased to have the opportunity. America had always been tipless. When the owners returned from Europe with their new staffs, they introduced tipping into America—claiming it was an established European practice.

At the same time that the great influx of immigrants were arriving in the United States, Delmonico's opened in New York City (in 1832). This restaurant gets the credit for teaching the American public how to enjoy fine dining. It also set the standard for elegance that all other restaurants in the United States tried to match. Delmonico's offered the first a la carte menu, courteous service, private dining rooms, flowers, music, and fine wines to its guests.

Oscar Tschirky, employed as the maître d'hôtel at the Waldorf-Astoria, worked exclusively in the dining room. He elevated service to the highest standards in America. No waiter was allowed to have chin whiskers or a mustache, as he considered facial hair to be unsanitary. He also got American restaurants to cut down on the abundance of food.

Thanks to Delmonico's, Oscar Tschirky, and European immigrants, America now had its own unique type of service, which took the best parts of French and Russian service and combined it with American ingenuity.

American Service

American service is characterized by portioning all the food on the dinner plate in the kitchen. It is also referred to as plate service or German service. It is the fastest of all types, and requires the least amount of skill to wait on guests. One service person generally works a station (a group of tables in an area of the room) containing between fourteen to eighteen seats. The main difference in serving food in American service, as opposed to French and Russian service, is that all food is served from the guest's left side with the service person's left hand, and all beverages are served from the guest's right side with the service person's right hand. Raymond J. Goodman theorizes in his book *The Management of Service* that the practice of serving food from the guest's left side occurred because Americans consume more beverages and more varieties of beverages than Europeans.[3] Because the glasses are positioned on the right of the place setting, it was easier to serve the food from the left side, so as not to disturb the guest when he was drinking or reaching for his glass.

The advantages of American service far outweigh the disadvantage:

1. It is a simple service to teach and learn. The staff only has to put a plate in front of the guest. They do not have to know how to cook, carve, or flambé.
2. A skilled staff is not necessary. Almost anyone can be trained to serve American style.
3. The cost of equipment is small, as there are no gueridons or silver trays to purchase.
4. Service is extremely fast.

FIGURE 3-11

Advantages and disadvantage of American service

ADVANTAGES AND DISADVANTAGE OF AMERICAN SERVICE

Advantages

1. A simple service to teach and learn.
2. A skilled service staff is not necessary.
3. Cost of equipment is small.
4. Service is fastest of all three methods.
5. Less dining room space is required for guests.
6. More guests can be served.
7. Menu prices can be lower than in other services.
8. Quality control can be excellent.

Disadvantage

Service is not as elaborate as in French or Russian service.

5. Less dining room space is required for each guest.
6. Because service is fast and less space is required per guest, more guests can be served during the meal period.
7. Menu prices can be lower for the same meals compared to other services.
8. Portion and quality control are excellent, as all foods are plated in the kitchen.

There is just one main disadvantage in using American service: the service is not as elaborate as the other two.

American service is widely used in restaurants around the world today because the advantages far outweigh the disadvantages. Most restaurant managers will borrow parts of French and Russian service and incorporate it into their particular service style. For example, many restaurants in the United States offer salads made tableside (French); or they may serve a dish like lobster Newburg, portioning it out in front of the guests (Russian). American service is the best type of service to use for most restaurants.

Banquet Service

A **banquet** is a meal where all the food has been preselected by the host before the guests enter the room. Banquets are served using American, Russian, or buffet style. All have advantages and disadvantages. The key factor in serving banquets is that the service person have as much needed equipment on the guests' table before they enter the room. The purpose of banquets is to serve guests faster than in a la carte dining. This is because most banquets are arranged for a special purpose—a dance, testimonial, or awards presentation—not just to eat. A brief description of all types of banquets are given below.

Origin of the Word *Banquet*

At large dinners in medieval times, the seating arrangements were precise. The feudal lord and lady sat on a raised dais at one end of the room. The children and relatives sat on removable benches along the walls. The term *banquet* comes from the French work for bench, which is *banc*. Servants stood behind the chairs of the wealthy couples to make certain that the food was not poisoned. At medieval and Roman banquets there were not many spoons, so the diners used their fingers or short, pointed daggers to bring the food to their mouths. There were no forks or napkins or place settings.

American Banquet Service

Like American service, this is an easy service to serve. One waiter can usually serve from sixteen to twenty-four guests. The service is the same as American, except for the place setting.

AMERICAN BANQUET SERVICE PLACE SETTING

The place setting for **American banquet service** is similar to American a la carte service. However, the place setting changes with every banquet. A separate utensil is needed for each course. Because the purpose of the banquet is to serve guests as quickly as possible, the utensils should be preset.

Therefore, the meal illustrated in Figure 3-12 needs two forks, three spoons, and two knives. The place setting appears in Figure 3-13. Note that the coffee cup and saucer is preset with the cup up and the handle in the correct position.

Figure 3-13 is the correct place setting for the menu as it appears in Figure 3-12. However, a banquet house may not have enough spoons to place three at each setting. Therefore, a banquet manager might be forced to use only two spoons.

TIP$

To Insure Proper Service

Develop positive relationships with your competition to borrow equipment and with a business that rents equipment for banquets.

However, if a restaurant is going to be in the banquet business, it is strongly recommended that the establishment purchase enough equipment to do the job properly.

FIGURE 3-12

The menu for a typical banquet, with the utensils needed to serve one guest. Two forks, three spoons, and two knives are needed. A bread and butter plate, cup and saucer, napkin, and water glass are needed as well.

TYPICAL BANQUET MENU

Item	Utensil Needed
Fresh Fruit Cup	Teaspoon
Salad, House Dressing	Fork
Prime Ribs	Knife to cut, fork to eat
Baked Potato, Green Broccoli	
Rolls and Butter	Butter spreader
Chocolate Mousse	Teaspoon
Coffee	Teaspoon

AMERICAN BANQUET PLACE SETTING

A   Coffee Cup
B   Fruit Spoon
C   Coffee Spoon
D   Dessert Spoon
E   Dinner Knife

F   Main Course Fork
G   Salad Fork
H   Bread and Butter Plate
I   Water Glass

FIGURE 3-13

An American banquet place setting

History of Forks

The first types of forks had two prongs. They were used to hold sacrificial meat, not for eating. People ate by picking the food up with their fingers or the pointed end of a knife. Two people are credited with introducing the fork to modern society. A Byzantine princess introduced the fork in the eleventh century to the people of Venice, Italy. Queen Catherine de Medici was the second person. She introduced it to the aristocrats of France after returning from Italy in the mid-1500s. At first, it was used more as an amusement than as a serious eating utensil. By the 1600s, forks became fashionable and were more acceptable than eating with one's fingers.

Like spoons, forks became very elaborate. These forks sometimes were as elaborate as a piece of jewelry. When people were invited to dinner, they carried their precious forks with them in special cases. Forks were introduced to

England by Tomas Coryate, who brought back samples of them from Italy, where he first used them.

Governor John Winthrop of Massachusetts brought the fork to America. When he came to the colonies in 1630, he brought it along with his personal knife in his personal case.

By the 1800s, forks had become acceptable throughout the Western world. Some restaurants started to provide all utensils for guests.

Russian Banquet Service

Russian banquet service is the most elegant of banquet services. Two service people are generally assigned to work in pairs, serving a total of twenty guests. Food is served from platter to plate. One server serves the main course, while the other follows with the potatoes and vegetables. A skilled staff is needed for this type of service.

RUSSIAN PLACE SETTING

Like the American setting, all utensils are put on the table. However, each guest has his own set of salt and pepper shakers. The dessert fork and spoon are set above the place setting. As in American banquet service, the amount of silverware needed changes with each banquet, depending on the menu.

Buffet Service

Buffet service is characterized by the guests obtaining either their whole meal or parts of the meal from food that is displayed in the dining room. One service person can be assigned as many as thirty-five guests. The place settings for banquets have only enough utensils set to do the job.

There are three types of buffets. The first is simply called **buffet**. In this service, guests obtain all their own food and drinks. The service person has only one job: to clean up dirty dishes.

The second is called **modified deluxe buffet**. Tables are set with utensils and guests are served coffee, and perhaps dessert, by the service person.

The third is the most elegant, called **deluxe buffet**. The guests are served the first and second course, as well as their beverages and dessert. They obtain their main course from an elegant buffet. The service person must serve and clear many courses. They must have all the dirty plates cleared before the guest returns from the buffet table. One service person is needed for twenty guests in this style of buffet service.

Because it is a banquet, the place setting of the buffet is determined by what food is offered on the buffet. Management should train their staff not to allow guests to bring back used plates and utensils to the buffet line. Instead, the guests should be given a new plate each time they come to the buffet line. In addition, there must be enough utensils on the buffet line so the guests do not use their fingers to pick up food or dip bread or raw vegetables into the food. By taking these precautions the establishment will prevent cross contamination. However, the manager must use common sense in determining how many utensils to set.

SUMMARY

1. There are many styles in which to serve food and beverages to guests.
2. No one style is correct for all establishments.
3. Each restaurant and banquet house has to decide the type of service it will give.
4. The style of service provided depends on the restaurant's menu, decor, and pricing.
5. Some establishments serve their food on silver platters, while others serve their food on paper plates. You have to choose which is best for your operation.

REVIEW QUESTIONS

1. How did American service first begin, and how did it evolve?
2. Describe the differences in the three types of a la carte services.
3. Compare the advantages and disadvantages of the three types of a la carte services.
4. Diagram correctly the place settings for French, Russian and American a la carte service.
5. Describe the different banquet styles: American, Russian and buffet.
6. What are the advantages and disadvantages of the three buffet services?

7. What must a manager know before he or she can diagram the place setting for American, Russian, or buffet banquet services?

8. What is a cover, and how were eating utensils introduced?

9. Explain how to change tablecloths during a busy period.

10. How many guests is a service person expected to serve in each of the following services: American, French and Russian a la carte; American and Russian banquet; buffet, modified deluxe buffet and deluxe buffet?

11. How would you as the banquet manager for a party solve this equipment shortage problem: Each person should have three forks at his or her cover: one for salad, one for main course, and one for dessert. You need six hundred forks, but have only four hundred. In addition, the rental company sent you only two hundred bread and butter plates, while you need six hundred: two hundred for the first course (melon), two hundred for the place setting, and two hundred for the last course (pie).

REFERENCES

1. Janet McKenzie Hill, *The Up-to-Date Waitress* (Boston: Little, Brown, and Co, 1906), vi.

2. Christine Terhunne Herrick, ed. *Consolidated Library of Modern Cooking and Household Recipes* (New York: Bodmer, 1904), 25.

3. Raymond J. Goodman, Jr., *The Management of Service for the Restaurant Manager*, 2nd edition.

4

Proper Guidelines for Service

OBJECTIVES

At the completion of this chapter, the student will be able to:

1. Define competency as it relates to proper service
2. Understand how to properly pick up, load, carry, and put down a tray
3. Define a sidetowel and explain its purpose
4. Recite and properly use the seven guidelines for providing competent service
5. Understand how to properly serve coffee and tea, and change ashtrays
6. Explain the different ways in which food is served in American, French, and Russian service
7. Explain the proper method of serving guests at tables and booths

Excellent Service

All restaurants and banquet halls strive to give their guests excellent service. Some of them succeed; but many of them fail miserably. It is a known fact that one of the major causes of restaurant failure is poor service. As was stated in Chapter 1, survey after survey has shown that the American public values good service and despises poor service.

Many people, including restaurant reviewers, restaurant owners, and guests, have stated that excellent service can compensate for average food; but great food cannot compensate for bad service. Excellent service is the result of the two factors, competency and friendliness. Competency is serving food and drinks to the guest in the correct manner. Friendliness is a characteristic that the dining room and/or banquet manager must encourage in service staff. At times, the manager has to be concerned if the service staff become too friendly with the guests. This friendliness leads to informality and then sloppiness. Friendliness, if done correctly, is an extremely important aspect of excellent service. However, the service staff must also be competent in order to provide excellent service.

Importance of Competency

The manager must teach and reinforce correct serving methods to the service staff so that these methods become second nature. *The Random House Dictionary* defines competent as "having suitable skill, experience, etc., for some purpose."[1] Competent service in a restaurant has one main purpose: the guest will leave the establishment pleased with the dining experience. Competency in a restaurant can best be described in the following way: Competency occurs when the customers do not have to ask the service person for any item during a meal. The water glasses are refilled. The meals are served without the service persons asking which guest receives which menu item. In short, the guests know they have had a great dining experience because the service person brought all items to them before they could think of asking for it.

How to Obtain Competency

Great restaurants instill competency in their service staff through great attention to details, training, and follow-up. The success of a restaurant depends on the manager. If the manager overlooks the little details, the service staff will also overlook the little details. However, if the manager pays attention to details, the service staff will consistently follow the manager's lead.

Competency comes from management. Management must teach their staff the proper way to serve their guests. As previously stated, training at Walt Disney World concentrates on the competent service methods. In addition, management continuously monitors their service. The staff must be reminded about what they are doing correctly and incorrectly.

Anything being done incorrectly must be corrected immediately. Managers are taught to be coaches, and to coach cast members in the correct way to serve. The key to competent service is training. A customer will immediately notice things that are right and wrong about the establishment. Restaurants that have all details in place usually are excellent at service. Places that look disorganized usually give merely adequate or even poor service.

T I P $

TO INSURE PROPER SERVICE

As a manager, keep in mind the old Irish saying, "If you don't know where you are going, any road will take you there."

A How-Not-To Story

A wedding reception was held at a country club in one of the richest and most elegant communities in America. The first thing that was noticed when entering the dining room was that all the tables and covers were set in a haphazard manner. Some coffee cups had their handles at the four o'clock position, some at the five o'clock. The cups were placed at the top of the place setting, mixed in with the bread and butter plates. It appeared that there was a problem with taking care of details. Sure enough, the concerns were justified. After being served an adequate meal (nothing outstanding, nothing poor), the wedding cake was served. However, the tables had not been totally cleared of the dishes from the main course. Nevertheless, the service staff brought the cake to the table and pushed the dirty dinner plates to the center of the table. What was an adequate meal turned into a disappointment for the guests as they had to eat their wedding cake while staring into leftover broccoli, stuffed baked potato skins, and fried chicken.

THE KEY TO COMPETENCY

In an issue of *Connecticut Magazine* is a story about the Copper Beach Inn in Ivoryton. This restaurant, voted best in the state of Connecticut by the readers of the magazine, was owned by Jo and Bob McKenzie. One reason for their success was their training methods. They did not just hire someone and call him or her a service person. The owners set policies for their staff and trained them thoroughly.

All new service staff and bartenders were required to study a sixty-page service manual and to pass a written test on the McKenzie method. Included in the manual were all the minute details through which service is accomplished. For example, the placement of tomatoes on the salad dish was explained, as well as how to remove dishes. Even the proper way to stand in the dining room, upright and with hands behind the back, was covered.

Their key to excellent service, however, was the constant supervision and implementation of their policies. Manuals and training are worthless if the manager does not enforce the guidelines set forth in those books. Colleen Sherman has worked in four different types of restaurants. In an interview with the author, she compared the type of training and follow-up methods she has received. She noted that all of the restaurants varied in their training. At the family restaurant, she was told she was a waitress. That was the extent of her training. Her next job was at a chain restaurant. She had to study and memorize menus and policies, and was then assigned tables to serve. When she worked at a franchise chain restaurant she had to pass three written tests before being assigned as a waitress. However, at all these places there was no follow-up to her training. She considers her most successful training to have been at Walt Disney World, because of the follow-up training she received.

Walter Conti at Cross Keys Inn also uses follow-up. He notes the errors made by staffers and corrects them, thus maintaining excellent service. The key to a competent serving staff is good training plus excellent and consistent follow-up training. As in all learning, repetition is the key to success. The dining room and banquet manager must stress and reinforce the competent way to serve the guest.

THE KEY TO COMPETENCY

Training by management

plus

consistent observation of the service staff

plus

coaching and complimenting

and

repetition of proper serving methods

by

the manager

FIGURE 4-1

The Sidetowel

All professional service persons must have with them a napkin to use as a sidetowel. As the veteran waiter Sam Bubonia at the DeWitt Clinton Hotel in Albany, New York, used to say, "You are not a professional waiter unless you have a sidetowel with you."[2] Unfortunately, use of a sidetowel is a rarity at most establishments. The sidetowel has two purposes.

First, it can be used as an insulator; the service person can pick up and serve dinners with the sidetowel rather than risking getting burned from handling hot plates.

Second, if there is any type of spill, the service person has a cloth to clean up the spill. There is no need to waste valuable time running back to the kitchen to obtain cloths to clean up the mess. Therefore, the sidetowel becomes a time-saver.

When the sidetowel is not used for any of the above purposes, it should be placed over the service person's left arm, not stuck in the back pocket like a handkerchief. It must always be clean. If the service person is not using the sidetowel as an insulator to serve food, then the sidetowel should be placed over the right arm. Figure 4-2 shows three service staff ready to greet guests.

FIGURE 4-2

A service staff ready to greet guests. The first server has the sidetowel properly positioned over the arm. The second has the sidetowel improperly positioned on the shoulder. Photograph by Randall Perry.

Trays

A wonderful invention was made for waitpeople: the tray. Two basic types of trays are used in the restaurant industry. Large trays, called hotel ovals, are used to carry food and plates to and from the guest. The other type are small round, rectangular, or oval trays (called tea trays) which are generally used to serve drinks.

Large trays enable the service person to carry many items at once, as opposed to delivering food as they do in diners and coffee shops, item by item. It may be impressive to see a service person carrying eight dinners stacked up on both arms. However, using a tray is much more professional looking, efficient, safe, and sanitary than using the style called arm service.

Many of the best establishments insist that waitpeople use a tray to carry all items. The server must use a tray even if it is to carry a water pitcher or one coffee cup. Waitpeople should not be allowed to serve guests directly from the tray without putting the tray on a traystand, as it creates a safety hazard.

Easter Dinner

As the family approached the restaurant for their Easter dinner, they saw an ambulance at the entrance. Entering the restaurant, they heard a child screaming.

Once the child was taken to the hospital, they were told what had happened. After the child's family (grandparents, parents, and children) had finished their meal, the mother asked for coffee. The service person carried the hot, steaming cup of coffee to the table without a tray. The mother swung around in her chair, hit the server's hand, and the hot coffee spilled on the child, causing second-degree burns.

Not a pleasant way to celebrate a holiday! All because the server did not use a tray.

Dining room and banquet managers who insist that the service staff use trays will have a much more competent service staff than managers who do not. Once the service staff form the habit of using trays, it becomes second nature. Soon their service improves, because they are carrying more items on each trip between the dining room and the kitchen. As a result, they make fewer trips and save themselves a most valuable commodity: time.

Besides enabling servers to carry more food and beverages to tables, using a tray is safer and more sanitary than using arm service. The tray is bigger than a plate. Therefore, anyone walking past will most likely see the tray and avoid a possible accident. Using a tray is more sanitary because the plates do not slide down the server's arm into one another.

When this happens, one guest's gravy ends up on the other guest's plate. Using a tray is more eye-appealing and pleasing to the guest because the plates do not slide down the server's arm into one another.

However, the greatest reason for using a tray is that all the food can be delivered to the guests' table at the same time. This makes the guests' meal more enjoyable, and the restaurant more efficient.

Small trays are used to bring drinks from the bar or one or two items from the kitchen. Some establishments will allow their servers to serve the guest directly from the tray, but that may create a safety hazard. Other establishments, like Walt Disney World, insist that the servers place the tray on a sidestand and serve from the sidestand to the guest.

Whatever the policies of the establishment, using a tray to serve food is much more efficient than using arm service.

TRAYSTANDS AND/OR SIDESTANDS

There must be a place for the waitpeople to place their trays. Trays can be set down on a permanent table in the dining room called a sideboard or service station. Or they can be placed on lightweight devices called traystands.

Traystands are excellent for use in a restaurant or at banquets because they are light enough to be carried by the server in one hand, while carrying a tray of food in the other hand. Therefore, the service person can carry the stand right to the guest table. This saves the service person time and extra steps, because the tray is right next to the table instead of being located a distance from the table. Traystands open easily and are secure, so they are easy to use and safe. Using trays and having traystands located near the guests' table is the most efficient way to deliver food to the guests.

THE CORRECT WAY TO LIFT AND PUT DOWN A TRAY

There is a correct way to lift and put down a tray on the traystand. First, when training the staff, they should be taught the parts of the traystand. Make certain that they know all the parts and how they operate.

There are two legs which open up and have cloth supports which hold the traystand together. The service person's body must be lined up parallel with the cloth supports. If the waitpeople line up correctly, their hands will not get tangled with the metal supports when they put down or pick up the tray. Figure 4-3 shows the proper way to line up to pick up a tray from the traystand.

FIGURE 4-3

The proper body position to pick up a tray from the sidestand. The server's body is parallel with the cloth supports. This position makes it easy to slide the tray onto the shoulder without getting the hands tangled up in the wooden supports. The server is squatting, not bending over to pick up the tray. Photograph by Randall Perry.

PROPER WAY TO LIFT A TRAY

Waitpeople should be taught to line their body up even with the traystand. The opening of the traystand should be at a right angle with the server's body. They should bend down at the knee, as if they are about to kneel, as illustrated in Figure 4-3. Figures 4-4 and 4-5 illustrate proper and improper ways to pick up a tray. In order to protect their clean shirts from the dirty tray, service persons should place a clean napkin or cloth on their shoulder. The tray should be in balance before reaching the shoulder. The tray is then slid onto the service person's shoulder. Most waitpeople pick up the tray with their left hand under the tray and slide it onto their left shoulder because they control the tray with their right hand. However, it does not matter which shoulder the tray is carried on as long as it is carried properly.

The service person's hand (if the tray is going on the left shoulder, it should be the left hand, as shown in Figure 4-4) should be placed under the tray. The larger tray or hotel oval is usually carried while it is resting and balanced on the palm of the server's hand. More experienced waitpeople will balance the tray on their fingertips. The inexperienced server should grasp the front of the tray with the free hand (as shown in Figure 4-4) for stability. The service person lifts the tray by

FIGURE 4-4

The proper manner to pick up a tray. The tray is balanced correctly with dirty dishes neatly stacked. On the server's shoulder is the sidetowel which protects the shirt from getting soiled. The tray has been slid to the right shoulder, and the server is lifting the tray with her legs. A sidetowel is placed over the tray to prevent spillage. Photograph by Randall Perry.

FIGURE 4-5

The improper way to carry a tray, positioned in front of the server and poorly balanced with dirty dishes. In addition, the server has no sidetowel. Photograph by Randall Perry.

using leg muscles, not back muscles. A tray should never be carried as illustrated in Figure 4-5. This is too dangerous and may result in injury to the server.

TIP$ **TO INSURE PROPER SERVICE**

How to Carry a Large Tray

1. Line up your body parallel with the cloth supports on the traystand.
2. Bend down at the knee, as if you are about to kneel.
3. Slide the tray onto your shoulder and use the palm of your hand to balance the tray. If you are right-handed, you normally put the tray on your left shoulder in order to have your right hand free to control the tray (you may put a clean napkin on your shoulder to protect your shirt from getting dirty).
4. The arm from elbow to wrist should be at a right angle to the tray.
5. Stand up, using your legs to give you the strength to life up the tray. Your right hand is controlling the tray.

TIP$ **TO INSURE PROPER SERVICE**

How to Carry and Serve From a Small or Tea Tray

1. Carry the tray waist high.
2. If transporting a beverage, carry with your left hand; if food, carry with your right hand.

If your manager allows you to serve guests from the tray:

3. Serve beverages with your right hand from the guest's right side, holding the tray in your left hand.
4. Serve food with your left hand from the guest's left side, holding the tray in your right hand.

HOW TO PUT DOWN A TRAY

The procedure is the reverse of that for lifting a tray. The server must align his or her body so that the tray can easily be slid onto the cloth supports. The server should then bend down at the knee and slip the tray onto the traystand. Employees should be taught never to bend over at the waist. If they do, they may injure themselves because they are using their back instead of leg muscles. Once the tray is on the stand, the server takes the sidetowel off the shoulder and places it in the proper position (either over the arm or used as an insulator for the hot plates).

The smaller tray or tea tray is carried waist high. Because this tray is so light, the service person can place it on a sideboard without bending down. If the dining room manager allows drinks and food to be served directly from the tray, it must be held in the correct hand. With drinks, hold it in the left hand; with food, the right hand.

LOADING A TRAY

The first thing a server must do is to check that the tray is clean on both the top and bottom surfaces.

Trays are designed with either a nonslip surface such as an abrasive material or without it. If the tray does not have a nonslip material, the staff should be taught to take a damp, clean cloth, and put it on the tray. Even if the tray is made with a nonslip material, a clean cloth placed on the tray will make the service look more professional.

In loading a tray, the heaviest items should be placed on the side of the tray that will be closest to the server's body. This will allow the server's shoulder to bear the brunt of the weight and allow the server to have more control over the tray. When more experienced servers carry the tray by balancing it on their fingertips, they place the heaviest items in the center of the tray.

The lighter items and glasses are placed to the outside of the tray or away from the service person's shoulder. Items with spouts and handles should have their spouts and handles facing the center of the tray.

When serving food, the servers should be instructed to keep all hot items together. If it is necessary to carry both hot and cold food on the same tray, instruct their servers to separate the cold food from the hot food. Plates should never be stacked on top of each other unless plate covers are used. When serving soup, the cups should be placed around a stack of saucers. The soup should not be placed on the saucers until the server places the tray on the traystand.

When removing dirty dishes, the establishment should have an organized system for loading trays so that all plates are stacked neatly. This means all bread and butter plates are stacked on each other, instead of having a dinner plate on top of a bread and butter plate, with forks, knives, and spoons stuck in between them. Figures 4-6 and 4-7 illustrate proper and improper methods of loading dirty dishes onto a tray.

It must be emphasized that the only way the staff will load their trays properly is if they are taught correctly by the manager. Once the training is complete, there must be consistent reinforcement by the manager; that is, correction and reinstruction if done incorrectly, and praise if done correctly.

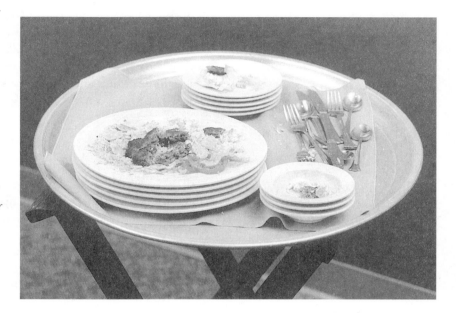

FIGURE 4-6

The proper way to load a tray of dirty dishes. The silverware is separated from the plates. The top plate has all of the leftover food on it. When the server brings the food into the kitchen, it will be easy to unload the tray. Photograph by Randall Perry.

FIGURE 4-7

The improper way to stack dirty dishes. The dishes are placed on the tray in no specific arrangement. This makes for a dangerous and hard-to-carry tray of dirty dishes. Photograph by Randall Perry.

Guidelines for American a la Carte and Banquet Service

For a restaurant to have competent service, certain standards must be met by all servers. The following guidelines have evolved over many years of serving. Originally, they were thought of as rules, but they should be renamed guidelines because rules are too rigid for the dining room business. Perhaps that is why they were not and are not enforced consistently. Often, because of circumstances beyond the server's control, common sense must prevail when serving guests. The server will often have to serve from the "wrong" side because of the physical constraints of the room or for the guest's comfort (for example, when the guest is talking to the person on the side from which you normally serve). However, these guidelines should be enforced whenever possible.

The Seven Guidelines Explained

1. LADIES ARE SERVED BEFORE MEN.

This means that if there is a party of two couples (two men and two women), the service person serves one woman and then the next woman. The service person serves in this order: woman #1, woman #2, man #1, man #2. If the server can easily determine who is the older woman at the table, she should be served first.

There are instances when the server would break this guideline. Children should be served before adults. Then serve the women, then the men. People always wonder if this can be done. Does it make any sense? When guests dine at The Publik House in Sturbridge, Massachusetts, they indeed see that it is possible to serve the children first.

THE SEVEN GUIDELINES OF SERVICE

1. Ladies are served before men, (if children are present, they should be served first, then ladies, then men).
2. Food is served from the guest's left side, with the service person's left hand.
3. Beverages are served from the guest's right side, with the service person's right hand.
4. All guests' food must be brought to the table at the same time.
5. Do not remove guest plates from the table until all guests are finished eating their meal.
6. Never stack or scrape dirty plates on the guests' table.
7. Dirty dishes are cleared from the guest's right side with the service person's right hand.

FIGURE 4-8

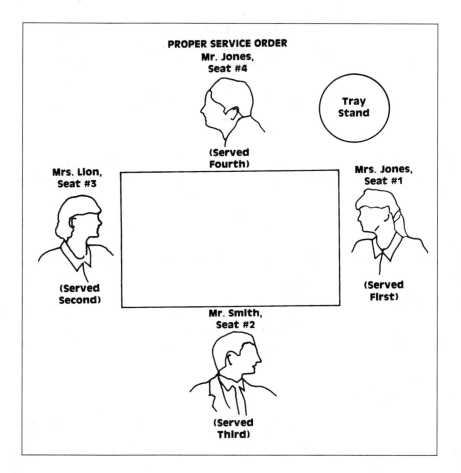

PROPER SERVICE ORDER

Mr. Jones,
Seat #4

Tray
Stand

(Served
Fourth)

Mrs. Lion,
Seat #3

Mrs. Jones,
Seat #1

(Served
Second)

(Served
First)

Mr. Smith,
Seat #2

(Served
Third)

FIGURE 4-9

The proper sequence to serve a table. The server should serve the table in order 1, 3, 2, 4. The women are served first, and then the men are served.

The server first took the order for drinks. She returned and served the youngest child his cola. Then she walked past the mother to serve the older son his soda. She returned to their mother to serve her drink. And finally, the father was served his drink. It did not take that long to serve all four guests. She served all drinks from the guests' right side with her right hand. Throughout the meal, service was performed quickly and competently. The dining room (which seated over 100) was filled and the service was superb. It added to the great food and pleasant atmosphere of the restaurant.

Another exception to this guideline is when serving a banquet, where the room is set up with long banquet tables seating more than ten people. With long banquet tables it makes little sense to skip over the men because there are so many guests at the table. If a server is working at a banquet where the banquet table has ten or more people on each side of the table, it is more logical to serve the guests in sequential order.

2. FOOD IS SERVED FROM THE GUEST'S LEFT SIDE WITH THE SERVICE PERSON'S LEFT HAND.

There is a logical and practical reason for this guideline. If the service person served with the right hand from the left side of the guests it would create a potentially dangerous and awkward situation. The service person is putting his or her arm right in the faces of the guests. This could be most unappetizing if the waiter has body odor. Also, the guests would have to back away in order to prevent the service person from brushing or hitting them with his arm. It is also dangerous for the service person. Figures 4-10 and 4-11 illustrate proper and improper ways to serve food in American service. There are times when a guest does not pay attention to the service person and moves unexpectedly. When the service person sees the guest moving quickly, the server's arm can be swung out and away from the guest if the service is being done correctly. The chance of an accident is reduced by proper service.

Because the service person is serving with the left hand, service should proceed in a clockwise direction. Many people have trouble with the concept of clockwise and counterclockwise; a simple way to

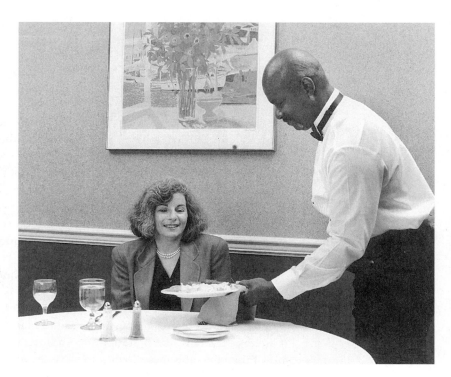

FIGURE 4-10

The waiter is serving food properly to the guest. He is serving from the guest's left side with his left hand. His sidetowel is used as an insulator between his left hand and the hot plate. His right hand is behind him. Photograph by Randall Perry.

FIGURE 4-11

The waitress is serving food incorrectly to the guest. She is serving with her right hand from the guest's left side. Her sidetowel is on her shoulder and her hair is flowing onto the guest's plate. Photograph by Randall Perry.

remember the correct direction is "to follow your nose." Proceed in the direction that your nose is pointing. Serve food from guest's left side with your left hand and follow your nose. Figure 4-12 illustrates the proper direction in serving a party of four.

There are a couple of exceptions to this guideline also. Serving food to guests seated at a booth or a table positioned against a wall requires a different set of procedures. The service person must serve and pick up with the same hand. Look at Figure 4-13. The server should serve the guest in seat A, using the left hand. The guest in seat C is served using the right hand. Removing dirty dishes, the service person would use the same hand that was used to serve the meal. This allows the server to keep his or her arm out of the face of the guest. The same rules of serving women before men apply.

When two guests are talking to each other, the service person does not interrupt their conversation by serving the food properly. Instead, he or she serves one guest from the left side, the other from the right side. When serving from the right side, the right hand should be used. If there is a physical item in the way (like a pole) or the table is positioned in such a way that makes it impossible to serve the guests from their left, they should be served from their right side.

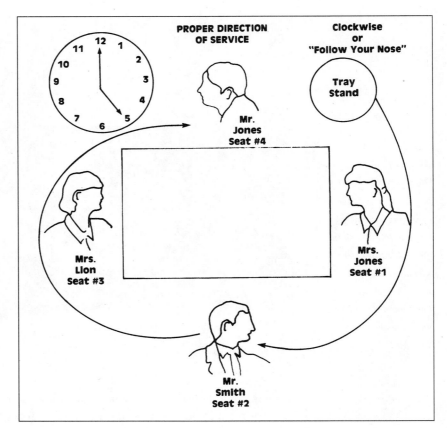

FIGURE 4-12

The proper direction of serving a meal. The service person would serve guest 1, then 3 going in a clockwise direction. Returning to the tray, guest 2 would be served followed by guest 4.

3. BEVERAGES ARE SERVED FROM THE GUEST'S RIGHT SIDE WITH THE SERVICE PERSON'S RIGHT HAND.

Because a large majority of people are right handed, the glasses and cups for beverages are put on the right side of the guest. It is logical that the service person would pour beverages from the right side of the guest. Therefore, to be consistent, all beverages are served from the right side.

When serving an alcoholic beverage, a cocktail napkin should be placed in front of the guest. The beverage should then be placed on the cocktail napkin. If there is a meal in front of the guest, the service person will place the beverage above the spoons and knives on the right side of the guest.

When service persons have to pour water, wine, or coffee into a glass or cup already on the table they must not pick up the glass or cup, unless leaving the glass or cup on the table would create a safety hazard.

FIGURE 4-13

Service at a booth. The server serves and picks up with the same hand. Guests in seat A and B will be served and dirty dishes picked up with the left hand. Guests in seat C and D will be served and dirty dishes picked up with the right hand. The same rules for serving women before men apply.

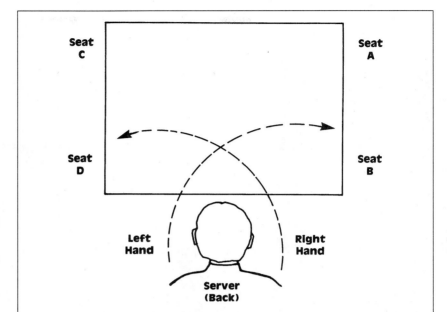

The proper way to pour water is to pour with the right hand, keeping the left hand folded behind the back. Some establishments prefer that the service person hold the sidetowel (with the left hand) under the lip of the glass to catch any drips or spills. Water glasses should be filled three-quarters to the top of the glass. Figure 4-14 shows the proper way to pour water.

T I P$

To Insure Proper Service

Leave glasses and cups on the table when pouring beverages into them.

Coffee should be poured with the right hand while the left hand holds a coffee shield. This shield (bread and butter plate) is placed at an angle between the coffee pot and guest to protect the guest from coffee spills and steam from the hot pot. Figure 4-15 illustrates the correct way to pour coffee.

Tea should be brought to the guest in a small pot and be placed above the coffee cup. The teabag should be in the pot, steeping.

However, a good service person is always aware of a guest's needs. If a guest is left-handed, he or she will switch the water glass or coffee cup to the left side. When this occurs, the server should serve from the guest's left side with the left hand. One important rule is never to reach

FIGURE 4-14

The waitress is pouring water the correct way, from the guest's right side with her right hand. The glass is not removed from the table.

FIGURE 4-15

The waitress is pouring coffee the correct way. Served with a coffee shield, from the guest's right side with the service person's right hand. The sidetowel is on the right arm. Photograph by Randall Perry.

in front of the guest. For example, when the service person is pouring coffee and the guest has moved the cup to the left side, the service person would never reach across the guest. The proper way to serve is to move to the left side of the guest and pour coffee into the cup on the left side of the guest. However, generally, all beverages are served from the right side with the right hand.

4. ALL GUESTS' FOOD MUST BE BROUGHT TO THE TABLE AT THE SAME TIME.

One of the most annoying situations for a guest is to be served first and then have to wait for others at the table to be served their food. This creates two problems for the guests. Guests with proper manners will wait for the whole table to be served before they begin to eat their meal. Most likely their food will get cold, as the service person has to return to the kitchen to obtain the rest of the food. Colleen Sherman says that "the supervisors at Walt Disney World never let a service person go to a table without the complete order."[3] It is also embarrassing and annoying for the guests.

The manager should insist that all food reach the table at the same time. This is especially true at banquets when the guests have their choice of two main entrees. All guests must be served the meal at the same time even if half of them are eating chicken and the other half beef. The manager must devise a system (which is explained in Chapter 12) by which all guests are served at the same time.

5. DO NOT REMOVE ANY GUEST'S PLATES FROM THE TABLE UNTIL ALL GUESTS HAVE FINISHED EATING THEIR MEAL.

This guideline means exactly what it says. It is a mystery why wait-people remove plates from guests before all the guests at the table are finished eating their meal. This implies to the guests who have not finished their meal that they are taking too long to eat and must hurry and finish their meal. Of course, if a guest is done and pushes the plate to indicate he or she wants it to be cleared away, then take the plate away even if the others have not finished their meal.

Another part of this guideline is that a new course must never be served until the dishes from the previous course have been removed from the table. This is another of the strict competency rules that are enforced at Walt Disney World: A server must remove the soup course before being allowed to serve the salad course.

The only exception to this guideline may occur during a banquet. Because most banquets are on a strict time schedule, if the banquet manager waited for all guests to complete every course it could put the banquet behind schedule. If a guest has not finished eating his or her salad course and the main course is ready to be served, the banquet manager could instruct the service staff to do the following: Have the service staff remove all the finished salad plates. If the guest is finished eating his or her salad when the service person brings out the entree, the service person should remove the dirty dish before serving any of the main entrees. If the guest is still not finished with the previous course, the service person should ask permission to move the plate. The server should move the dish above and to the left of where the entree will be placed.

6. NEVER STACK OR SCRAPE DIRTY PLATES ON THE GUESTS' TABLE.

This is the most irritating and unappetizing habit a service person can have. Some waitpeople take the dirty dishes and stack them-one on top of another-right in front of the guests, as is illustrated in Figure 4-16. It is even

FIGURE 4-16

The improper way to clear a table. The server has the guest's dishes stacked in front of the guest. In addition the server is picking up from the guest's left side and has the sidetowel over the shoulder. Photograph by Randall Perry.

FIGURE 4-17

The waitress is using common sense to remove the dirty bread and butter dish from the guest. She is removing it with her left hand from the guest's left side. Photograph by Randall Perry.

worse if the service person scrapes all the leftovers onto one plate in the center of the table. Some of them will even dump the cigarette and cigar ashes from the dirty ashtray into the leftover mashed potatoes.

If the restaurant or banquet establishment allows smoking, there is a proper way to change the ashtrays. The service person should bring to the table a clean ashtray. The clean ashtray should be turned upside down and placed over the dirty (capped ashtray). This acts as a cover, so as the service person removes the ashtrays, no ashes will spill onto the guests' table or into their food. The server places the capped ashtray behind his back and with his free hand places the clean ashtray (the cap) back on the table. Figure 4-17 illustrates the proper way to cap an ashtray.

7. DIRTY DISHES ARE CLEARED FROM THE GUEST'S RIGHT SIDE WITH THE SERVICE PERSON'S RIGHT HAND.

The guest's dirty dishes must be cleared with the service person's right hand, except when it makes more sense to clear from the left side (then it should be done with the service person's left hand). Figure 4-19 illustrates how the waitress uses common sense by removing the bread and butter plate with her left hand from the guest's left side. She does so because if she removed the bread and butter plate from the guest's right side, she would have to reach in front of him. A service person should never reach in front of the guest, as in Figure 4-18.

TIP$

To Insure Proper Service

Do not pick up a dirty plate without removing the utensils first.

The correct and efficient way to remove dishes from the table is as follows: From each guest, the service person will first remove the silverware with the right hand and transfer it to the left hand. Next, the dirty plate will be removed, and it will be transferred to the left hand. "Following your nose" (going counterclockwise), the service person will remove the next guest's silverware and dirty plate. The server will step back, out of view of the guests. The leftover food will be scraped from the plate just removed onto the first one removed. The new plate will be shuffled to the bottom of the stack held with the left hand. The silverware should be held in the fingers of the left hand and laid across the

FIGURE 4-18

The waitress is clearing the dirty dishes incorrectly from the guest's left side with her right hand. The sidetowel is improperly positioned on the shoulder. Photograph by Randall Perry.

FIGURE 4-19

The correct way to crumb a table. Crumbing from the guest's left side using her left hand, the server uses her sidetowel to brush crumbs off the table into a bread and butter plate held in her right hand. Photograph by Randall Perry.

top plate with the food scraps. The dirty plates should be placed on a tray in the neat organized manner that was discussed in the tray loading section. This procedure takes practice to master, but it is the most efficient way to clear a table.

Before serving the dessert course, the server must "crumb the table." The server would take either the sidetowel or a crumbing device and brush the crumbs from the table into a bread and butter dish, as illustrated in Figure 4-19.

OTHER HELPFUL HINTS FOR SERVING

Whichever hand you are using to serve or pick up, place that foot forward for balance. For example, if serving food with your left hand, place your left foot forward.

If a guest places a dirty dish on his or her left side (to the left of the fork), the service person should remove the dish from the guest's left side with his left hand.

Keep in mind that the above are guidelines, not rules. The most important criteria are the comfort and safety of the guest. If you have to serve from "the wrong side" for the guest's comfort, do it.

Guidelines for French and Russian Style Service

The guidelines are basically the same as for American service, with the exception of guideline number two.

1. Ladies are served before men.
2. In French service, food is served from the guest's **right side** with the service person's **right hand**; in Russian service, food is served from the guest's **left side** with the platter in the service person's **left hand**, while serving with the **right hand**.
3. Beverages are served from the guest's right side with the service person's right hand.
4. All guests' food must be brought to the table at the same time.
5. Guest plates should not be removed from the table until all guests are finished eating their meals.
6. Dirty plates should never be stacked or scraped on the guest's table.
7. Dirty dishes are cleared from the guest's right side with the service person's right hand.

GUIDELINE NUMBER 2 EXPLAINED

In French service, food is served from the guest's right side with the service person's right hand.

In French a la carte service, the service person has to transfer food from a pan at the guerdon to plate. The plate is then served to the guest from the guest's right side with the waiter using his right hand.

In Russian service, food is served from the guest's left side with the platter in the service person's left hand, while serving with the right hand.

This is the most confusing and contradictory of all the guidelines. In Russian service, clean plates are put down from the guest's right side with the service person's right hand. The food is then brought out on a silver platter. After the food has been presented to the guest, the service person transfers the food from the tray to the plate. This is accomplished by holding the tray in the left hand. The service person should serve the guest from the left side with the right hand. Even though this method will make the service person put an arm in front of the guest, making the guest back away, this is the method that has been taught since the beginning of Russian service.

The method probably originated because it is easier for the service person to transfer food from the platter to the plate. At times it can be difficult to manipulate the serving fork and spoon. There is a chance that the food may slip out of the fork and spoon. In order to be consistent with proper serving techniques, Russian service should be changed to have the service staff hold the tray in their right hands and serve the food with their left hands from the guest's right side. This would be safer and less awkward than the current system.

SUMMARY

1. The dining room and/or banquet manager who learns and insists that the guidelines of competency be followed will have an establishment with excellent service.
2. If the manager can combine this competency with the staff's friendliness, the establishment will be successful from a service standpoint.
3. Competency in a restaurant means that the guest does not have to ask the service person for anything.
4. Following the seven guidelines for serving guests will ensure competent service.
5. Proper methods for using traystands and trays are necessary for both efficiency and safety.

REVIEW QUESTIONS

1. Define competency as it relates to the service staff.
2. Can excellent service compensate for average food? Explain your answer by giving examples to justify your position.
3. What problems must the manager foresee regarding the friendliness of the staff with the guests?
4. How does the dining room manager obtain competency from his staff with regard to proper service?
5. What is a sidetowel, and what is its purpose for a service person? How should it be carried when it is not in use?
6. Describe the proper manner in which a tray should be loaded with dirty dishes. What is a traystand, and how should a tray be picked up from the traystand?

7. Why should trays be used to carry food or beverages?
8. List and explain the seven guidelines of service.
9. Are there any differences between the American and the other types of a la carte service with regard to the guidelines of service?
10. Why are the guidelines of service called guidelines, not rules? Is there any part of the guidelines that is a rule?
11. You, the manager, have an excellent waiter. Guests like him; they always tell you he is an asset to your establishment. He constantly outsells all the other staff in desserts and wines. However, he breaks all the guidelines of service. He serves from the wrong side, picks the glasses off the table to pour water, etc. In short, he ignores proper guidelines of service. How would you get him to adhere to the guidelines? Or, do you think it is not necessary for him to adhere to the guidelines since he is such a great waiter?

REFERENCES

1. *Random House Dictionary*, S.V. "competent."
2. Sam Bubonia, interview with the author in Albany, New York, 15 February 1969.
3. Colleen Sherman, interview with the author in Schenectady, New York, 2 April 1987.

Chapter 5

The Styles of Service

OBJECTIVES   At the completion of this chapter, the reader will be able to:

1. Give the names and responsibilities of the four typical service positions in a dining room for a restaurant that provides American service
2. Describe and explain the three service options in a restaurant that provides American service
3. Define the term *station*, and demonstrate the proper method of setting up stations
4. Explain the importance of and how to assign sidework in order to have a smooth-running operation
5. Describe and organize a dining room using the team method of service for the service staff
6. Explain the advantages and disadvantages of the three types of service (team, individual stations, and captain) in the American restaurant
7. Teach the service staff the proper sequence of serving a meal
8. Describe how to serve wine to guests

American Dining Room Service Styles

The American dining room is unique in the world of service. In other countries, such as France, there are clear rules that each restaurant follows to provide its guests standard service. A standard has been set and all restaurants follow the same standards concerning service.

Because the United States is a melting pot of cultures and different types of service, there is no one style used by the restaurants. One restaurant may have a captain to take orders and service people to serve the meal, while another just a block away eliminates the position of captain and has the service person do all the service. A third, a few doors further on, has three people waiting on one table of two guests. All three restaurants are successful, yet all use different styles of service.

Dining Room Service Personnel

In American restaurants, there are four traditional job titles for individuals who serve the guests. They are: the **service person**, the **busperson**, the **captain**, and the **wine steward**.

Because there are no firm standards followed by American restaurants, establishments may call their employees by one title and combine them in other job descriptions. Therefore, job titles and responsibilities change with each restaurant. In some restaurants, a captain will be assigned to take food and wine orders. Another restaurant will have a wine steward to take and serve the wine selections.

All restaurants must have people, called the service staff, who serve the meal. Many restaurants have a person, called a busperson, to assist the service staff. In some types of services, the jobs of captain, wine steward, busperson, and service person are combined into the service person's job. In other restaurants, a team of two or three works together to give the guests service.

The following sections describe the responsibilities of each job and the qualities needed by dining room personnel.

Qualities of Successful Dining Room Personnel

Certain qualities are needed that will make the dining room personnel successful in dealing with the guests. The manager must be aware of these qualifications when hiring service personnel.

The personal appearance of the applicants must be excellent, as stated in Chapter 2.

They must have excellent communication skills, both oral and written.

Dining room personnel must be sensitive to their guests' and fellow employees' feelings and needs.

TIP$

The personnel must be able to work well under pressure. Being a service person is an extremely stressful job. They will have to be able to gather a variety of information, understand it, and make correct decisions, often in a split second.

In addition, they must be organized and efficient.

TIP$

CAPTAIN

The job of captain is usually found in restaurants with high-priced menus. The surroundings are generally nicer than in an average restaurant and the clientele is usually willing to spend a great deal of money for a meal. One establishment that uses the captain system is the New York Racing Association at its Aqueduct, Belmont, and Saratoga racetracks. The captain is usually responsible for an area of the dining room (called a **station**) with as many as sixty seats and four service persons. Because the tables are only used for one meal period (called a **seating**) and time is not a factor, the station at the racetracks is larger than normal. A more typical station has between thirty-five and forty seats, a captain, and two service persons.

Captains have the following responsibilities and duties:

- Supervising the service staff and buspersons in their station
- Greeting guests who have been seated at the tables in the station
- Merchandising (selling) and taking all drink and food orders
- Tableside preparation, if called for
- Sometimes serving the meal (but more often the service person does the serving)
- Ensuring that the service staff and buspersons clear the dirty dishes and reset the tables

The captain has been a service person and has been promoted to this position after demonstrating proficiency in selling and serving.

This job is a selling job. As the captain is the first person the guest talks to about the meal, the captain must be personable. Also, he or she must be able to manage employees, because this position also is a supervisory one.

WINE STEWARD

As the name implies, this person is responsible for suggesting and serving wines to all guests in a restaurant. This job requires a personable individual with a knowledge of wines. The wine steward must know which wine will complement which food on the menu. It is the responsibility of the steward to suggest, sell, and serve wines to the guests. Usually, one wine steward is sufficient for a restaurant. If there is no wine steward, this job becomes the responsibility of the captain or the service staff.

BUSPERSON OR DINING ROOM ATTENDANT

The busperson or dining room attendant is basically an assistant to the service staff. For many years, this job was filled by individuals who were unskilled and/or illiterate. It was unfortunate, because many managers placed individuals in this position who had no idea of how critical the job was in the successful operation of the dining room.

The specific jobs of the busperson seem easy enough. They are:

- Setting the place settings on the table
- Clearing the dirty dishes from the dining room and bringing them into the kitchen
- Assisting the service person whenever necessary in clearing away dirty plates from a table and restocking the service area with condiments, plates, glasses, and other items needed for the smooth running of the dining room

Because the above jobs seem so straightforward and easy, managers usually assigned one busperson to work with two or as many as four service staff. The busperson was usually poorly trained, if trained at all. That is when the so-called easy job turned into a problem for the manager, service staff, and guests. The busperson could not keep up with the pace of a busy dining room. In the middle of the rush hour, the service staff would find themselves with dirty tables and not enough clean linens or plates or condiments.

The busperson should not be an unskilled worker, but a person who is training to become a service person. The busperson must be as organized and efficient as a service person. If the busperson is not organized, then the whole dining room will suffer and the guests will receive poor service.

THE SERVICE PERSON

Service persons are the eyes and ears of the dining room manager. They interact directly with the customers. The guests are more likely to tell them what is good or bad about the restaurant than tell the manager. In the eyes of the guests, the person who waits on them is the restaurant. The chef of the restaurant could have been awarded three stars by the Michelin guide; the restaurant could have won an award for interior design; the manager can have excellent financial and managerial skills; but if the service staff do not perform up to the guests' expectations, the restaurant is bad. The guests are the ultimate critics. If they leave dissatisfied, they will tell many of their friends. Therefore, the manager's number one priority must be hiring, training, and supervising the service staff for the purpose of providing service that excels. It has been proven over and over again that proper service can make a restaurant successful. Even more reliably, poor service can ruin a restaurant.

What Do You Think?

A couple had an eight o'clock reservation for dinner. They were seated right at 8 P.M. As they looked around the beautifully designed room, they noticed the fresh flowers on the white-clothed tables. Classical music was being played in the restaurant by talented musicians. The food being served to the tables around them was attractive and plentiful. It was obvious by the looks on the faces of the other guests that the food was excellent and many people were enjoying themselves. However, it was ten minutes before anyone approached their table to take their drink order. Finally, an order was taken and delivered. The service person put it down and disappeared for fifteen more minutes. At 8:32 the service person came back and took the order. The wait between the courses seemed like an eternity for the couple. Finally, the main course was served at 10:03. It was served to them in a very formal, non-caring manner by the service person. The food was excellent and plentiful. What do you think the couple told their friends about the dining experience? Will they ever return to this restaurant for another meal?

The service persons have very specific duties. They are responsible for the total service of the meal. In most American restaurants, the service persons work alone. They have no one else to assist them in serving the meal. If the host seats too many people at their table at once, or if there is a complaint about the food, they find themselves unable to serve and attend to all their guests' needs, or they are (as it is known in restaurant slang), "**in the weeds**." They have no one else to rely on. They must greet the guests and from that point serve the guests flawlessly through the end of service. Their only assistance comes from the (probably) untrained, unskilled busperson. They generally have a station with anywhere from four or seven tables seating between sixteen and twenty-four guests.

Specific responsibilities of the service person are:

- Obtaining any specific instructions about reservations and policies for the meal period
- Preparing the station, checking chairs and place settings for cleanliness, and making certain all tables are set correctly
- Greeting customers
- Suggesting menu items
- Taking orders for and serving food and drinks
- Inquiring about the guests' satisfaction with the meal
- Clearing dirty dishes
- Refilling drinks and bread by anticipating customers' needs
- Suggesting desserts
- Serving dessert
- Preparing and collecting bill
- Offering to the guests a closing remark
- Doing preparation work for the next day

Each restaurant has its own specific tasks for the service person. The tasks should be outlined in an employees' manual. The Barnsider Restaurant chain requires its employees to know all the facts covered in its 228-page training manual. The chain tests the employees for proficiency, in an extensive training program that may last up to one year. There is a constant reinforcement of the policies by veteran service staff employees.

The manager must know all the job tasks of the service person. Once the manager knows and understands the tasks of the service person, another task is at hand: understanding how implementing and assigning stations makes a dining room run smoothly.

All restaurants should divide their dining room up into small sections called **stations**. Each station has between sixteen and twenty-four seats, depending on the size of the tables and other factors. By using this

Stations

method, the service people are responsible for one part of the restaurant rather than for the whole dining room.

Many restaurants assign one service person to one station. Other restaurants assign a captain and two or four service people to a station that may have up to sixty seats. Still other restaurants use a system that has a three-person team responsible for up to sixty seats.

A manager should organize the stations to maximize excellent guest service. For example, a dining room has four tables of four seats and two tables of two seats with a view of the ocean. Even though this is only a total of twenty seats, it should *not* be one station. These tables will be requested by the guests first, so it is best for the manager to split up these tables into two or three stations. But the tables in the station must be together. Look at Figures 5-1 and 5-2. If you were a manager, which plan would give your guests the best service?

Several factors must be taken into consideration when the manager divides the room into stations. These factors are:

1. Distance of the guest tables from the kitchen
2. Number of guests seated at each table
3. Physical attractiveness of the station
4. Amount of food preparation required at the table

FIGURE 5-1

Stations set up for a ninety-six-seat dining room. Five servers all have their tables close to one another. John has the most tables because his station is closest to the kitchen door. Jim is an inexperienced service person. Tom is the best service person, so his station has more tables, but his area also has the rest rooms, which are not a desirable location. Lisa has twenty seats, and Pam has twenty-two seats to serve. This is the correct manner for setting up stations.

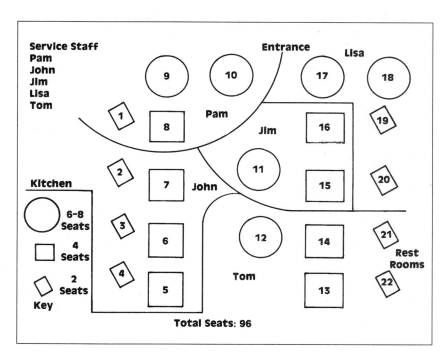

FIGURE 5-2

This dining room also has ninety-six seats. Each service person should have twenty-four seats to serve, because there are only four of them. All four have their tables scattered over the dining room. The service in this restaurant will be poor, mainly because of poor station assignment by the manager. This type of station assignment is incorrect.

5. Union contract requirements
6. Competency of the staff
7. Tables most frequently requested by guests
8. Location of waitstaff work stations (if not in or by the kitchen)

DISTANCE OF THE GUEST TABLES FROM THE KITCHEN

The station that has the fewest number of tables should be the one farthest from the kitchen. Because of its location, it will take the service person longer to obtain the food. Therefore, fewer guests can be accommodated in this station than in the other stations.

NUMBER OF GUESTS SEATED AT EACH TABLE

A mixture of small tables that seat two (called **deuces**) and larger tables (called tops—four people, **4-top**; six people, **6-top**) is ideal for organizing a station. There should be a maximum of twenty-four seats in a station for one service person to serve. The twenty-four seats should not be made up of twelve deuces, however. That would be almost impossible for a service person to serve, because there are too many parties to wait on at once. Ideally, the station should consist of a

6-top, three 4-tops, and three deuces. Of course, this station must be close to the kitchen area. All stations should be designed with a variety of tables that seat different numbers of guests.

PHYSICAL ATTRACTIVENESS OF THE STATION

In every restaurant, there are tables that are more desirable to the guests than others. Traditionally, tables by the kitchen or rest rooms have been designated as the poorest tables. Tables by the windows, with a view of nice scenery, are considered the best. If there is entertainment in the restaurant, tables closest to the entertainment will be the most popular. The popular station should be smaller than the one by the kitchen door, because many guests will request the popular tables.

FIGURE 5-3

Popular stations, such as ones by a fireplace, should be smaller because many guests will request these. Photograph by Randall Perry.

Managers should rotate the assignment of the desirable tables to all servers.

AMOUNT OF FOOD PREPARATION DONE AT THE TABLE

If the menu of the restaurant has a lot of items that will be prepared or finished off at guest tables, the number of seats at the station should be fewer than twenty-four. Because the service staff has to do a lot of tableside cooking and tossing of salads, they will spend more time at the guest tables. Tableside cooking (usually with French service) will require more space between the tables because of the cart and food preparation equipment. The stations should be smaller than in American service. However, if the restaurant has a set menu (as often is the case on holidays), the number of seats in the station can be increased.

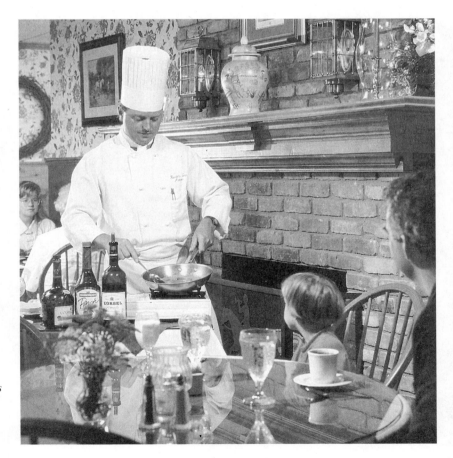

FIGURE 5-4

Tableside cooking requires extra space between tables. Photograph by Randall Perry.

UNION CONTRACT REQUIREMENTS

A union contract generally states the number of guests a service person can serve at a station. If that number is exceeded, a per-person bonus must be paid to the service person who has served the extra guests. One of the purposes of a union is to provide jobs for their members. It is in the best interests of the union (and management) to keep the size of the stations reasonable. Therefore, this bonus fee discourages management from making the stations too large, as the fee will generally be more expensive to the restaurant than employing another service person.

COMPETENCY OF THE STAFF

Every manager will realize that some service persons are more competent than others. These service persons can serve more guests than others. A manager must take this into consideration when assigning stations to his or her staff.

A caution to future managers: Many a well intentioned new manager has made erroneous changes in stations without asking for input from the staff. A manager should always obtain input from staff and customers before making changes. Since tips make up most of service staff's wages (as opposed to a set hourly wage), planning and consultation with the staff is vital before changes are made.

Assigning Stations

There are two methods of assigning stations after all the relevant factors have been considered. The first is the seniority method, the second is the rotation method.

SENIORITY METHOD

In the seniority method, service people with the most seniority are assigned permanent stations. The station truly becomes their little restaurant. On their day off they are replaced with a relief service person, usually one with little seniority. Normally, in this system, the best stations are assigned to the service staff who have been employed at the restaurant for the longest time. This system is used in restaurants where guests "lunch" daily at the same restaurant. The guest has a standard reservation for the same table and wants the same service person to serve him or her every day. Once this method is put into place, it is almost impossible to change.

ROTATION METHOD

This method is favored by many restaurant mangers and employees. The service staff is rotated among all the stations on a daily basis. Mary, our service person, is responsible for station one on Monday, station two on Tuesday, and so on throughout the week. This system allows the manager to close off the poorer stations when business is forecasted to be bad. It requires more planning and organization than the seniority method, but it allows all service staff to have the better as well as the poorer stations.

Whichever method is chosen for a restaurant, guest satisfaction must be the determining factor. Because much of guest satisfaction depends on the attitude of the service staff, the method selected must satisfy the needs of the restaurant, guests, and service staff. Once the decision concerning stations has been made, the next problem that managers have to deal with is that of sidework.

Sidework

Sidework is one of the necessary jobs that must be done by the service staff. It is a job that is not well liked, because it does not produce tips directly. However, the manager should explain to the staff that sidework is a positive factor in making the restaurant a success. For instance, if the salt and pepper shakers are filled before the guests enter the restaurant, the service persons will not have to interrupt service to fill up the shakers during the restaurant's busy time. Therefore, the service persons can serve more guests, and the income of both the restaurant and the service persons will increase. The restaurant is displaying competency, and service persons are less pressured and able to spend more time talking or doing suggestive selling with their guest. Sidework can be defined as all the extra jobs that service persons must do to get the restaurant ready to serve the guests. Sidework can be assigned before the shift or after the shift. Examples of sidework are filling salt and pepper shakers, restocking condiments, cleaning the coffee stations, and folding napkins.

Sidework can create many problems for a restaurant if the manager does not establish a policy. If a restaurant manager has to staff for more than one meal period (breakfast and dinner), there are often disagreements between the two shifts over which one is doing more sidework. The restaurant's policy must define the exact duties and responsibilities of the service staff concerning sidework. Employees must be taught about the importance of and need for sidework and the reason why it contributes to the success of the restaurant. They must understand that the tasks must be completed, but that the guest is still their most important responsibility. The restaurant manager should not allow any staff member to finish a shift and leave until his or her sidework is completed.

How do You Solve this Problem?

One evening a couple went out for dinner at a local diner. The food was served quickly and correctly by an efficient waitress. Because it was near closing time, as soon as the food was served, the waitress went to an area where there was a lot of stainless steel equipment. She proceeded to wipe it down and make sure it was clean for the next day. She was a master at doing this sidework. The stainless steel was shining and the condiments were replaced. However, she did not return to the guests' table to see how the meal was or to offer dessert. It took a long time for her to bring the check. But her sidework was completed.

Scheduling Sidework

The manager must plan out the specific tasks needed in the restaurant and decide how many people are required to do the tasks. Sidework should be scheduled on a daily basis. All assignments concerning sidework, just like stations, have to be posted for all the employees to see. The sidework can be rotated, just like the stations are rotated. In some establishments, the sidework becomes a part of a certain station. For

FIGURE 5-5

A sidework chart designed for a restaurant with stations. By organizing the sidework duties in this manner, all employees know their responsibilities.

SIDEWORK DUTIES	
Station	**Daily Duties**
1 & 2	Fan fold 50 napkins
3	Refill salts & peppers, sugar bowls
4	Wipe down all stainless steel
5	Flowers
6	Dust woodwork and window sills
Note: On days when there are fewer employees, sidework duties will be combined.	

example, the service people assigned stations one and two have to fan fold one hundred napkins each day. Therefore, if Pam is scheduled for station one today, she knows that she must fold fifty napkins. This method creates accountability for both the manager and employees.

Each restaurant has its own specific jobs for sidework. The key is that the manager must be organized and follow up to make certain that the sidework is completed. When the manager does this, sidework becomes an integral part of the success of the dining room.

Restaurant Success

One of the main reasons for the success or lack of success of a restaurant is the service that the guest receives. The dining room manager is the key person to insure that the guests receive this level of successful service. The manager is responsible for hiring and training the service staff. The training should not be a one-time session, but continuous. The manager must follow up on the training through observation and evaluation. Service standards must be explained and maintained. As repetition is the best teacher, here again are the seven guidelines of service:

1. Ladies are served before men (if children are present, they should be served first, then ladies, then men).
2. Food is served from the guest's left side with the service person's left hand.
3. Beverages are served from the guest's right side with the service person's right hand.
4. All guests' food must be brought to the table at the same time.
5. Guest plates should not be removed from the table until all guests are finished eating their meal.
6. Dirty plates should never be stacked or scraped on the guests' table.
7. Dirty dishes are cleared from the guest's right side with the service person's right hand.

Serving the Meal

The sequence of serving a meal is relatively the same from restaurant to restaurant. It generally is served in the following sequence:

• Drinks
• Appetizer
• Rolls and Butter

- Salad
- Entree
- Coffee/tea
- Dessert
- Wine is served when requested, either with dinner or immediately when ordered.

In some restaurants, the salad course is served in the European tradition, after the entree.

Special instructions should be given by the manager to the staff concerning substitutions; furthermore, menu items should be clearly explained and the service staff should know them.

However, people occasionally do not learn the material unless they know they will use it. More and more restaurants have tests as part of their training program. Passing a test is one of the criteria for obtaining a job with the restaurant. This makes the applicant and the employees realize that the restaurant is serious about providing proper service.

Waiting Tables: A Three-Part Job

Bruce Griffin Henderson states in his book, *Waiting*: "There are three main components to the job of waiting tables. 1. Selling food and beverages; 2. Delivering food and beverages to the table; and 3. Representing the business to the public. Any restaurant consultant will tell you that a waitstaff can make or break a restaurant; the chef or owner will tell you that their unique genius is responsible for any success the restaurant has, but the waitstaff is responsible for any and all failure. Most restaurant customers never have any contact with the chef or the owner, so their impression of how they were treated is created by their interaction with the waitstaff."[2]

Methods of Service

Staffing in an American dining room depends on the management of the restaurant. There are three ways in which the dining room can be organized for service. The most common method has one person waiting on a specified number of tables, aided by a busperson. The second is borrowed from the French system, which has a captain responsible for an area of the restaurant. The captain is assisted by service persons and buspersons. The third method is a relatively new system, the **team system**. As the name implies, a great amount of teamwork is needed to make this system succeed.

The manager needs to know how each of the above systems works, in addition to their advantage and disadvantages. It is then up to the restaurant manager to decide what type of system will work best in his or her restaurant. The critical part of making any system work is training and follow-up. All of the systems explained below will work if the manager trains and reinforces the policy constantly.

Regardless of the method of service a restaurant uses, all follow the general sequence stated above. Lists of the advantages and disadvantages of each system follow.

INDIVIDUAL SERVICE PERSON METHOD

The service person is assigned a small area of the restaurant called a station. It is the sole responsibility of that service person to provide expert service to all the guests at the station. The service person must be extremely organized. If any mistakes are made or if the service person

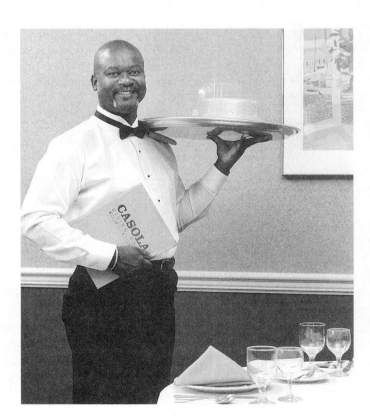

FIGURE 5-6

The individual service person. He is responsible for presenting the menu, taking the order, and serving the meal and beverage. Photograph by Randall Perry.

cannot handle all the problems in the station, the guests will receive poor service. The station generally has between sixteen and twenty-four seats. Many restaurants provide buspersons (one for every two to three service staff) to assist in clearing the dirty plates. Figure 5-6 shows a service person and his responsibilities.

The advantages of the individual service person method are as follows:

1. It is an easy method to teach and learn.
2. The guests know their service person.
3. The manager knows who is responsible for service.
4. The service person gets to keep all of the tips.
5. The service person knows that he or she is responsible for the serving and guest satisfaction of the total meal.

However, this method has disadvantages as well:

1. If there is a problem, the service person can become overwhelmed and the result will be to provide poor service.
2. Service people may have no one to rely on if there is a problem. However, many times servers will back each other up if there is a problem.
3. Because training is so simple, employees can easily move from job to job. This system does not encourage loyalty to the restaurant.
4. The service person is responsible for serving the entire meal. If the service person is performing poorly, the guest will have a poor dining experience.

CAPTAIN METHOD

This system is characterized by having a captain responsible for a double or triple station. The captain has been promoted from service person. The service staff assist the captain in serving the station. There may even be a busperson to assist the service staff and captain. The captain is usually in a supervisory position, and acts as a sort of public relations person. Captains generally stay in the dining room, while the service staff obtain and serve food from the kitchen.

The advantages of the captain method:

1. The restaurant has other supervisors besides the host or manager in the dining room.
2. The guests will have more than one person to serve them.
3. If a problem develops, the captain can assist the other service staff in the station.

4. The guests will have the benefit of having an experienced—and, most likely, a personable—individual to take their order.

The disadvantages:

1. A restaurant must have an individual experienced in both supervision and waiting to fill this position.
2. The job descriptions and roles are clearly defined; thus, not much flexibility is built into this system.
3. The guest is expected to leave a larger tip because if must cover both the captain and service staff.

TEAM SYSTEM

A system that was characterized as an idea whose time has come was highlighted in *Nation's Restaurant News*: the team system.

Ross Sponder owns the forty-eight-seat diner restaurant called the Palace Café in Santa Barbara, California. In his system, a service person takes the initial order and informs the customers that any of the twelve waiters or waitresses can help them with whatever they want. Each table has a pamphlet that states: "Our staff works as a team in order to better serve you. You need not look for the person who initially took your order for additional service. Just ask anyone! This system of service is designed to help you enjoy your time here by making everyone on our staff available to take care of your table."[3]

Sponder has virtually no employee turnover. His biggest challenge was breaking the service staff of the habit of sticking to their individual territories or stations. But the problem was overcome by requiring dining room servers to pass an intense practical examination.

The teamwork concept has turned out to be a highly efficient style that makes jobs easier, provides better service, and results in higher gratuities.

FIGURE 5-7

The typical number of guests a service staff should be responsible for at a station

SIZE OF STATIONS	
Type of Service	**Number of Seats at Station**
Individual Service Person	16-24
Captain	48-72
Team	40-45

La Paloma in North Miami, Florida uses a similar system. A service person takes the orders and gives them to the kitchen staff. Speed runners bring food to the tables, while the service staff answers customer questions. The result is speedier and more efficient service. Michael Hurst of 15th St. Fisheries believes that restaurants should keep servers at their stations. He uses runners to bring food from the kitchen at his restaurant.

HOW THE TEAM SYSTEM OPERATES

The team is divided up into three positions, an **Aid**, a **Lead**, and a **Follow-up**. The two critical jobs are the Lead and the Follow-up. Normally, a team is responsible for a station with between twelve and fourteen tables and forty to forty-five seats. A restaurant of 150 seats usually has three teams serving the guests. It generally takes five months to master the concept of team service. Because of the long training period, this reduces the normally high turnover of service people.

The Aid

The first job that is learned is that of the Aid. Of the three positions, the Aid training takes the longest to master, about three to four weeks. This is because the new employee must learn the policies, menu, and organization of the restaurant. The Aid has the following responsibilities:

1. The normal duties of the busperson
2. Picking dinners up from the kitchen and delivering them to the guests (this is the only part of the meal in which the Aid participates)
3. Taking dirty entree dishes from the guest table, if the Lead requests

The Lead

The Lead is the first member of the team that the guest comes in contact with in this system. The Lead should be personable and a suggestive salesperson. The two main duties of the Lead are suggestive selling and timing of placing dinner orders into the kitchen. The duties of the lead are as follows:

1. Suggestive selling for drinks and appetizers
2. Serving drink orders
3. Taking the guest's drink and dinner orders
4. Obtaining additional drinks for the guest

FIGURE 5-8

The team system. The Lead presents the menu and takes the order. The Follow-Up is holding the tray, and the Aid is holding the water pitcher. Photograph by Randall Perry.

5. Selling and serving wine
6. Setting the place of service for the other two team members
7. Turning the dinner order into the kitchen and timing the dinners

The Follow-Up

The Follow-Up is the quarterback of the section, making sure the station runs smoothly. This is the most mentally demanding of the three jobs. This person must run the section, making sure the guests are satisfied and solving problems. The Follow-Up is the one member of the team who should never leave the station. If it is necessary to leave the station, the Follow-Up should have the Aid and Lead assume the duties. The Follow-Up has the following responsibilities:

1. Checking the guest satisfaction with the meals
2. Conversing with the guests about their meals
3. Assisting the other two members of the team in taking orders (Lead) or serving meals (Aid), if necessary
4. Solving any problems concerning the meals
5. Clearing dirty dishes from the guest's table
6. Suggesting and selling dessert
7. Totaling up and presenting the check to the guests
8. Collecting the money for the guest check

ADVANTAGES AND DISADVANTAGES OF THE TEAM SYSTEM

The team system, done properly, provides the guest with the best service. The reason for this is that there is always a service person available if the guest has a problem. One member of the team is on the floor of the restaurant at all times. The team members are always available, but they are not hovering over the guest, as is the case with the individual service person.

The biggest problem for the guests is that they often get confused because they are being waited on by three people. Guests don't understand how the team system works and are confused over who is getting the tip.

The advantages of this system:

1. There are three people to take care of the guests' needs.
2. A professional service staff is obtained through a thorough training program
3. It provides an organized system for anticipating guests' needs.
4. There is a consistent peer evaluation of service.
5. Jobs are clearly defined, but flexibility is built into the system.

Its disadvantages:

1. An extensive training period is needed.
2. The system may be difficult for experienced service to accept.
3. Guests become confused about who is serving them.

The team system has nontraditional job titles and names. But the job descriptions resemble the traditional jobs found in restaurants that provide their guests with American dining room service. Once the team system is mastered, restaurants are reluctant to go back to the old method of service.

Wine Service

Regardless of the type of service a restaurant uses, the staff would be instructed in the proper method of serving wine. Knowledge of wine and wine service by the service staff is essential for guest enjoyment.

Restaurant patrons should be encouraged to enjoy wine with their meal by the service staff. In order to do this, the service staff must be knowledgeable about wine. For instance, the staff must know what wine best complements what food, and how to present and serve wine properly. This section will not cover what wine complements what food, but it will discuss wine service. Service people should take courses on wine and sample wine with foods to become confident and knowledgeable on the subject.

As a general guideline, red wines complement foods that are hearty, like prime ribs and steak. White wines are generally served with lighter dishes, but are used mostly for celebrations. If a guest asks for the "wrong" type of wine with a meal, the service person should not challenge the guest's choice of wine. There are some white wines that complement a hearty dish, or the guest may have a favorite wine that is drunk with every meal. The service person may suggest a selection that complements the food, but this depends on the service person's feeling about the guest. After determining that the guest indeed wants the particular wine requested, it should be brought to the guest.

T I P $

TO INSURE PROPER SERVICE

Every time you try a wine, keep a note about what you liked or disliked about the wine. The note should include the name of the wine, along with the vintage and what food you ate with the wine. This is a great method to build up your knowledge of wine and food.

FIGURE 5-9

The correct way to present a bottle of wine. The bottle is held with the sidetowel, with the label facing the guest. Photograph by Randall Perry.

PRESENTING WINE

Once the guest has selected a wine, the server should bring it to the table and present it to the guest for inspection, as illustrated in Figure 5-9. The bottle should be presented with the label facing the guest, so the guest can ascertain that the bottle is exactly what was ordered. The server should present the bottle resting on the sidetowel for two reasons: One, if the bottle is wet, the sidetowel will keep the bottle from slipping from the server's hands. Two, the sidetowel acts as an insulator and will not transmit as much of the server's body heat to the wine. Serving wine at the correct temperature adds to the enjoyment of the wine.

As soon as the guest approves of the bottle, the server should open the bottle—at the service stand, not the guest's table. The cork should be presented to the person who has ordered the wine, and a small tasting should be poured into the glass. The guest samples the wine and either approves of it or tells the service person it is not acceptable.

You First!

The purpose of having the host taste the wine first is steeped in history. In ancient times, the way to eliminate your enemy was to invite him or her to your dwelling to share a bottle of wine. It was easy to hide the poison in the wine. The guest was offered the wine first, drank it, and died. Before long, guests demanded that their host sample the wine first, reasoning that if the host drank first, the wine would be safe to drink. The tradition carries on today.

UNACCEPTABLE WINE

If the wine is not acceptable, the service person should ask if the guest would care for another bottle of wine. The service should not challenge the integrity of the guest, but should inquire what is wrong with the wine. Depending on the policy of the restaurant, the guest may or may not be charged for the wine.

Restaurants that have expensive bottles of wine often employ a different method of handling wine service. When a guest orders an expensive bottle of wine, the manager is called to the guest's table. The guest is told the conditions of the purchase. For instance, the manager may say, "You have made an excellent choice on the 1898 Chateau Lafite Rothschild. However, because the wine is so old, the restaurant cannot guarantee the quality of the wine. If we open the wine for you, you must pay for it." The guest then has the option of accepting or refusing the wine.

SERVING WINE

When the guest approves the wine, the server should pour the wine into the guests' glasses using the guidelines for serving beverages. Red wine glasses should be half-filled. White and sparkling wines should be poured three-quarters to the top of the glass. Sparkling wines should be served in two steps. The service person should pour an amount into the glass so the bubbles and foam will not overflow the glass. Then the other glasses are poured in the same manner. The service person should then go back to the first glass that was poured and continue to fill up that glass so the guest receives a glass that is three-quarters filled. As the service person finishes pouring any type of wine, the bottle should be rotated to the right to prevent the wine from dripping.

Red wines should be placed on the guest's table. The sparkling and white wines are placed in a container to keep them at their proper temperature. This container is either an ice bucket placed near the guest's table or a container that retains the cold temperature and sits on the table. Throughout the meal, the service person should return to the table and refill the guests' wine glasses when needed.

PROPER SERVING TEMPERATURE OF WINE

Serving wines at the proper temperature is essential for guest enjoyment. When wines are served correctly they offer incredible perfumes and bouquets. Proper temperature balances the sweetness and acidity in wine.

White, rosé, and sparkling wines should be served chilled. Sparkling and sweet dessert wines should be served at 35° to 45° Fahrenheit. Rosés and dry white wines should be served at 45° to 55° Fahrenheit. These wines should be stored in a cooler for at least two hours. If they are not, and the guest orders a wine that should be served chilled, the service person can put it in a bucket with ice and water. It will be the proper temperature in about fifteen or thirty minutes. However, any restaurant that sells wine should have proper refrigeration.

Red wines should be served at the old European temperature of 55° to 65° Fahrenheit. A red wine served too warm goes out of balance and

PROPER SERVING TEMPERATURES OF WINE

Name of Wine	Serving Temperature (°Fahrenheit)
Wine coolers, Rosés, Beaujolais, White Wines	45 to 55
Red Wines	55-65
Sparkling, Sweet White Dessert	35-45

FIGURE 5-10

The proper serving temperatures of wines

becomes overwhelming. Particularly robust reds that contain more than 13 percent alcohol begin to smell like ether. It also causes a slight warm sensation in the wine drinker's throat. If red wines are served too cold, they lose their aroma and bouquet. Coldness brings out the astringency in the tannin and makes the wine taste harsh. It if is possible, a red wine should be opened for half an hour before serving to let it breathe. This breathing makes the wine taste smoother.

Serving wine with a meal adds to the pleasure of the dining experience. Restaurants with service staffs that are knowledgeable concerning wines and wine service offer their guests an additional benefit.

SUMMARY

1. There are four typical service positions in American service: captain, wine steward, busperson, and service person.
2. There are three methods of service: the individual service person, captain, and team methods.
3. Six important factors are taken into consideration when a room is divided into stations.
4. Sidework is essential for a smooth-running operation.
5. The proper serving sequence of a meal and the proper method of wine service are of the utmost importance for the maximum enjoyment of the guests.

REVIEW QUESTIONS

1. What is the best system for your restaurant? Now that you have read and know about the three systems, which one would you choose for your restaurant? Give specific reasons why you would choose one system over the others.

2. What are the four traditional job titles for dining room service personnel? Explain the duties of these employees.
3. List and explain five qualities that applicants must have to be successful as dining room service personnel.
4. What is the main difference between the captain system and the team system in dining room operations?
5. Explain the jobs of the wine steward and dining room attendant.
6. What are the stations? What factors contribute to assigning stations?
7. What are the two methods for assigning stations? In your opinion, which is the better method? Explain your answer.
8. What is sidework? Why is it necessary in a restaurant? What are its benefits for the service staff?
9. Explain and list the seven guidelines of service.
10. What is the sequence of courses in a typical American a la carte restaurant? Is there ever any change in the sequence of courses? If so, explain when and why.
11. What are the three positions in the team service, and what are the individual responsibilities?
12. What should a service person know about wine service? What are the proper temperatures at which wine should be served to guests?

REFERENCE

1. "Ivy Operators Share Tips For Cultivating Staff," *Restaurant & Institutions*, 30 May 1992, 115.
2. Bruce Griffin Henderson, *Waiting: Waiters' True Tales of Crazed Customers, Murderous Chefs, and Table Side Disasters* (New York: Plume/Penguin Press: 1995).
3. Charles Bernstein, "Teamwork Service: An Idea Whose Time Has Come," *Nation's Restaurant News*, 10 August 1987, 13.

Part Two

Dining Room Management

6

Training the Service Staff to Serve the Meal

OBJECTIVES

At the completion of this chapter, the reader will be able to:

1. State the importance of thorough knowledge of the menu
2. State why service persons should know the ingredients of all menu items
3. Write down and organize food and beverage orders so that there will be no question of who gets what
4. Explain the importance of cooking times
5. Understand the importance of suggestive selling and merchandising
6. Define the term *86*, and tell how to avoid problems with 86 items
7. Order food from the kitchen
8. Give the serving sequence of a meal
9. Explain the importance of training, testing, and evaluating employees
10. Explain the purpose of a substitution or no substitution policy
11. Understands the value of a computerized register system

The Manager's Role

The dining room manager is the key to a successful restaurant. The manager sets the tone and the pace of the establishment. The success or failure of the restaurant is determined by the manager. The manager should not be at the restaurant twenty-four hours a day, or even eighteen; but the restaurant should run as if he or she were.

How do successful restaurant managers make their businesses run effectively, even when they are not present? By proper selection, teaching, training, and continuous evaluation of all employees. A dining room manager is like an orchestra leader. The orchestra leader does not play an instrument; the dining room manager does not serve food; but both of them are responsible for their guests' enjoyment. They both have to select, teach, train, and evaluate their talented employees, so the guests will have an enjoyable experience. In addition, the restaurant manager's attitude is passed to the patrons by the employees.

The importance of competency and friendliness have been emphasized in the previous chapters. There are many types of service available for the restaurant manager to choose. But all this does not make good service. The final important element in providing excellent service occurs because the staff *knows* and *communicates* information that adds to the guests' enjoyable dining experience.

Parts of the Meal

All dining experiences can be broken into three parts, as it relates to service. The first part is getting prepared to serve the guests. The next part is merchandising and taking the meal order. Finally, comes the actual service of the meal.

It does not matter if a restaurant offers French, American, or Russian service to the guests; nor does it matter what the style or service (team, individual service person, or captain) is. The following information will apply in all settings.

Learning the Menu

The dining room manager should insist that all employees know all the information about items on the menu. Employees should know which foods or beverages are offered, their pronunciation, and their ingredients. It is the responsibility of the manager to prepare this information for the employees. The information must be clearly written in a manual and given to all of the employees. Many restaurants, such as Specialty Restaurants and Casa Lupita Mexican Restaurants, are using this type of training method.

True Food Experts

Up until now, I don't believe the service staff has received as much education as it needs. We concentrate so much on training the kitchen staff. The servers aren't taught about the food, and yet they are the people who have contact with the customers. I think it's time that changed. I think the time has come to educate servers and turn them into true food experts," said Reimund Pitz, a Certified Master Chef at the MGM Studios Theme Park at Walt Disney World.[1]

In order to make certain that the employees become knowledgeable, they are tested on the material. Casa Lupita stresses to its employees that customers have no idea about what it is like to open a restaurant. Guests don't think about the problems of a restaurant; they simply want good food and service. Applicants should be told when hired that knowledge of the material in the training manual is a requirement to start and keep the job. The Barnside Restaurant chain manual states clearly the purpose of knowing the information. They inform their applicants that they must know the material before they are allowed to work on the floor of the dining room, because they do not use their guests as guinea pigs for training the service staff. Therefore, before any person becomes a service person he or she must know the material required by the chain. The appendix of the manual contains a series of tests that may be asked of the applicants. The applicants are required to know 90 percent of the answers to the questions before they are allowed to work on the dining room floor. All managers should set up a policy of testing employees on material. There should be a test covering all the items that the manager feels are important to make the guests' meal an enjoyable experience.

Lack of Knowledge

A couple went out for dinner in an area noted as a summer vacation resort. The waiter approached the table to inquire if the guests wanted a before-dinner drink. The woman ordered a whisky sour and the man asked, "What kind of ale do you have?" The waiter thought for a moment and then blurted out "Ginger, sir." The man had to explain to the waiter that he was inquiring about an alcoholic beverage, not a soft drink! Obviously, the service person had very little or no training. He certainly did not know all the items on the menu.

The training manual must cover areas such as general policies, food prices and descriptions, beverage prices and descriptions, and specific information about the restaurant. Is it hard to set up a training manual? Is it hard to evaluate employees? Does it take a lot of the manager's time? Of course, it does. But it pays off in guest satisfaction, return business, and—in the long run—profits!

Dining Out: What Went Wrong?

A party of six had dinner at a restaurant. The restaurant seated about 150 on several levels. There was a large rectangular bar with tables surrounding it. About four tables were occupied, with a total of fifteen guests in the restaurant. One bartender, a hostess, and six service persons appeared to be staffing the restaurant.

The guests were seated at an 8-top. Next to the table were two round tables, both 6-tops. One of the guests asked the hostess if the group could move to one of the 6-tops, and the hostess instructed the waitress to move the party.

The waitress moved the menus and place settings to the new table. She then asked for their orders. They ordered salad and asked her what the salad dressing choices were. She said she didn't know because that was her first night on the job, though she had worked at the restaurant during the summer, before she went away to college. She asked the waitress next to her for the choice of salad dressings and then repeated them back to the guests. One of the guests was reading her menu and did not hear the choices. When she ordered her salad, the whole process had to be repeated, with their waitress again asking the other waitress the choice of salad dressings.

It was now time to order the main course. The first guest ordered a burger without a bun and a Diet Coke (she had asked for her dressing to be served in a separate dish for her salad). The other guests ordered their main courses also.

Five of the six meals were delivered to the table. The order for the first guest (the hamburger) was served on a bun. There were three other meals, besides the hamburger, which were to receive French fries as an accompaniment. Each meal had on the plate, the sandwich, an orange garnish and a sprig of parsley, plus a large area of white space left on the plate. Five minutes later, the waitress brought a community basket of French fries to the table, explaining that they had not been ready when she had brought out the other food. The sixth meal (Cajun-style shrimp) was finally brought to the table along with the French fries.

Coffee was asked for and brought. The coffee was served with a napkin between the cup and saucer. The coffee spilled all over the napkin. The waitress asked the customer if she wanted a new napkin. The customer felt like saying "No, I'd rather slop it over my dress."

What is wrong with this restaurant and who is responsible for this mess?

What Should the Service Person Know?

Before a manager allows employees to wait on guests, there are many facts they should know. The first group of facts deals with specific policies about the restaurant. Acceptable standards of appearance, dress, and attendance should be explained before the service person has been hired. Additional items, such as what time to report to work, food and drink policies concerning consumption both on and off the job, and serving hours, should also be explained to the employees. These facts must be reinforced in a training booklet.

The next set of facts should deal with the establishment. The purpose of having these facts known is so the service people can answer any and all questions that guests ask. The guest will feel good about the service person if he or she is able to answer questions intelligently and confidently.

A third group of facts should be concerned with the physical layout of the restaurant. It should also explain how to order and pick up food and beverages. There should be an area that explains how to write and read guest dinner checks. The list is long but important for a successfully run restaurant.

KNOWLEDGE ABOUT THE RESTAURANT

Guests perceive service persons in two ways: Are they nice, and can they answer questions? Guests will ask many questions. Most of them are legitimate, but others may seem silly. However, they are not silly to the guest.

All of the employees must know the history of the business. For example, questions will be asked concerning the ownership of the restaurant; how long has it existed; and what are the names and locations of other restaurants in the chain.

Other facts employees should know are the days and hours of operation of their restaurant. If there are any other restaurants on the premises or in the hotel, the employees should know their hours of operation, type of foods served, the general price range, and the dress code.

One area in the manual should outline trivia and historical information about the community and the restaurant. For instance, room 1140 of the DeWitt Clinton Hotel in Albany, New York, was where Thomas Dewey spent election night in 1948. When he went to bed that November evening all the pollsters had predicted that he had won the presidential election in a landslide. When he awoke, Harry S. Truman was the new President of the United States.

There should be a daily listing stating what events are occurring in the restaurant, hotel, and community.

All of this information is vital for the service person to be able to answer questions intelligently and to converse with guests. This knowledge demonstrated by the service person will made the guest feel comfortable and confident in the server's ability. Occasionally there will be a question asked to which the service person does not know the answer. Management should provide a method for service people to obtain the answer. Many establishments compile a "fact book" that is kept at the host stand or, in a hotel, at the front desk.

PHYSICAL LAYOUT OF THE RESTAURANT

In order for the service staff to take orders and deliver food correctly to the guest tables, all employees should receive a floor plan of the dining room. The floor plan should have the size and number of each table in the dining room. The diagram should be planned so that the employees will be able to understand it. Confusion should be kept to a minimum. For example, instead of numbering the tables in a haphazard manner, all tables in the first row would be labeled from 10 to 19, the second row from 20 to 29, and so on. As most dining room tables remain in the same location day after day, the staff will know the location of each table. It is much simpler for a manager to say, "Check table 21 for a problem," than to say, "The guy over at the table by the window has a problem." All employees will know exactly where table 21 is located by memorizing the floor plan.

FIGURE 6-1

A numbered floor plan diagram. The tables are numbered in a logical pattern to make it easier for the service staff to do their job efficiently. Tables illustrated with a circle (#20) seat from six to eight guests; those with a rectangle (#2), four guests; and those drawn at an angle (#10), two guests.

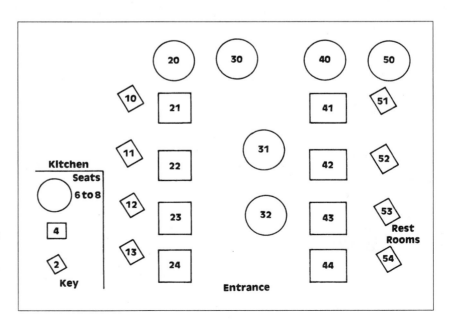

It is also important in the floor plan to label the size of the tables. However, most service people are not concerned with the size of the table (e.g., 60 inches in diameter); instead they are concerned with how many guests each table seats. The diagram must state the number of guests each table seats. The diagram must state the number of seats at each table. An easy method for diagramming the size and numbers of the tables is illustrated in Figure 6-2. Notice that all tables are numbered in the manner described above. Some of the table numbers have a circle around them, others have a rectangle, while still others are drawn at an angle. In addition, some tables are drawn larger in size than the other tables—another helpful visual reminder. By designing the floor plan carefully and making the employees memorize it, service will run more smoothly.

WRITING AND READING THE ORDER

The manager should stress to the employees the correct way to write and read a guest check. The manager must translate all the menu items into *standard abbreviations*. Each item must have its own abbreviation.

All employees (including kitchen staff) are required to know and use the abbreviations when ordering food from the kitchen or serving food. This is to prevent any confusion in the restaurant. For example, what does *SS* on the check mean? Would the guest receive shrimp scampi, sirloin steak, or swiss steak? Abbreviations are used for all menu items, including accompaniments. For example, *BAK* would mean a baked potato, while *BAKy* means that the guest has requested sour cream with the baked potato.

Many times restaurants offer a children's menu. The children's portion would be abbreviated with the letter *C* in front of it. For example, if *SS* means sirloin steak, a *CSS* is a child's portion of sirloin steak.

With the advent of computerized systems, which transmit orders directly to the kitchen, does a service person still need to know the importance of using abbreviations? Yes. It will help the service staff know which guest gets which meal, for one thing. Also, in the case of an electronic or computer failure, the service staff should know how to use this method.

TIP$

TO INSURE PROPER SERVICE

Joseph Pierce of Pierce's 1894 Restaurant in Elmira Heights, NY, a Nation's Restaurant News Hall of Fame Restaurant, says, "Detail—little things make the big difference. Stay within your capabilities."[2]

KNOWLEDGE OF THE MENU

Many times guests are not familiar with your menu, so they ask the service person about the entrees. For example, a guest will ask "What is the shrimp scampi?" The service person should know the names of all items, how to pronounce them, and how to describe them. The training manual should have a description of all menu items. Shrimp scampi is as follows:

Shrimp Scampi

Pronounced *Shrimp Skamp-ee*
Abbreviation SKP
Five sized 15/18 shrimp, sautéed in garlic butter and served over a bed of wild and white rice.

All items on the menu should be described in this manner and the staff must know all of them before they are allowed to wait on guests.

Ingredients

Many people are allergic to certain spices and foods. In the description about the shrimp scampi, the ingredient garlic is mentioned. The manager should list any spices or ingredients that are predominant in the recipe. For example, when a guest asks if there are any sulfates in a food item, they are asking for a specific reason. In addition, the manager should also instruct the service persons to ask the chef about the ingredients in the food if they do not know them. The service person should not guess about ingredients in food. Many guests have gotten ill because a service person guessed rather than knew the ingredients of a dish.

Many people have severe allergic reactions to some types of foods, spices, additives, and other ingredients. Allergic reactions have killed individuals who unknowingly or accidentally ate a particular food item or ingredient.

TIP$

To Insure Proper Service
Make certain your service staff know all the ingredients in menu items!

If your staff do not know the ingredients, the consequences could be serious. The family of Janet Walker of Plaistow, New Hampshire, sued

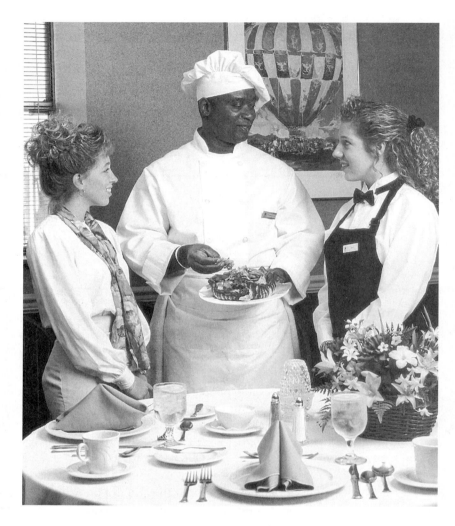

FIGURE 6-2

Having the chef explain particular items is a good way for the service person to learn the menu. Photograph by Randall Perry.

Bertucci's Inc., a Wakefield, Massachusetts restaurant chain, for $10.4 million in Massachusetts state court, claiming the woman was killed by an allergic reaction to its pesto sauce.

She went into a coma in January 1994 after she ate part of a chicken pesto sandwich at a Bertucci's in New Hampshire. She died a week later.

Mrs. Walker's lawyer, J. Albert Johnson, said Mrs. Walker specifically asked her waitress if the pesto sauce contained nuts. The waitress allegedly told Mrs. Walker that the sauce contained only basil and other herbs, failing to mention that it also contained walnuts and pine nuts, both of which Mrs. Walker was allergic to.

The lawsuit claims Bertucci's withheld from the waitstaff a list of the ingredients for the "secret sauce."[3]

Figure 6-3 shows a variety of food presented on a buffet. The service staff should know the names and ingredients of all the foods.

Garnishes and Substitutions

In the manual, there should be an area that explains how each food item should be garnished. A diagram or picture of where the garnish is placed and how it looks is helpful. For instance, the manual would state that all hamburger plates are garnished with a leaf of romaine lettuce and with an orange slice at the three o'clock position on the plate, as shown in Figure 6-4.

At the end of the food item section, there should be an explanation of what each guest receives in the form of accompaniments with a meal. For example, all beef items will be served with *BAK*. It is a good idea to use the abbreviations in the manual so that the employees will realize the importance of learning and using them. Of course, management should include in the manual a definition page for all abbreviations.

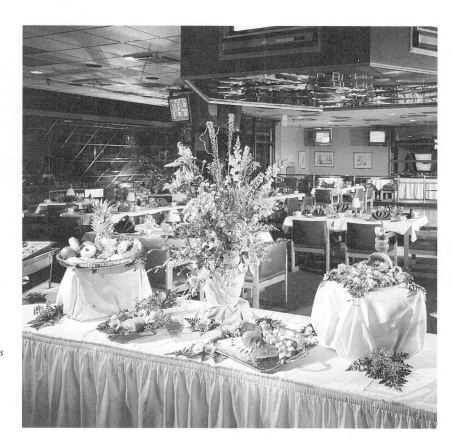

FIGURE 6-3

For a buffet, the service staff must know the names of the items and the ingredients used to make them. Photograph by Randall Perry.

FIGURE 6-4

Diagram of the positions of items on a plate, using a clock as a guide. The hamburger is placed from 4 to 8 o'clock, the French fries from 9 to 1 o'clock, and the romaine and orange at 2 and 3 o'clock, respectively. When served to the guest, the orange is placed at the 3 o'clock position.

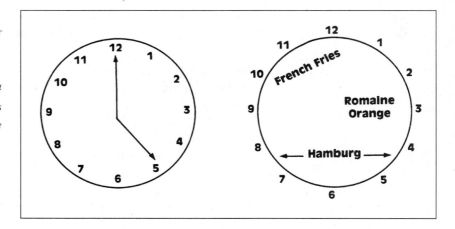

Finally, in this section there should be an area that states what (if any) the substitutions are for each item. For example, *RIC* (rice) can be substituted for any *BAK*. It is important to have a clearly stated policy for substitutions. Some guests will have a legitimate reason for asking for the substitution; others only do it to get more food for their money. If the service persons have questions about what items may be substituted, they should be instructed to ask the person in charge of the restaurant.

No matter how large or small the restaurant is, if the manager writes out the policies, the guest will receive the same meal and the same answers to the questions, regardless of the service person. Most likely, the restaurant will be more profitable, because guests will feel comfortable knowing there is consistency every time they dine at the restaurant. They will not be frustrated because one time they are allowed to substitute *RIC* for *BAK* and the next time they are not.

Cooking Methods

Guests often inquire about terms on the menu that are unfamiliar to them. For instance, a guest may ask the meaning of *sauté*. Each employee should know the more common preparation methods of cooking foods. There are at least twelve methods. This information is also needed in the manual. An example of two cooking methods: *Baked*—cooked by dry, continuous heat in an oven; *sautéed*—browned or cooked in a small amount of hot fat.

Preparation Time and Cooking Doneness

This is a critical part of the service person's training. Knowing how long it takes to cook an item and knowing what "medium" or "pittsburgh" means is important for ordering and picking up food from the kitchen.

A chart of the cooking times of all menu items should be listed. The chart should range from pittsburgh to well done, with the normal cooking time for each item.

To Insure Proper Service

Knowing the approximate cooking time of an item may make the service person a star to the guest who is in a hurry!

In addition, there should be a description of what the terms for cooking doneness mean. A diagram of all the types of cooking doneness that the chef can prepare is most helpful. For example, a steak ordered medium would be described as having a pink hot center. One unusual way to cook meat is referred to as pittsburgh. A steak done in this manner is raw on the inside and black on the outside. It is cooked by having the cook drop fat onto the fire. This cause a big flame to rise through the grill. The cook chars the outside until it is black; the inside is raw and cold to touch.

ALCOHOLIC BEVERAGES

As with the food, there should be a description of every beverage the restaurant has available. In addition, there should be a description of how the drinks are made, the glass the drink is served in, and the proper garnish. The brand names of all wines and beverages must also be included in the section on alcoholic beverages. Here is an example of a drink description:

Margarita

Pronounced *Marg a rita*
Abbreviation MARG
Made with tequila, triple sec, lemon, and lime. Served in a fiesta grande, straight up ( ) or on the rocks (v). Garnished with salt around the rim of the glass and served with a lime wheel.

Glasses

There should be a diagram or a picture of all the glasses used for drinks. Underneath the picture should be the name of the drink that is served in the glass. There should also be a description of the glass. For example, a *fiesta grande* glass would be described as a 16¾ ounce glass used for all frozen margaritas.

Pricing

Because menus are constantly being changed, a separate price sheet should be distributed with the current prices. Owing to the fluctuation of prices, putting prices into the manual would be a waste of time and money. The prices will most likely change more often than any other information in the manual. When done on a separate sheet, the manager only has to print the new prices instead of the entire manual.

TASTING THE FOOD AND BEVERAGE

This is another part of the training for the service staff that must be continuous. However, many restaurant managers refuse to let their staff taste the food. Instead, they serve them an employee meal each evening. The feeling is that it is too expensive to serve to the staff. In reality, it is too expensive not to serve it to the staff. The guests are going to ask the service person how the food tastes. If they have never been allowed to sample the food, how will your service staff know what to tell the guests? The service staff should taste all food and beverage items as soon as it is practical. This does not mean that each night, the service staff should have a gourmet meal; but they must taste the food that they will be recommending and serving to their guests. One way of accomplishing this is by having meetings where the service staff sample the menu items. Or management could encourage the service staff to entertain their families at the restaurant and purchase their meals at a discount.

Once the service staff has mastered the knowledge concerning the restaurant and menu by the testing criteria set up, it is time for them to move on to the second part: serving the meal.

Has this ever happened to you?

At a restaurant, you are asked by the service person if you want a salad. You reply, "Yes." The service person says, "And what would you like on your salad?" That's it: that's all they say. They figure you must be a mind reader. The next time someone says that to you, reply "Poppy seed vinaigrette," or some other made-up salad dressing, and watch the expression on the person's face!

Merchandising Food and Beverage

Merchandising food and beverage is simply another term for selling. Selling occurs because the guest likes and is confident in the service person's ability. This part of the training program should concentrate on getting the guests to like your staff.

This should be done by placing the service staff in common situations that occur daily in the restaurant. This is called role playing. For instance, have the service staff ask the "guests" what type of salad dressing they want, using the example of the problem stated on the preceding page.

The service person should assess the mood of the guests as they approach the table. Are they celebrating and in a festive mood or do they appear somber, as if they have just returned from a funeral? Once the service person has assessed the situation, the behavior should be appropriate for the situation.

Each guest deserves and expects a warm, sincere greeting. If the staff person knows the guest, the guest should be addressed by name. Furthermore, the staff should acknowledge the presence of the guest immediately and take care of any requests as soon as possible. This will make the guest feel as if the restaurant appreciates his or her patronage and will help make the dining experience a positive one.

ASSISTING THE GUEST WITH THE ORDER

Many times guests will know exactly what food they wish to order; other times they cannot make up their minds. There is a trick that experienced service persons use to sell items and help guests make up their minds. If guests are asked for their order and they hesitate, count backwards from seven. If the guests have not made up their minds by the time the server reaches zero, then they need help. And that opens it up for the service staff to sell suggestively.

SUGGESTIVE SELLING

The first step in suggestive selling is having the guests like the service person. Once this happens, the guests will respond to the service person's suggestions. The guests now trust the service person's knowledge and judgement. He or she has answered all the guests' questions about the restaurant, told them what is happening in the area, and is perceived as knowledgeable.

The next question the guests usually ask is, "What's good on the menu?" "Everything," is a poor response. Instead, train your staff to turn the question around and ask the guests what type of food they like, fish or beef? The service person may then describe a meal that tastes and looks great based upon their preference. This is the main reason why employees should be required to taste all items on the menu. They are then able to describe how the food tastes and can base their recommendations on what the guest desires.

No Soup Today

After the server stated the soup special, a guest asked how it was. The reply, "It's OK." No orders of soup were sold at that table!

The key to suggestive selling is for the service person to keep a positive attitude. The staff must put themselves in their guests' place, then use mouth-watering descriptions of the menu item for the purpose of selling the item. The service person shouldn't say, "Would anyone care for dessert?" Instead, he or she should describe the desserts available.

Chocolate, Anyone?

A typical suggestive selling job occurred when a veteran waiter was removing the dinner plates at the end of the meal. While he was crumbing the table, he said, "May I get you coffee?" As soon as the guests said "Yes," he added, "By the way, if you like chocolate, I tasted our great new decadent dessert, the triple chocolate cake. I'll be back with your coffee and a dessert menu." The service person had obtained the guests' trust; they liked him, and he put the idea of a specific dessert in their minds. They all ordered desserts.

If a service person does not suggest desserts, or merely asks the guests if they care to see a dessert menu, too often the answer is "No." By suggesting a specific dessert and using mouth-watering descriptions, the rate of success of selling desserts will be greatly enhanced.

Another technique used by experienced salespeople is to suggest last the item they wish to sell. This is because people usually remember the last thing said to them.

Suggestive selling can build the profits for the restaurant by encouraging guests to order extra items that they normally would not have ordered. It also builds up the check total; and as most guests tip on the total bill, the amount of tip for the service person increases.

THE SPECIAL OF THE DAY

What is the special of the day? If you are shopping in a supermarket or for clothes, a special means reduced prices for that item. Does a special in the restaurant mean reduced prices? Contrary to that, it usually means a special item prepared by the chef. The price is special. In some areas it is lower priced, or "best buy," and in other areas it is higher than a normal menu item.

A manager might do well to change the name of the special of the day to the *chef's creation*. Then the service staff can approach the table and explain the chef's creation to the guests. Should the service staff be instructed to inform the guests of the price of the chef's creation?

In an Ann Landers column, a reader wrote in for advice about etiquette in a restaurant. The reader stated that the service persons rattle off the specials of the day, and while they all sound wonderful, they don't tell you the price. When the bill comes, it is a lot higher than if you had ordered from the menu. Would you buy a shirt or blouse without knowing the price?

No one has ever satisfactorily explained the reason why prices are not given when a special item is offered. In keeping with the premise of this book, that the restaurant's job is to please the guests, the service staff must *recite* the prices to the guests. This is another positive factor that builds up the trust of the guest. Another annoying custom is for restaurants to instruct their service staff to offer an item (such as blue cheese dressing), and state it is "a la carte." Most guests have no idea what a la carte means. The service staff should inform the guests the price of all items.

WINE, DESSERT TABLES, GIMMICKS

Other techniques may assist the service staff in selling additional items in a restaurant. These are usually associated with wine and dessert sales.

More and more restaurants include wine glasses at the place setting. Others sell a sample two-ounce portion of wine to the guests. Still others put a bottle of unopened wine on each table to encourage guests to order wine with their meal.

Desserts provide the opportunity to increase sales enormously. Even though the American public is becoming more nutrition conscious and eating lighter meals, survey after survey has found that guests will order desserts. Many restaurants display their desserts so the guests can view them before they begin their meal. This technique has been used successfully by many restaurants for merchandising desserts. If the desserts are kept attractive and eye-appealing, the guest will usually order dessert. However, if the cart or table becomes messy and unappetizing, it does the restaurant more harm than good.

Another excellent way to merchandise desserts is to bring out a sample tray of all desserts. The service person brings the trays to the guests' table and describes the desserts to them. This method eliminates the problem of the desserts looking unattractive, because the desserts on the tray are not served to the guests. Instead, the service person obtains the desserts from the kitchen. As soon as a dessert on the tray looks unappealing, it is replaced.

One of the best selling gimmicks that has been used for ages is initiated by the manager. If done properly, it can increase sales and repeat business dramatically. It involves the manager giving away an item that will call attention to that item. For example, a restaurant sells flaming coffee. The manager should approach a table in the center of the dining room, where other guests can see the coffee being prepared. The manager should introduce himself or herself to the guests, inquire about their meal, thank them for their business, and offer to buy them an after dinner coffee. Once the coffee is being prepared, all the eyes in the dining room are attracted to the coffee presentation. This display will encourage other guests to order the coffee after their meals. This can be done with a fancy dessert, large glass of beer, or any type of fancy entree. The cost of this to the restaurant is the cost of the item. In addition, the guest will feel special, because the manager gave away an item (back to Maslow's Hierarchy).

The manager must encourage the service staff to sell extra items. The guests have already made the decision to patronize the restaurant. With suggestive selling, the service staff can increase profits for the restaurant. However, one word of caution: the manager must make certain that the service staff do no push so hard that the guests become upset with their selling aggressiveness and have a bad dining experience.

Taking the Order

Training your staff to take a guest's food and beverage order correctly is critical. There are many correct methods to take the order. All of them should have one goal: to serve the meal to the guest without having to ask who gets what.

The manager should teach the service staff how to talk to the guests and how to take meal orders. The staff should not be allowed to say to the guest, "Whadda ya want?" instead of "May I take your order?" Avoid addressing guests by "hon," "doll," "fella," "madam," and other words that can be interpreted as derogatory. The staff should be encouraged to address people by their names; always by the last name, unless the guests tell the service people to call them by their first names.

The manager must impress upon the service staff that they should treat the guests as if they had never dined at the restaurant before. They do not know how the specials are made or what the salad dressing is that evening. It must be impressed upon the service staff that this will be the first time the guest hears the specials. Even though the service staff may have repeated them one hundred times that evening, employees should be taught to explain every item to each guest.

The manager must train staff to explain in detail the chef's creation of the evening. When it is time to offer the guest the choice of salad dressings or vegetables, explain what they are. Rather than let the staff say, "And what would you like on your salad?" encourage them to say something like: "A salad is included in the meal. Our choice of dressings are: blue cheese; Russian; Italian; and our house dressing, which is a sweet and sour dressing made with mustard and honey." The same should be true for vegetables, potatoes, and chef creations, especially if the item is new or one that is not normally served in the area where your restaurant is located. Included in the explanation can be the ingredients, how it is prepared, and the price.

Finally, the order should be repeated back to the guest. By doing this, your service staff will avoid any misunderstandings of guest orders. However, the method used should not be annoying to the guests. For instance, a service person who echoes every single item that the guest orders will be annoying. It is much better to wait until the complete order is taken and then repeat the main course back to the guest. Should one guest change his order, the service person, in order to avoid a misunderstanding could say, "Your final choice was _____" or "am I clear you wanted _____?"

The job of the service staff should not just be to serve the food, but to be the human link between the kitchen and the guest. This is why the importance of verbal communication between the service staff and the guest must be stressed. It gives the restaurant a personality.

WHERE TO STAND

There are two opinions on where the service persons should be standing when they take the guests' order. Both agree that order taking should follow the proper guidelines of service: children first, then women, then men. There is an exception, when one person is the host of the party and he or she is ordering for the entire table.

The first method states that the service person should stand to the left of the guest and take the order, then move to the next person, following the proper guidelines of service, and take the order. The problem with this method is that if the service person takes the order by following proper guidelines, it may be necessary to skip over one male guest to take the next female's order. The service person will then have to return to the man, and move back and forth, creating much unnecessary confusion.

The second method is to have the service person stand in one spot and take all the guests' orders from that spot, following the proper guidelines of service. This works well at a table with two to four guests. However, for more than four guests, especially with rectangular-shaped tables, the service person may have to move to different spots in order to hear the order.

Whichever method is used, the management should set guidelines for their own restaurant, keeping in mind that guests should be served smoothly and efficiently.

86 ITEMS

The term *86* in the restaurant business means to be out of an item. When a restaurant sells all of its orders of prime ribs, the chef will tell the service staff, "Ribs are 86ed." Before a service person takes the dinner order from the guests, they should know what items are 86ed. Managers must set up a system that provides a list of 86ed items to the service staff, through either oral communication or a blackboard. The manager should train his chef and kitchen staff to inform the service staff when there are ten servings of a particular entree left. The service staff will then be able to inform the guest that they think that the dinner item is available, but will have to check with the kitchen. This will avoid embarrassing the service person and annoying the guest. It is a bad situation to have the guest decide on shrimp scampi, have the service person take the order, and then come back to say, "I'm sorry we are out of the shrimp, what would you care for now?" It gets even more annoying to have the guest then decide on another item, only to find that the kitchen is out of that too. Who will make the third trip to the table to tell the guest?

HOME BASE

Many of you have experienced the auction game. The service person comes to the table with two dinners and asks "Who's the beef and who's the shrimp?" It does sound funny, but it can be embarrassing and insulting. This should never happen. The most common way of taking orders to avoid this is referred to as *home base*.

The home base system works in the following manner: The manager decides on one focal point in the restaurant as the home base. It may be a clock, the kitchen door, or some other satisfactory item in the restaurant. Management has all the tables numbered. At each table, chair one is designated by management so there is no confusion among the service people. Confusion could occur because of a table placed at angle to home base. Once every staff person knows the location of chair one, the chairs are numbered clockwise. This allows any staff member to serve food or drinks to the guests without having to ask who gets what item. Figures 6-5 and 6-6 illustrate how this system works. Figures 6-5 and 6-6 illustrate home base at a four-top with only two guests at the table. In Figure 6-6, using the clock as home base, chair A would be the first chair.

ORDER FORMS

Once the staff know where the home base is, the next thing the manager must teach them is how to write the guest orders. The system must be explained simply enough so that any employee who picks up the food order can deliver it to the guests without having to ask who gets what.

Each person should be provided with some sort of form with which to take orders. The service person must be organized; but it is up to the manager to devise this policy in such a way that all employees will know who gets what item. Some managers, in addition to using the home base

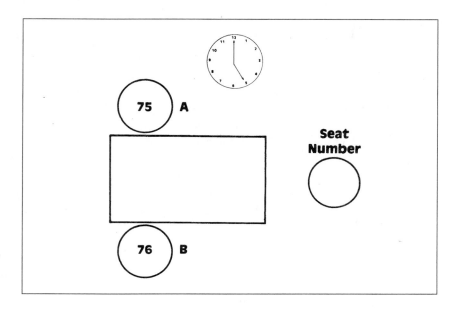

FIGURE 6-5

Using the clock as home base, the seat closest to the clock is home base. Seat A is home base.

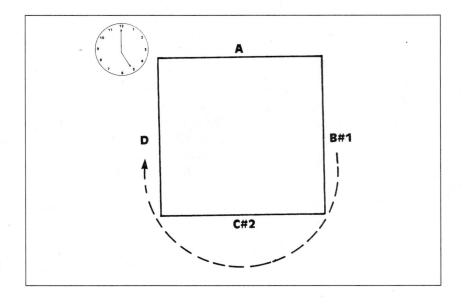

system, will have their staff put an X next to the seat number of the women. This is a variation on the system called *code order*.

Here is an example of a guest's order form:

Order Form

Table Number 49						Time 7:02
Seat	D	App	MC	Sal	Pot	Veg
1	ws	sc	ss	bc	b	gb
2x	ws	os	NYS	it	m	c

In the above example, the woman is seated at seat 2. By putting an X next to her number, all employees will know that an X means a woman is seated there. Because all employees know the standard abbreviations, this form can be used by all staff. The time and table number are also on the form to tell the service person what time the order was taken. This form can be expanded to include desserts and after-dinner drinks; however, it would be preferable to use a new form for these items. Across the top of the form is *D* which stands for before dinner drink; *App* for appetizer; *MC* for main course; *Sal* for salad; *Pot* for potato; and *veg* for vegetable. Because more restaurants are using computerized systems to order food in the kitchen, the manager would be wise to institute the system. The computer system provides for the food order to be transmitted directly to the kitchen, without the service persons entering the kitchen. The printer is programmed to print orders based upon cooking time priority (the longest item to cook is shown first). Even though the computer system relays the order to the kitchen, when it is ready, the restaurant has to have a system in place in order for the employees to know what guest gets what food item.

Training in Evidence

At the Old Homestead Restaurant in Burnt Hills, New York, the competent staff delivers orders quickly and efficiently, without having to ask who gets what item. Every course and every drink are served to the guests properly. The training is evident. No wonder this restaurant is one of the highest grossing restaurants in the Capital District area of New York state.

ORDERING ON THE GUEST CHECK

Some restaurants use a system that has the guest check remain at the table, in a slot provided in each table. The duplicate check (**dupe**) is brought into the kitchen to order the food. The guest check can have the system of "who gets what" directly written on the check. The service staff will write the check in the following manner: The seat immediately to the left of the slot is the number 1 seat. Going in a clockwise direction, the seats are numbered consecutively, 2, 3, 4. The management arranges the tables so that the slots are always in the same position relative to the home base.

On the bottom of the check, the server writes in the table number and the last three digits of the check. This information appears on the dupe which is turned into the kitchen. An example of a check follows:

Sect 5					245666
Chair				**Food**	**Bar**
1	NY	mr	Xs	14.95	
2	Rib	end m	BQ	15.95	
3	Smp +S	r	p	10.95	
4	FsOs	m	1p	16.95	
	Amarone 1–4 (3)				45.00
2	Bq2,4			4.50	
1	mk 3			1.95	
2	c cho 1,3			2.50	
2	wit 2,4				4.50
1	vo w 1				2.25
1	jb v 3				2.25
26/666					

An Explanation of the Check

This check combines many different techniques for taking orders. The service staff must know what all items and abbreviations on the check mean. Working from the bottom of the check up, the 26 represents the table number. As the staff know the layout of the restaurant, they will all know where 26 is located.

The last three numbers of the check 245666 are represented by the 666. Any person who picks up the food in the kitchen will know that the food will be delivered to table 26. Once the food is placed at table 26, the staff member can verify that it is the same check by comparing the last three numbers on the dupe with the guest check in the slot at the table. If there is a problem at table 26, such as food not being served quickly enough, the manager can go into the kitchen and check on the status of the dupe.

The *1 jb v 3* for $2.25 means that there is one order of J & B scotch served with Vichy to the guest in seat number 3 for $2.25. The server can see that it is a drink because the price is listed under the bar column.

Reading up the check, the first food item is the *2 c cho 1,3* for $2.50. This means that there are two orders of clam chowder served to the guests at seats 1 and 3. The total price of $2.50 ($1.25 each) is placed under the food column.

Continuing up the check to the *Amarone 1-4(3)* , the service staff knows that the table ordered one bottle of this red wine, with four glasses. The *(3)* means that the guest seated in seat 3 ordered the wine.

Above the line, the ordering is different. The chair numbers are written, and then the entrees are ordered. For instance, the guest seated in chair 1 is to receive a *NY mr Xs* for $14.95. Translated, this means a New York sirloin, cooked medium rare with baked potato (*x*) with sour cream *(s)*.

These are two methods for writing guest orders and determining who gets what order. There are other methods, but they all have one thing in common: They are set up in an organized manner than can be easily learned. The key is to have the manager decide on one system and have all of the staff use the same system.

CODE ORDER

Another system for determining who gets what is the code order. This system is not recommended, because too much confusion and embarrassment can result. The code order system was used in the past when a single service person was responsible for the station. The service person would write next to the order a code to identify the guest. The code would represent some distinguishing feature that made one guest stand out from the other, such as blue tie or red hair. This system can create problems because not all the service staff would understand the system. It also could be embarrassing if the service person uses a code order that was derogatory toward the guest—such as fat person, bald, or grey hair.

PLACING ORDERS IN THE KITCHEN

Correct ordering in the kitchen is a must for guests to receive their dinner cooked and served properly. As the service staff know the time it takes to cook every item, they should submit their orders based on the mood of the guests and how long it will take to cook the meal. In most restaurants, the time to submit the order is when the service person picks up the guests' salad from the kitchen. In restaurants with a salad bar, the service person is instructed to turn the order into the kitchen when the guests go to obtain their salads from the salad bar. However, each manager can determine what is best for his or her individual unit.

Depending on the type of system, the service persons may be required to order all the entrees at the top of their check. They may put all the cold items at the bottom. Others may have a computerized system that prints all the orders in a priority based on cooking times. It does not matter how it is done, as long as all members of the staff use common abbreviations and the same system.

Serving the Meal: Timing is Everything

This is the critical part of the meal. If the meal is served incorrectly, the evening can be ruined. The service staff has ordered the meal correctly. It has been cooked properly, and the kitchen is waiting for the service person to serve it to the guest in the dining room. But instead of being picked up and delivered to the guest, it sits in the kitchen, becoming colder and less appetizing. Timing is of the essence. The staff must get the meal to the table as soon as it is ready. If the dinners sit too long, the quality suffers, and the guests become impatient.

More and more restaurants are using electronic means to notify the service person that the meal is ready. These electronic devices may include a light system, a vibrating beeper, or other methods to let the service person know that the order is ready to be picked up. As soon as the food is ready, the service person should pick it up and bring it to the table. But before doing so, the service person should take a few seconds to check that all the food items on the dupe match those that have been prepared by the kitchen. He or she must also check to see that all special instructions on the dupe have been followed. The tray will be loaded by placing the cold items first, then the hot items. (The hot items should be placed on the tray last, so they will not cool off fast.) The food on the tray should be arranged to serve the guests in the most efficient manner. Any condiments and garnishes should be brought to the guests' table along with the entrees.

SEQUENCE OF A TYPICAL MEAL

The sequence for serving a typical meal using the team system is as follows:

1. All the sidework has been completed, the service staff are prepared to receive their guests. The service staff know the chef features of the day; what items are 86ed. They have their guest checks and duplicate order forms to take orders.
2. Guests are seated by the host, presented with menus, both food and wine. Chef features are recited or given out using a printed daily chef feature menu.
3. The Lead approaches the table, greets the guests in a friendly manner; answers questions about the menu, and offers to take drink or wine orders.
4. Drinks are written on the check and the order form, using the system that has been taught to all service staff. In the team system, the check never leaves the table. The check is placed back into the slot in the table.
5. Drinks are served on a cocktail napkin in the center of the setting. If the setting has a show or starter plate, the drink is placed on the center of the starter plate. All drinks are served from the right side of the guest with the service person's right hand.
6. The food order is taken by the Lead. The Lead attempts to merchandise the additional items. After the order is taken, the menus are collected by the Lead.
7. The order is placed on a duplicate check; the Lead holds it in his or her pocket until it is time to turn it into the kitchen to order food.
8. The Aid picks up the appetizer (first course) from the kitchen and serves it to the guests. When an appetizer is served and there has

not been a piece of flatware included in the cover for an appetizer, it is brought with the food. For example, if a bowl of soup is served, the soup is served from the left side with the left hand, and the soup spoon is placed on the right side of the guest. The staff do not reach across the front of the guests but walk behind them to put the spoon in its proper location.

9. Rolls and butter are served by the Aid, who places them in the center of the table.

10. The first course is removed from the guest's right with the Aid's right hand.

11. Salad is served, or the guests go to the salad bar. If a guest requests salad dressing on the side, it is placed in a separate container and served on a bread and butter plate, called an **underliner**. The salad is placed in the center of the place setting or on the starter plate.

12. When salads are served, the Lead turns the check into the kitchen for the food to be cooked.

13. Wine is served at this point, or it was served as soon as it was requested. The Lead shows the label to the person who ordered the wine. Once the guest verifies that this is the wine desired, the Lead opens the wine and presents the cork to the guest. The guest should feel the cork (it should be wet) to determine if the wine was stored properly. The Lead then pours about an ounce into the glass of the guest. Once the guest approves of the wine, the Lead pours the wine into the glasses of the guests, using proper serving techniques. Glasses of red wine should be filled ½ full; white, ¾ full. The bottle of red wine is placed on the table, while the white wine should be placed in an ice bucket.

14. Salad plates are removed, as well as the starter plate. If guests tell the service staff they would like to finish their salad with the meal, the staff person should move it to the left of the place setting.

15. When the food order is ready, the kitchen informs the Aid to pick up food by calling out section 1, or by following whatever its system might be for informing service staff when the food is cooked and ready to be served.

16. The entree is picked up in the kitchen. The plates are placed in the same order as written on the duplicate check. The Aid compares the food to the duplicate check. If any mistakes are found, they are corrected immediately. It is the responsibility of the person picking up the food to make certain that the plate is eye-appealing, attractive, and the proper temperature.

17. Before food is served to guests, the service person makes certain that plates are the proper temperature, attractive (no gravy or juices slopped on the rim of the plate), and garnished correctly.

18. All entrees are brought to the table together. If the service person has more entrees than can fit on the tray, another service person carries out the remaining food. All guests receive their food at approximately the same time; no one has to wait while the service person returns to the kitchen to pick up the additional meals.

19. The entree is served without asking who gets what. If vegetables or potatoes are served in a side dish (called monkey dishes), they are placed above and near the main entree dish. The staff never puts one course in front of the guest before the previous course has been removed. If a woman is not finished eating her salad when the service person removes the other salad dishes, her salad dish is removed before her entree is placed in front of her.

20. Condiments that accompany the main courses (such as sour cream, catsup, and so on) are placed on the guests' table.

21. All meat items are placed in front of the guest with the meatiest part facing the guest (meat in front), so when the guest cuts the meat, they cut into the most tender part. If starch and vegetables are served on the same plate, they are placed the farthest from the guest.

22. As soon as all entrees are served to the guests, the service person checks the table to determine if more rolls and butter are needed or if more wine is to be poured, and inquires if there is anything else that the guests would like.

23. Throughout the meal, the Lead constantly checks the tables to determine if guests need more drinks. In order to save time, the Lead learns to take more than one table's order at once. Then the Lead can order ten or twelve drinks at once instead of having to make four separate trips back and forth.

24. The service staff check back at the table as soon as the guests sample their food to inquire if the food is done to their satisfaction. The question is not, "Is everything OK here?" because that assumes that it is not. Instead, it is "Is the steak cooked the way you ordered it?" Any problems are taken care of immediately. Food is returned to the kitchen and recooked if is is not done well enough. If food is done too well, the service person informs the guest that it will take extra time to cook the meal over and offers an alternative item that is already prepared and can be served immediately (such as prime ribs).

25. Once the guests inform the Follow-Up that the food is done to their satisfaction, the guest check is flipped over so the other members of the team can see that the table has been checked.

26. The service staff returns to the table to pour extra wine and water throughout the meal. Water glasses are filled as soon as they are half

empty. Any time a service person performs any service at the table, he or she converses with the guests.

27. As soon as all guests have finished eating their meals, (the staff can determine this as guests put their utensils across their dinner plates or push their dinner plates away from them) their plates are removed.

28. If any guests have not finished their main course, an inquiry is made to determine if the guests would like to have the remainder of the meal wrapped so they may take it home. If the answer is "Yes," the server takes one plate at a time to the sidestand to wrap the leftover food, and brings it back to the guest. This eliminates having the guest question whether the food they have received is their own. The service persons bring wrapping material with them when they are preparing to clear the dirty dishes.

29. The staff remove all the dirty dishes, including bread baskets, bread and butter plates, butter plates, dirty glasses, and wine glasses.

30. The service staff crumb the table with either the side towel or a crumbing device. The crumbs are swept into a bread and butter plate.

31. The staff inquire from the guests if they would like coffee or tea. They merchandise dessert by using descriptive words, such as "our triple chocolate dessert."

32. Coffee is served by the service person, using a coffee shield. Tea is served by placing the teapot above the coffee cup. Cream, sugar, and lemon are served with the tea and coffee.

T I P $

To Insure Proper Service

Always tell the guest which coffee cup is the decaf. Don't make a mistake, because if you serve regular coffee to a person who wanted decaf they will be awake all night! Also, there are people who have been advised by their doctors not to drink regular coffee.

33. Dessert is served to the guests. If one dessert is ordered for two people, the staff bring two forks. If the dessert is gigantic, they inform the guest, and bring extra plates for other guests to share the dessert.

34. The staff serve second and third cups of coffee and tea before the guests have to ask for additional beverages. Once the dirty entree dishes have been cleared and the coffee and dessert served, the meal is not over! The guests deserve as much attention at the end of the meal as they receive at the beginning of the meal.)

35. The check is presented to the guests. If the staff cannot determine who is the host of the party, they place the check face down in the center of the table.

36. When the guests pay the bill, they are thanked for their patronage and encouraged to return.

37. After the guests leave, the staff reset the table for the next party of guests.

38. Throughout the meal, the service staff are always thinking of ways to save time. They never go into the kitchen empty-handed or come out empty-handed. They are attuned to when and how to change the ashtrays if the guests are smoking tobacco.

The preceding illustrates a typical sequence of serving a meal using the team system. (However, this typical meal will work with any system.) Depending upon the restaurant's menu, steps may be changed to fit the individual needs of the operation.

Computerized Systems

There are many computer systems designed to make a restaurant more efficient. Some of these point of sale systems allow the server to transmit the order directly to the kitchen with a hand-held electronic order pad. Other systems have computer terminals throughout the dining room to allow the waitstaff to enter information to the kitchen. All of the systems are a benefit for the guests, servers, and management.

Traditional face-to-face service is being transformed by technology. *The Wall Street Journal* reports that at the Stinking Rose in San Francisco, waiters record orders on a hand-held computer. With the push of a button, the order is zapped to the kitchen, where it is printed out for the chef. The wireless ordering shaves as much at ten minutes off a meal. "We can handle more diners at night, because everything comes out faster." says Edward Saravia, the restaurant's general manager. And each waiter now handles a dozen tables a shift, twice the load handled before adopting the hand-held devices.[4]

Other restaurants are using electronics to better address customer tastes. With technology becoming more affordable, independent restaurants can compete with chain operations. For instance, the Chilli's chain, owned by Brinker International, Inc., has instituted a frequent-diner program. When a guest makes a purchase at a Chilli's, credits are placed toward free meals or prizes. The same type of program has been put in place in independent restaurants.

As with any computer system, management must train the staff properly and the more a server uses the technology, the easier it is to understand. The computer has changed the way restaurants, managers, and servers do business.

A Glimpse Into the
Restaurant Industry Computer World

Modern technology has made paper pad ordering, barking orders in restaurant lingo to the cookie, "86 the onions," and manual price-entering on clanging cash registers practically obsolete. The wait staff of the '90s punches their orders on touch-screen monitors which lead them through transactions to focus their attention on what is required for each point of ordering. For example, selecting "Entree" on the screen would pull up a list of all the available options. Choosing "rib eye" from those options would prompt the computer to ask how it should be cooked—rare, medium, etc.—similarly, the computer would lead the server through all the dressing options on salads, baked potato toppings and the bar order. Some systems even have "Help" screens to assist the wait staff in explaining specials of the day, wine lists, or any other personalized information custom-tailored by a particular restaurant.

As items are ordered, they are printed out to the appropriate preparation area. Bar orders are automatically fed to the printer behind the bar. The rib eye order goes to the grill, other items may go to the pantry area. No need for the server to physically go to these areas until the order is ready to be picked up and served.

The bartender and cooks benefit from uniformity in ticketing, abbreviations and legibility. Employees in each area of service become more efficient, and less apt to make mistakes. Orders are identified by table number and even seat number, so that when they are ready, a runner stepping in for a waiter knows exactly which meal goes where. When it comes time to present the check, the server simply presses the table number and the check prints off the printer.

Computerized point of sale (POS) systems save time for management in many ways—in taking inventory, making reports, handling accounting, cutting training time for wait staff, etc. It is easy to see that investment in a point of sale system is quickly repaid in saved labor costs, greatly reduced losses from inaccurate ordering, and enhanced security. Orders cannot be prepared or served until they are rung up, which occurs simultaneously upon ordering, thus protecting the establishment from the common losses incurred by such instances as forgetting to enter the sale of an item added after initial ordering. Some systems have developed inventory control tied to the ordering process; the computer knows the ingredients in each item ordered and reports the depletion to its inventory database with every order entered. Special access cards are commonly used to allow managers to easily run reports, authorize a comp, or add employees by swiping the card's magnetic strip through the same slot that reads credit cards.

In choosing any type of computer equipment for a food service establishment, it is important to consider the practicality of the system for its environment. No industry could be more hostile to sensitive equipment. Sticky liquids, food crumbs, and multiple users will put the equipment to a daily durability test. Understandably, there is a great argument for choosing hardware developed specifically for the restaurant industry. Squirrel™ and Micros® Systems offer some of the most advanced point of sale computer systems, with sophisticated software integrated into their own hardware systems.

Micros has recently made a great improvement to hand-held touch screens. Using a Spread Spectrum radio frequency, derived from a military application, the Micros system signal transmission is declassified, eliminating the need for signals to be licensed by FCC. It transmits on multiple frequencies for greatly improved directional properties. The Micros hand-held units are approximately the size of a pocket daytimer and allow the server to enter data at the table as the customer orders without having to go back to a central touch screen. Hand-held units are especially useful for patio table service and poolside service in country club or hotel establishments. Circus Circus, the MGM Grand, and the Luxor in Las Vegas use hand-held units to increase bar orders in casinos. The server punches in the slot machine number and the drink order, and the information prints to the bar.

Other manufacturers offer hardware that meets the restaurant durability test while allowing the flexibility for the restauranteur to choose the software to input into them. Panasonic will release a new touch screen this year engineered for the restaurant industry, and Sharp has aligned with Comtrex to offer a restaurant proprietary system.

For cost savings, some establishments choose an open architecture system using PC-based standard hardware and can choose from a multitude of various types of restaurant industry software. The Right Touch™ from Spector Software, Inc. is a touch screen program which operates on PC-compatible hardware and allows the restauranteur to use the network he is most comfortable with. Its open architecture also allows data transfer to other software. Digital Dining™ from MenuSoft Systems Corporation integrates cash registers to back office computers and includes comprehensive inventory control and a full accounting system rolled into one easy-to-use software program. MenuSoft has also developed Digital Delivery™ to meet the needs of delivery service as the fastest-growing segment of the food service industry. Most systems allow the credit card authorization system to be programmed into them. Competitive credit card processors are anxious to align themselves with the point of sales systems manufacturers as well as proprietary systems to develop software which integrates credit approval access into any system's dial-up terminals. New terminals such as the VeriFone Omni 380 and Hypercom now dial directly to American Express to save the 15 to 20 cent switching charge that was previously charged by a processor to access American Express. New Hub-PC products are being used in the lodging industry, which allow enriched data to be captured and transferred to a credit card running tab for better billing control and to qualify for the lowest processing rates.

Check acceptance in restaurants has also gained popularity. TeleCheck can now be accessed using existing credit card authorization terminals to process authorizations quickly, with only one ID to accept any check from the U.S. or Canada.

Another consideration for your equipment budget is computerized seating management programs. Rock Systems has introduced ProHost, which operates on a standard personal computer with touchscreen, light-pen, mouse or keyboard options. It provides a graphical view of the restaurant floorplan, consistently displaying the status of all tables. A hostess simply selects the table on the screen to assign it to an incoming party. It will also suggest table assignment to improve station balancing. Remote clearing terminals allow servers and buspersons to notify the hostess of table availability.

Your options are many. Look for a professional computer systems dealer in your area who specializes in restaurant computer equipment. Of course, one who represents a number of options will be best able to help you with the selection that meets your needs and budget. If you're sure about which system you want, a manufacturer's representative may be able to offer you an increased level of training and support.

Welcome to the vast computer generation![3]

SUMMARY

1. The manager must select, train, and evaluate the employees.
2. Guests expect two qualities in service personnel: politeness and the ability to answer questions.
3. The service staff must know the physical layout of the restaurant, the menu, the ingredients in all food items (including garnishes and substitutions), cooking methods and cooking times, and all alcoholic beverages offered by the establishment.
4. The service staff must be well versed in suggestive selling, particularly of desserts and chef's specials.
5. In serving the meal, timing is everything.

REVIEW QUESTIONS

1. A check for $15.97 was presented to a guest, who paid it with a $20 bill. The service person brought three cents change back to the table, having kept the four one-dollar bills without the guest's offering the tip. Is there any problem here? And if there is, how would you as a manager handle the complaint from the guest and make certain that it never happens again?

2. What would you do as a manager if the guest refused to pay the bill because it is the policy of the restaurant not to tell the guests the "special prices"?
3. Why should the service person have a thorough knowledge of the menu?
4. Why is it important that a service person know all the ingredients of all menu items?
5. The cooking times of all menu items are important for a service person to know. Explain why you believe this is true or false.
6. What is suggestive selling, and what is its benefit for the restaurant?
7. What does the term *86* mean? How can servers avoid problems when an item is 86ed?
8. What is the home base system? Describe how it operates.
9. Should guests be allowed to substitute items on the menu?

REFERENCES

1. *Restaurant & Institutions*, 12 August 1992.
2. *Nation's Restaurant News*, 4 May 1987, F4.
3. "Restaurant Chain is Sued in Death Blamed on Pesto," *The Wall Street Journal*, 8 August 1995, sec. A, p. 2.
4. G. Pascal Zachary, "Restaurant Computers Speed Up Soup to Nuts," *The Wall Street Journal*, 25 October 1995, sec. B, pp. 1, 7.

Chapter 7

Organizing the Dining Room to Accept Guests

OBJECTIVES

At the completion of this chapter, the reader will be able to:

1. Give a historical background of the host's job
2. List the qualities that make a good host
3. Explain the importance of stations and sidework as they relate to the host's job
4. Recite the five Ps of management and know what the saying means
5. Discuss the factors that affect scheduling
6. Organize a dining room to accept guests

The Host

The key person in the dining room is the individual who greets the guests. This person may be called the maître d'hôtel, the director of service, or the host or hostess (called the **host** in this chapter). Regardless of the name, this job must be staffed by a competent individual. In most instances this is the first human contact the guest will have with the restaurant. Therefore, the host represents the restaurant to the patrons.

Guests often decide to patronize a restaurant based upon the greeting and attention they receive from the host. The mood for the evening is set by the actions of the host. In addition to greeting the guests, the host is responsible for the operation of the dining room. This person is the one who must ensure that the guests have an enjoyable dining experience and must solve any problems that may arise in the dining room.

TIP$

To Insure Proper Service

Give customers the free gifts they cherish most: recognition, recommendation, reassurance, says Michael Hurst of the 15th Street Fisheries.

AN HISTORICAL OVERVIEW

The job of the host has evolved from the classical restaurant. In this type of restaurant, the job titles were as follows: *directeur du restaurant*; *maître d'hôtel*; *deuxième maître d'hôtel*; and a *maître d'hôtel de carré*. This type of staffing had a host for each area of the restaurant.

The directeur du restaurant had complete charge of the restaurant, including the kitchen and dining room staff. He was also responsible for long-term planning, food and beverage cost controls, and service.

The maître d'hôtel was the host of all the dining rooms in the hotel. The operations may have been in many different restaurants. He was

FIGURE 7-1

A host at a restaurant, which in some cases may be the owner, is often the first person that the guest comes into contact with. Photograph by Randall Perry.

responsible for what occurred in all the different restaurants in the hotel. He was in charge of the dishwashers, cleanup crew, and linen service. If the hotel was large, there may have been a second (deuxième) maître d'hôtel, who was responsible for one dining room.

The maître d'hôtel de carré had the responsibility of a section of the dining room, similar to the captain of today.

Because of the high labor cost involved in employing a large number of individuals in a restaurant, many operations have consolidated the above jobs into the position of host. However, there are some larger restaurants that still have a director of food and beverage, and also a host. Figure 7-2 compares the early job titles to the responsibilities of restaurant personnel today.

AUTHORITY OF THE HOST

The authority and respect of the host has deteriorated over the years. As service became more and more lax in America, the job of the host was considered an entry level position. Restaurant owners paid the host at the minimum wage rate because the owners felt that this person did not directly produce money as a service person. Consequently, the person who was given this job was poorly trained, if trained at all. This position changed from being a job of prestige, power, and respect, into a job that restaurant owners felt anyone could do. Instead of having experienced waitpeople striving to become the host, they avoided it because it did not pay as much money as their tipped position. Guest service and the industry suffered tremendously.

Today, the pendulum has begun to swing back to the experienced and respected host. Restaurant owners are realizing the importance of

FIGURE 7-2

The early job titles compared with the responsibilities of restaurant personnel of today

THE HOST'S POSITION

Early Days	Responsibility	Today
Directeur du Restaurant	Total Restaurant Operation	Food and Beverage Manager or Host
Maître d'Hôtel	All Dining Rooms	Food and Beverage Manager or Host
Deuxième Maître d'Hôtel	One Dining Room	Host
Maître d'Hôtel de Carré	One Section of the Dining Room	Host or Head Service Person (often called Captain)

having a well-trained host. A well-informed and personable individual holding the job of host will make the restaurant a success. Restaurant owners are now compensating their hosts at a higher pay rate than the minimum wage. As the laws regarding tip reporting and taxes become more stringent on restaurant owners, more and more are instituting a fixed service charge. From this fixed service charge, the host is being paid a much higher wage than minimum. Other restaurants, which still have a voluntary tipping policy, make the service staff contribute part of their tips to the host.

Restaurant owners are, once again, realizing the importance of having a competent, personable host to greet their guests.

HOST SELECTION

Selecting a person for the host's job is important and challenging for the manager or owner of the restaurant. This is because a major portion of the job is dependent upon the host to observe a situation or problem, weigh the positive versus the negative aspects, and make a decision—all in a few seconds. Because the ability to think quickly and react to situations positively is a necessary qualification, the manager must try to select an individual who is personable and can work well under stress. The selection process should be structured in such a manner as to determine the personality of the applicants and how they handle stressful situations. Figure 7-3 lists the criteria for selecting a host. In addition, the manager should look for some additional specific qualifications that have been identified with excellent hosts. These qualifications are discussed in the next section.

TIP$

TO INSURE PROPER SERVICE

To determine the personality of his applicants, Michael Hurst asks, "What is the funniest thing that ever happened to you?"

CRITERIA FOR HOST SELECTION

Individual Selected to Be a Host Must:
1. Be personable
2. Work well under stress
3. Be able to think quickly
4. Be able to make decisions

FIGURE 7-3

QUALIFICATIONS TO BE A HOST	
Physical	**Behavioral**
Positive Appearance	Personable
Able to stand on feet for	Outgoing
long period of time	Ability to work well with others in all situations

FIGURE 7-4

QUALIFICATIONS OF THE HOST

The qualifications for a host fall into two general categories: physical and behavioral (see Figure 7-4). The first relates to the appearance of the individual. The second refers to the manner in which a person interacts with people.

The host is the first person guests see when they walk into a restaurant, therefore the physical appearance of the host must be positive. Figure 7-5 shows a host outside his restaurant. This host makes a positive physical appearance. As with the service staff, cleanliness is essential. Any uniform (tuxedo or evening gown) must be neat and clean. These uniforms are a symbol of professionalism. The host should be proud of wearing the uniform.

The second qualification, behavioral, is the ability to deal with people. The host has to be able to meet the needs of the restaurant's guests and employees. Sometimes this is not easy. Many guests are not pleasant, because they may be having a bad day, are not used to waiting for a table, or for a myriad of reasons that the host has little, if any, control over. Employees provide another challenge. They will complain about the amount of tips that the guests have left and about their stations, for example. The host must have the ability to satisfy all the employee and guest complaints, whether they are legitimate or not.

USEFUL BEHAVIORAL TIPS

For the host to do the job effectively, other behavioral traits are needed. The book *The Professional Host* lists some of them as attentiveness, courteousness, dependability, economy, honesty, knowledge, loyalty, preparedness, productivity, quietness, sensitivity, tact, persuasiveness, and skill.[1] Even though it would appear that every person has the common sense to know and use these traits, many do not. The following information will give examples of the importance of the specific traits.

Attentiveness

Like the service staff, the host must be ubiquitous. He must know what is occurring in the dining room at all times, and must appear to have eyes in the back of his head. The host has to know the status of all tables at all times; whether table 3 has been served the main course; if table 5 needs more wine. An absentminded person or daydreamer does not belong in the position of host. This job requires a person who will be consistently alert to the guests' needs.

TIP$

TO INSURE PROPER SERVICE

Sirio Maccioni, the founder and owner of Le Cirque in New York City, tells everyone on his staff that if a guest calls them over, the thing to say is, "What can I do for you?" Do not ask, "Is everything all right?" That is very pretentious. When you ask, "What can I do for you?" people open up.[2]

Courteousness

The host must treat the guests as though they were guests in his or her home. Words such as "please" and "thank you" are thought by many people to be magic words. Guests appreciate hearing these magic words, and the host is encouraged to use them whenever appropriate. Greeting the guests by name and addressing the guests by name throughout the dining experience, the host should return to the table to show his genuine concern about their satisfaction. By using the magic words "please," "thank you," "excuse me," and especially the guest's name, the host will not only impress the guest by his courtesy but will provide a positive model for the service staff to follow.

Courteousness also includes assisting guests with little things that show concern. These little things are not something that will make a person jump up and down and say, "Wow, did you see what the host did!" Instead, they are displays of courteousness that will make the guests feel that the restaurant really cares about them and is happy to receive their business. Examples of courteousness are: assisting guests in removing or putting on their coats; pulling out the chairs for guests as they are shown to their table; and checking back with guests to determine if the table or temperature of the room is pleasing. Pulling the shades down so the sun will not shine in the guests' eyes is another example. The difference between a great restaurant and a good restaurant is taking care of the details—and courteousness is a detail.

Dependability

Dependability is a trait that is valued highly by restaurant owners. It is a sign of maturity. Basically, it means that the employees will be responsible for their own actions. It also includes the fact that the employees will accomplish the goals that have been set, either by management or by the employees themselves on their own without needing to be checked on. This trait is important in all positions, but is extremely critical for any person who will hold the responsible job of host.

T I P $

To Insure Proper Service

Offer to take pictures of guests, with their own cameras, when you see them taking each other's picture.

Economy

Economy means keeping costs at a minimum. This will be the host's responsibility. The dining room is an area where costs can rapidly get out of control because of improper scheduling, improper use of linen, and food waste. If the host schedules too many service staff, the labor cost will be a drain on the restaurant. If staff are allowed to use extra equipment (like extra sidetowels) when they are not needed, money is lost. Common sense is important in keeping waste to a minimum. An example of economy is to save and reuse individual packaged jellies if they have not been opened.

Efficiency

Efficiency means finding the quickest and easiest way to do a task without jeopardizing the guests' satisfaction. The ability to organize reservations in a systematic manner is an example of efficiency. By having an efficient reservation system, the host can take reservations correctly. This will allow the host to spend more time in the dining room (or working the floor) instead of trying to straighten out a mess caused by an inefficient reservation system. The more organized the host is, the more time can be spent with the guests.

Honesty

A person who deals with the public, especially in the host's job, will have to make many decisions that will test his honesty. For example, a guest approaches the host and asks for a table. The host has all the tables reserved and informs the guest of this. The guest produces a $50 bill and asks, "Are you sure?" The host and the guest both know that the patron is buying the table. What should the host do?

Other opportunities will arise to deceive the customer as well as the employees. In all instances, if the host is dishonest and allows the staff to be dishonest, word will spread that the establishment is dishonest. This will result in negative word of mouth from both guests and employees, and the business will suffer.

TIP$

TO INSURE PROPER SERVICE

Danny Meyer of the Union Square Cafe says "It's less appropriate to 'grease the palm' of a maitre d' to get a better table on your way in. Maitre d's who 'sell' good tables for tips are not providing good service for other guests."[3]

Loyalty

Loyalty is another highly rated behavioral trait of a host. It can be defined as being (or giving the impression to the public of being) totally supportive of the ideas and philosophies of the restaurant. An example of not being loyal is downgrading the establishment to the guests by such comments as, "Management has no idea of how to run this place."

Knowledge

As with the service staff, the host has to know all facets of the operation of the restaurant. In fact, he must know more about the operation than the service staff, because the guests perceive the host as the key figure in the restaurant. The host should know all the facts about the operation of the restaurant, including the preparation and service of food and beverage. In addition, the host has to be aware of the physical layout of the restaurant, how to deal with credit card charges, and the accounting procedures of the restaurant. With today's ever changing technology, knowledge of computers and computer systems is critical.

Knowledge of community events and area attractions is an important part of the host's concern. If a guest asks a question and the host doesn't know the answer, he or she will have to find out the answer and return to the guest with it.

Service, Indeed!

A couple invited two friends to dinner and a play on Saturday evening. A reservation was made at one of the couple's favorite restaurants; in addition, that restaurant provides the catering for the theater where the party of four were to attend the play. While driving to the restaurant, the host turned to the invited couple and said, "Well, we won't be late for the play, but we will be a little early, because our tickets are for next Saturday. I called and tried to exchange the tickets and get us seats for tonight; but as the theater only seats two hundred people, they are sold out." When they arrived at the restaurant, the host/owner greeted them warmly and inquired whether they were going to the play or "were there for a leisurely dinner." The guest explained the problem. The owner asked for the tickets and said "Let me see what I can do." By the time the salad arrived, the owner was back at the table to inform the group that he had secured tickets for that evening's performance.

Preparedness

Nothing is more frustrating for guests than to have to wait for something: a reservation, food, or drinks, The host has to be ready to accept guests into the dining room at its stated opening time. If a guest is promised a 3 P.M. reservation, then the table should be ready for them at 3 P.M. Preparedness is the act of planning and organizing all equipment and supplies so the guest will not have to wait for service.

Procrastinators do not belong in the hospitality industry. The host should have a plan for each situation and be considering alternative plans in case of a problem.

Quietness

A good host is always available when needed. However, the host has to be aware of the proper time to talk to guests and when to leave them alone. When talking to the guests, it is done in a nice manner, not in a loud or boisterous one. The host must act with dignity, and do the job quietly.

Sensitivity

Restaurants are where many special occasions are celebrated, such as engagements, wedding anniversaries, births, and job promotions. Unfortunately, it is also the place where many marriages and relationships are ended. People often choose a restaurant in which to tell their spouse or lover that the relationship is finished, because they think that the hurt party will not make a scene in so public a place. The host has to be sensitive to the needs of the guests and observe their actions to determine how much attention they want from the host. Sensitivity is a two-part trait: first to observe what is occurring between the guests or to the guests, then act appropriately. If the guests have just become engaged, congratulations should be offered. A dessert or drink may be offered, compliments of the restaurant. If the couple obviously is having a fight, then staying away from the table is best. Going to the table asking how the food is would not be appropriate. That would show a lack of sensitivity.

TIP$

Skill

A skillful host knows how to "work the floor." He knows how to obtain the most efficient or effective use of the tables in the shortest period of time. The skillful host knows how to keep the guests happy and how to motivate them to return. Skill also involves making salads tableside, carving meats and poultry, and pouring wine.

Tact

The ability to say the right phrase at the right time without offending the guest would be a definition of **tact**. Saying to a guest, "Where have you been, I haven't seen you in a long time," can be interpreted by many guests as tactless. A more tactful way of saying this would be, "It's nice to have you patronize the restaurant, we're glad to have you here again." This says the same thing, but it will not offend the guest.

Tact is also involved when inquiring about the guests or their families. The host has to be aware of what is happening in the community. Reading the local newspapers will give the host information needed to avoid embarrassment and appearing tactless. For example, in last week's newspaper, the host read that John Smith had been cut from the professional baseball team. When Mr. and Mrs. Smith come to the restaurant, the host would not ask them, "How is your son's baseball career going?"

Productivity

Productivity is defined as the ability to get the maximum amount of tasks accomplished in the shortest period to time. There are times when the host must take reservations, greet guests, take their orders, and return to their table to see if the meal is to their satisfaction. In addition, the host must monitor the service staff's performance, seeing that the sidework is being done and that the dining room is operating to its maximum potential.

Persuasiveness

This is another important behavioral trait, especially when dealing with guests who have problems. Persuasiveness could be used to convince the guest to take a different table, or to take a different time because the restaurant is sold out (booked solid). Convincing the guest to change his or her mind about something requires persuasiveness.

There are many more behavioral traits that the reader will be able to identify; however, an individual has to exhibit some, if not all, of the traits stated above in order to be an excellent host.

The Host's Responsibilities: The Five Ps of Management

In order for any restaurant to run efficiently, the host must be prepared. The key to having a successful restaurant or banquet are the five Ps of management: *P*rior *P*lanning *P*revents *P*oor *P*erformance.

This phrase and the meaning of it are important for all restaurant employees. However, this philosophy is especially critical in the host's job. The five Ps of management mean that if all tasks are planned in advance, problems will be kept to a minimum.

Therefore, a plan is needed to use before each meal period. This plan may be in the form of a checklist, as illustrated in Figure 7-7. Each restaurant may design one that fits the needs for that particular unit. By completing it, the host ensures that the restaurant is prepared to accept guests. The following are some examples of what items may be on the checklist and why they are important.

The list should include checking both the men's and ladies' room for all paper products and for cleanliness. If the host does not do this, it will have to be attended to during a busy time, taking valuable time away from the guests.

Another important area to check is the physical cleanliness of the dining room. Are the floors free of crumbs or lint? If the floor is dirty, it will have to be cleaned or vacuumed before the guests arrive. All light fixtures are inspected for burned out bulbs or cobwebs. The host may think "It's not my job," but the host is responsible for the operation of the dining room. The guests want to feel that they are eating in a clean and safe restaurant. Burned out light bulbs, dirty floors, and cobwebs send a message to the guest that the restaurant does not care about cleanliness.

THE FIVE Ps OF MANAGEMENT
PRIOR PLANNING PREVENTS POOR PERFORMANCE

FIGURE 7-5

HOST'S DAILY CHECKLIST FOR OPENING THE DINING ROOM

1.   Inspection of the service staff for proper grooming guidelines.
2.   Men's room and Ladies' room
        Clean
        Paper products
3.   Physical cleanliness of the dining room:
        Floor free of crumbs and lint
        Light fixtures clean and no burned out bulbs
4.   Printers have enough paper to complete meal period
5.   Menus are clean and chef's creations have been added
6.   Reservations have been blocked
7.   Computer system has been programmed with the chef's creations
8.   Host is neat and clean, ready to accept guests

FIGURE 7-6

A sample checklist for the host, to be done daily

For restaurants with a computer system, printers have to be checked first thing to see if there is enough paper to last though the meal period. With some computer systems, if the paper runs out, the computer will not work. All prices and new items should be put into the memory of the computer before the staff take their first orders.

The host may assign an employee to complete any task not completed. The first responsibility of the host is to prepare the dining room to accept guests. The host must have the dining room ready to accept guests when it is scheduled to open its doors. As has been said before, the difference between a good and a great restaurant is attention to details. A good host will anticipate and avoid problems. A great host will use the five Ps of management to have an excellent restaurant.

Organization of the Dining Room

Knowledge of the menu, pricing, ingredients, and all facts essential to the smooth and profitable operation of a restaurant is as essential to the host as it is to the service staff. In addition, the host has to supervise the service staff.

The host is responsible for making the service excellent. Successful restaurants constantly evaluate service throughout an employee's career. The host is responsible for the training and performance of the service. In addition, the host has to schedule employees and assign stations and sidework to make the dining room operate at its maximum efficiency.

FACTORS THAT AFFECT SCHEDULING

Have you ever been to a restaurant where you are served slowly because there are too many guests and not enough staff? Sometimes there is an obvious shortage of service staff to serve the guests. For example, a restaurant has 120 seats filled and only two service persons to tend to the guests. The person responsible for scheduling has not scheduled enough service staff to meet the demand. The host must schedule the correct amount of staff to meet the demands of business, while not overstaffing the restaurant. Overstaffing causes a loss of money and, at times, even results in poor service. In order to schedule effectively, the host must take certain factors into consideration and then schedule the employees correctly. The first step begins with forecasting.

Forecasting

Forecasting is planning for anticipated business based upon previous history of the restaurant, reservations, and events that are planned for the community which will affect the business.

A formal written forecast of covers produced on a weekly basis is the most important aspect in scheduling.

Scheduling

There are many factors that affect correct scheduling. The first has to do with the qualifications of the individual waitpeople. The next has to do with the type of menu and style of service that the restaurant offers. The third involves events occurring in the community in which the restaurant is located. If the restaurant is located in a hotel, expected occupancy rates of the hotel will play a major part in scheduling. Another factor is based upon the history from previous years' business. The final factor would be the number of reservations from the meal period. Scheduling is one place where the five Ps of management are extremely important.

The first consideration is the qualifications of the individual waitpeople. For example, one service person may be able to work best waiting on a lot of small parties; another may work better with large parties. Knowing this information allows the host to compensate for the inadequacies of the staff.

Next, the host has to consider the type of menu and the style of service offered by the restaurant. If the restaurant uses American service, the number of guests that can be served efficiently by one service person is anywhere from sixteen to twenty-four. Individual restaurants determine how many guests a service person is required to serve. This depends on the menu, the meal period, and the atmosphere of the restaurant. The host can use this standard in forecasting and scheduling.

The third factor that affects scheduling is events occurring in the community that will positively or negatively affect the restaurant's business. For example, if there is a parents' weekend at the local college, and the restaurant serves breakfast, then it should be staffed to accommodate extra guests. If there is a youth sporting event scheduled in the community, and the restaurant appeals to that market, it will be busier than usual. The host, the service staff, and the cooks want to avoid surprises. No one likes to be swamped with business when they are not prepared to handle it.

TIP$

TO INSURE PROPER SERVICE

Manage your restaurant from the front door, not from the kitchen. In other words, be visible so that you can observe what is occurring in your restaurant and the guests can see you are in control of the operation.

The next factor is particular for restaurants located in a lodging establishment. Almost all hotels send out a forecast of the prospective **occupancy rate** (this is the anticipated number of guests staying in the establishment on a certain night). If the rate is expected to be 100 percent, then the restaurant will be very busy for breakfast. It is amazing that when a hotel has 100 percent occupancy, the restaurant is not staffed properly for breakfast. That is the meal that will be eaten most often by the hotel's guests. Effective staffing in this category also means scheduling employees to work at the correct time. Having employees come in from 8 A.M. to 4 P.M. would be a mistake if the hotel's clientele are business people. They want to be out of the restaurant by 8 A.M. It is easy to obtain advance occupancy figures, thereby reducing the probability of an insufficiently staffed restaurant.

The next factor is determined by the history of the restaurant. Every restaurant needs a book at the host stand (some people call it a log book) for the purpose of recording the history of that day's business. Included should be the number of meals that were served for each meal period, the weather, and special events that were occurring in the community (such as conventions). The guest history also includes how much money was generated per hours and per meal period. This will assist the host in forecasting the staffing for the same day of the week next year, not the date. In addition, it is recommended to have an area where the day shift host can leave messages for the night host concerning important items, such as, "Jane called in and she will be twenty minutes late tonight."

Finally, the manager reviews the number of reservations that are normally taken on that particular day. If the restaurant is booked up far in advance, all the reservations will be factored into the scheduling.

By no means is this a complete listing of the factors that the host must consider when staffing the restaurant; however, the above items will help the host in this regard. This planning allows the host to staff the restaurant properly for all types of business, including the least busy (slow) nights. For example, the night before Thanksgiving is traditionally not busy in a hotel dining room. However, the dining room must be open. Using the previous history, plus the expected occupancy rates, the host can schedule a skeleton crew. On the other hand, one of the biggest business days at a restaurant like Churchill Downs in Louisville, Kentucky, is Thanksgiving. At the racetrack, the restaurant must be staffed to accommodate the large group of guests. Taking into account all of the above factors, the host can develop a schedule to satisfy the demands of both businesses.

Scheduling the Employees

Based upon the factors that were discussed above, the host can determine how many service people are needed for a certain time period. This time period is usually a week. It is beneficial to the host and employees to have the work schedule completed and posted in advance. This lets all employees know when they are scheduled to work.

The restaurant industry has a reputation for not treating its service staff decently. Many times, restaurant owners engage in day-to-day scheduling. When service persons ask for their schedules, they are told to call at 10 A.M. the next day. Then they are told to work or not to work. This type of scheduling is bad, because it negatively affects morale. Posting the schedule on the same day every week for the same period of time will alleviate the problem.

The busiest days in the restaurant business are the times when everyone else is enjoying themselves (weekends and holidays). Employees should be told when hired that they will have to work weekends and holidays. However, the host should strive to give his employees two days off in succession.

There is a system the author designed in order to improve scheduling, and that resulted in improved morale. First, the schedule was made every Wednesday and posted every Thursday. As an example, the schedule went from Friday, April 1, to Sunday, April 10. The employees would know a week in advance who had to work the following weekend. The next week's schedule went from Friday, April 8, to Sunday, April 17. Using this method, the host is planning for seven days, but always scheduling for ten days. An example of the two weeks' schedule is in Figures 7-7 and 7-8. Notice that the last weekend (April 8, 9, 10) of Figure 7-7, and the first weekend (April 8, 9, 10) of Figure 7-8 are the same.

This method improves morale and it will allow the employees to plan in advance if there is a special event they wish to attend. For instance, Pam knows that she has the weekend of the 16th and 17th off, when the schedule is posted on Wednesday, April 6.

In addition, if the employees wanted a special day or weekend off, they were allowed to switch with other employees, as long as the host was told. However, it was made clear to the employees who were scheduled to work that they were responsible for covering the shift. If their replacement did not show up, then the originally scheduled employee would pay the consequences. This system made the host's job easy. The staff was motivated because they knew exactly when they had to work and knew that they could take a day off if some special event occurred. Of course, if employees knew far enough in advance before the schedule was to be made up that they needed a day off, they would inform the host and they would be accommodated.

FIGURE 7-7

A ten-day schedule for restaurant employees

WEEKLY SCHEDULE, APRIL 1-10

Name	1	2	3	4	5	6	7	8	9	10
	Fri	Sat	Sun	Mon	Tue	Wed	Thu	Fri	Sat	Sun
Pam	7-3	7-3	7-3	OFF	OFF	7-3	7-3	7-3	7-3	7-3
John	7-3	7-3	7-3	7-3	7-3	OFF	OFF	7-3	7-3	7-3
Bill	7-3	7-3	7-3	7-3	7-3	7-3	7-3	OFF	OFF	7-3

FIGURE 7-8

A ten-day schedule for restaurant employees

WEEKLY SCHEDULE, APRIL 8-17

Name	8	9	10	11	12	13	14	15	16	17
	Fri	Sat	Sun	Mon	Tue	Wed	Thu	Fri	Sat	Sun
Pam	7-3	7-3	7-3	7-3	7-3	7-3	7-3	7-3	OFF	OFF
John	7-3	7-3	7-3	7-3	7-3	OFF	OFF	7-3	7-3	7-3
Bill	OFF	OFF	7-3	7-3	7-3	7-3	7-3	7-3	7-3	7-3

STATIONS AND SIDEWORK

Regardless of how the stations are arranged in the restaurant (team or individual), stations and sidework responsibilities have to be posted. Sidework should be with the station. Figure 7-9 is an example of how stations and sidework can be planned. Notice that the sidework corresponds to the station assignment.

The host must be flexible, and on occasion must combine stations or service staff from different stations when it would benefit the guests. For example, a party of twelve went to a restaurant on New Year's Day. The host assigned two service people to take care of the table, even though it was on one station. The group was served more quickly than if one person had served them.

MENUS AND CHECKS

The host is usually responsible for making sure the menus are clean and ready to distribute to the guests. In some establishments, the host has to write (or type) and put the daily specials into the menu, and/or write them on the blackboard. When putting the specials into the menus, the host also checks the condition of the menus. Dirty, torn, or smudged menus should be discarded. If the restaurant serves three meals a day, the host checks that the menu is correct for that meal period. Have you ever received a menu that was for lunch when the other guests in your party had a dinner menu?

Guest checks are sometimes given out to the service staff by the host; at other times the job is assigned to a cashier. Regardless of who gives out the checks, all service staff should have to sign for the

FIGURE 7-9

A ten-day schedule of corresponding sidework for restaurant employees

STATIONS AND SIDEWORK, APRIL 1-10										
Name	**1**	**2**	**3**	**4**	**5**	**6**	**7**	**8**	**9**	**10**
	Fri	Sat	Sun	Mon	Tue	Wed	Thu	Fri	Sat	Sun
Pam	1	3	2	OFF	OFF	1	2	1	2	1
John	2	1	3	1	2	OFF	OFF	2	1	2
Bill	3	2	1	2	1	2	1	OFF	OFF	3

1. Fold fifty napkins
2. Salt and pepper shakers; perform sidework of station 3, when only two people are scheduled
3. Housekeeping of all coffee and beverage machines

checks they receive. At the end of the meal period, the host verifies that all guests' checks that were given out have been returned, either used or unused.

STAFF INSPECTION AND DAILY MEETING

Before each meal period, the host has to conduct a staff inspection and hold a daily meeting.

It is at this time that the host inspects the employees regarding the grooming and cleanliness policies set by the restaurant. If a member of the staff does not meet the grooming standards that have been set, the host cannot allow that individual to work. Allowing a service person to work who has not met the restaurant's standards will make it difficult to enforce the rules to the other staff members. Making exceptions will create problems with the other members of the staff. Once the service staff realize that the grooming and cleanliness policies will be enforced, they will comply.

The daily meeting usually consists of a short information session that the host conducts before each meal period. Information is shared with the staff, such as the description and price of the day's chef's creations. Any new wines or beverages that the restaurant is featuring will be explained. The soup or vegetable of the day and items that the restaurant is temporarily out of are also communicated by the host. Any special requests from the reservations (birthday cake with the Smith reservation at 8 P.M.) and any items such as new promotions are also explained.

This informational session should not last long. There will be regularly scheduled meetings for the purpose of tasting food and wine, reviewing policies in depth, and soliciting new ideas from the staff. This meeting is only informational in nature, so that the dining room runs smoothly for that particular meal period.

SUMMARY

1. The host must be attentive, courteous, dependable, honest, loyal to the establishment, tactful, knowledgeable, sensitive to guests' needs and moods, and persuasive.
2. The five Ps of management are essential to any restaurant's efficiency. These are: *Prior Planning Prevents Poor Performance.*
3. The three most important factors in planning effectively are organization, forecasting, and scheduling.

REVIEW QUESTIONS

1. You are the manager of the dining room. Your morning host is a bright, articulate, and personable individual. All the staff love him. You have received many letters from guests complimenting him on the way he treats them at breakfast. However, he has an alcohol problem. About once a month he goes on a binge and does not show up for work. His wife does call in for him. What do you do with him?

2. The host has all the tables reserved and informs the guest of this. The guest produces a $50 bill and asks, "Are you sure?" The host and the guest both know that the patron is buying the table. What should the host do?

3. What does the phrase, "The taste of the roast is determined by the handshake of the host" mean?

4. Compare the jobs of the host today with the four job titles of earlier times.

5. What qualities should a manager look for when hiring a host?

6. What behavioral traits should a person have in order to make a good host?

7. What are the five Ps of management, and why is this phrase important in the restaurant industry?

8. What is forecasting, and how does it affect scheduling?

9. What is the purpose of having a ten-day schedule? Do you think it is a good idea? Explain your answer.

10. What factors have to be taken into consideration when scheduling?

11. What is a log book, and what is its purpose?

REFERENCES

1. The Food Service Editors of CBI, *The Professional Host* (Boston: CBI, 1981), 11-13.

2. Mervyn Rothstein, "Sirio's Circus of the Chic," *The Wine Spectator,* 15 May 1995, 71-80

3. Meyer, Danny. *Union Square Cafe Newsletter,* Autumn/Winter 1994.

Planning Reservations and Blocking Tables

At the completion of this chapter, the reader will be able to:

1. Take reservations
2. State the advantages and disadvantages of a reservation policy.
3. State the advantages and disadvantages of a no reservation policy
4. Demonstrate how to block tables when reservations are accepted
5. Plan and organize a system to seat guests who come into the restaurant with a reservation.
6. Explain the problems that occur when taking guest reservations, and propose solutions
7. Recognize the problems with no-shows, and know how to reduce the number of no shows
8. Understand how call-ahead seating works

The Decision on Whether to Accept Reservations

Each restaurant has to decide whether it will accept reservations or rely on walk-ins to fill up its tables. A **reservation** is a promise for a table in a restaurant. **Walk-ins** are guests who patronize the restaurant without making a reservation; in effect, they walk in the door expecting to obtain a table.

Many restaurants will not take reservations. Instead, guests are seated on a first-come basis. However, before the decision is made not to take reservations, some facts have to be considered.

One of the most important considerations in not accepting reservations is the location of the restaurant. A restaurant that is located in an area where there is a large population, or in a busy tourist area, may prefer not to take reservations. A large population guarantees the restaurant the number of potential guests needed to fill up its tables. The same is true in a busy resort area that caters to tourists. If the establishment is located in the area where guests have to travel a long distance to reach it, this will be a negative factor.

A second negative factor would be the absence of other restaurants of the same quality in the general area. The guest will take both of these factors into consideration, and most likely will not attempt to patronize the restaurant. Why should a guest drive for a long period of time and not be assured of getting a table or even getting a decent meal?

The next factor is the size of the party. Because most restaurants have the majority of their tables as deuces and 4-tops, they are not equipped to

FIGURE 8-1

A restaurant, such as the one pictured, can take both walk-ins and reservations. Photograph by Randall Perry.

accommodate groups larger than six people. It would be difficult, if not impossible, to accommodate a group of ten people at one table. Imagine a busy night at a restaurant. All the tables are occupied. A large group appears at the door and wants to sit together. The host would have to wait until three tables next to each other become vacant all at once. Then the host would have to move the tables so they could accommodate the party. To avoid this problem, reservations should be accepted for large parties. The definition of large would depend upon the size of the tables in the individual restaurant. Usually, large is a party of six or more guests.

Reservations should always be accepted on holidays. Easter and Mother's Day are special days for families. The families want to be assured that they can arrive at a restaurant, enjoy themselves, pay the bill, and leave in a definite period of time. For many people, it is the only time of the year that all members of the family can have a meal together. Because of the great difference in ages of most family groups (young children, parents, and grandparents), having to wait for a table would not be tolerated or even considered.

Accepting Reservations

Once the decision is made to accept reservations, the restaurant needs to create a policy to deal with reserving tables for the guests. Some establishments only reserve a certain percentage of tables. Many restaurants prefer the restaurant to be reserved completely. A gourmet restaurant like Victoria and Albert's Restaurant in Walt Disney World's Grand Floridian Beach Resort only takes reservations.

A reservation is a promise for a table in a restaurant. The promise works in two ways. The restaurant promises to have a table available for the guest for a certain time period. The guest promises to show up for the reservation.

Reservations provide a mutual benefit to the guest and the restaurant. The guests know that they will have a table available to enjoy their meal. They will not have to wait for their table, or even worse, drive to the restaurant and find out they cannot be accommodated. Reservations have advantages and disadvantages for both the restaurant and guests.

The benefits for the guests:

1. The table is available when requested.
2. The restaurant can be informed of special requests and have them available when guests arrive.
3. The host learns the guests' names.

The benefits for the restaurant:

1. The restaurant knows how many guests to expect; forecasting and scheduling are easier.
2. The menus and service staff can be planned exactly.
3. The host knows guests' names and can use them to create ego gratification.
4. A mailing list can be developed for future promotions.
5. If reservations are taken correctly, the restaurant will run smoothly, because the restaurant controls when the guests dine. The restaurant can prevent too many guests from showing up at the same time, thereby avoiding a strain on the kitchen and dining room.

However, reservations can also be a disadvantage. Among the disadvantages for the guests:

1. If restaurants do not know how to take and plan them correctly, reservations may not be honored at the stated time.
2. Some restaurants reserve more parties than they have tables available. This practice is called **overbooking**. The restaurant does this to avoid losing revenue in case guests who have reservations do not show up. Others overbook because they do not know how to plan reservations.

The possible disadvantages for the restaurant:

1. When guests do not show up (called no-shows), revenue from that reserved table is lost.
2. When guests arrive late, the reservation plan may be put in disarray.
3. Restaurants that do not know how to block tables correctly lose money because they are not getting maximum use from tables.

Taking reservations are a benefit to the guest and the restaurant only if both know their responsibilities concerning reservations. Training the host in the proper way to take reservations is important. When guests make a reservation, it is an essential part of the host's job to explain to the caller their responsibilities.

TIP$ To Insure Proper Service

Another of Michael Hursts's tips: Greet customers by name; make a game of remembering names.

FACTORS THAT AFFECT TAKING RESERVATIONS

As was stated in the list of disadvantages for the guests, one of the main problems is overbooking by the restaurant. The first thing that will have to be established by management is a system that allows the people taking reservations to know exactly how many tables can be reserved for the day. Also, if the restaurant takes more than one seating for the meal period, the **residence time** has to be established. The residence time is defined as the time it takes a party to eat its meal and pay its bill. For example, ninety minutes will be required for a complete meal with appetizers, drinks, main course, and dessert for a party of up to four people. Thus, leaving enough time to reset the table, reservations should be taken every two hours. Guests who have larger parties will take longer to eat, so the residence time must be adjusted. Other factors also influence the residence time of the guests. Items such as music, lighting, decor, mood, ambience, and special events make the difference in how fast or slow the guests will eat. A menu that is easier to prepare will speed up the residence time.

Once the residence time and the system have been developed, the host can take reservations.

TAKING THE RESERVATION

Practically all reservations are taken via the telephone or in person. The people taking the reservation have to be trained properly so they will obtain all important information from the guests and explain to them the policies of the restaurant.

The person answering the phone must be competent in taking reservations, but also must have excellent telephone courtesy. This is the guest's first contact with the restaurant. To ensure this, management may check their reservation procedures by conducting mystery calls to determine the telephone courtesy and competency of the host. It is common telephone courtesy for the people answering the phone to identify the restaurant as well as themselves. A sentence such as this is appropriate: "Good day, thank you for calling the Specialty restaurant; this is Sue speaking, how may I help you?"

The reservations should be taken and placed on a preprinted form like the one shown in Figure 8-2, or directly into the reservation book. This depends entirely on the size of the restaurant. A small restaurant would be able to put the reservations directly into a book. A large restaurant would have to use forms and then transfer them to the book afterwards. Some restaurants use personal computers with software developed to manage the reservation process.

RESERVATION FORM

Day & Date of Reservation _____ Time _____

Guest's Name_____ Number of Guests _____

Phone Number, Home _____ Business_____

Special Instructions_____

Taken By _____ Date Taken _____

FIGURE 8-2

A typical reservation form. The host will fill in the information in the appropriate space.

Regardless of what type of form the restaurant uses, the information required from the guest is generally the same.

INFORMATION TO OBTAIN FROM THE GUEST

The Name of the Guest

Included in this step is the correct spelling of the guests' names.

The Date for Which the Reservation is Desired

Ask for the date that they request with the day of the week and date. For example, when the guests state, April 2, reconfirm it by saying, "Saturday, April 2." If the date is open, proceed with other questions. If the date is booked, suggest a different day. If the guests are adamant and insist on that date, take the guests' names and phone numbers and tell them they will be placed on the waiting list. Depending upon the restaurant, there should be a maximum number of parties that can be on the waiting list. Inform them that they will be called if an opening occurs.

The Time of the Reservation

If the time is booked, suggest other times. At this point, the host should explain the policy concerning holding reservations. For example, a restaurant may have the policy that when guests make a reservation they are told they must be at the restaurant fifteen minutes early. It is further explained to the guest that if their reservation is for 6 P.M., they must show up at 5:45. If the guest is not there at 5:45, the table is given to a walk-in.

Obtain the Number of Guests in the Party and any Special Requests

If they need a birthday cake, special seating, or anything else, this should be noted.

Ask for the Guest's Phone Number

Take both the home and business numbers, if possible. If there is a problem, the host can contact the guests. The host may want to contact them after the meal to find out how they liked their dining experience.

OTHER ITEMS ON THE RESERVATION REQUEST

There are other items that the person taking the reservations should place on the reservation form. By placing these items on the form, they can be used in case any problems arise, as well as for planning future reservations.

The Name of the Person Who Took the Reservation

The people who booked the party must sign their names. This makes people responsible, and if a problem arises, the host will know whom to ask. If the guest calls and changes the reservation in any way, the person who took the changes must also sign and date the reservation request form.

The Date the Reservation was Taken

Noting the date on which reservations have been taken allows the host to determine how far in advance reservations are demanded.

EXPLAINING POLICIES OF THE RESTAURANT TO THE GUEST

Before the person taking the reservation thanks the guest and hangs up the phone, the guest will appreciate being informed of any special policies of the restaurant. For example, if the restaurant requires jackets for men in the dining room, this is told to the guest. The guest can be told that a gratuity is automatically added to the check. Each restaurant should develop its own checklist for reservation takers to make certain that the guest is informed of all of the policies.

TIP$

TO INSURE PROPER SERVICE

Guests will be reasonable if policies are explained to them. The Schenectady County Community College restaurant takes reservations for its evening meal only two weeks in advance of the date starting at 9 A.M. When guests are told that the policy has been designed so it will be fair to all, they express their appreciation.

In order to avoid mistakes, the reservation information taken down by the person who answered the phone is repeated back to the guest. Finally, the guest is thanked for calling, and told something like, "We will be looking forward to seeing you on Saturday, April 2, Mr. Smith."

Not Accepting Reservations

ADVANTAGES FOR THE RESTAURANT

When factors warrant not taking reservations, the advantages for the restaurant are much greater than for the guest. (Many no-reservation restaurants will take reservations for larger groups—usually six or more.) There are four main advantages for the restaurant.

1. Maximum use of tables is obtained.
2. No overbooking occurs.
3. Little preplanning of reservations is needed.
4. No-shows are not a problem.

Maximum Use of Tables Is Obtained

Many restaurants that accept reservations will lose the use of tables for a period of time, because the host reserves the tables incorrectly. For example, if a party of ten has a reservation for 8:30 P.M., the host puts three tables together and sets the table up at 5 P.M. Those tables are lost for the first three-and-a-half hours. Even when the host reserves tables correctly, some time will be lost. When tables are not occupied because the table is reserved, and other guests are waiting for a table, a reservation policy loses money for the restaurant and service staff. With a no-reservation policy, the guests are seated on a first-come basis and the restaurant is not losing money from unoccupied tables.

No Overbooking Occurs

With a no-reservation policy, there is no danger of reserving more tables than the restaurant has to accommodate the guests.

Little Preplanning of Reservations is Needed

The host only reserves tables for large parties. At all other times, the host will seat the guests at any table that is available.

No-Shows Are Not a Problem

Because reservations are not accepted (except for large parties), there is no danger of holding a table and not having the guest show up to use the table. Even if the large party fails to show up, the host can reset the tables and accommodate the guests waiting for a table.

DISADVANTAGES FOR THE RESTAURANT

There are a couple of disadvantages for the restaurant that has a no-reservation policy:

1. Business may be lost because reservations will not be accepted.
2. Guests may refuse to patronize the restaurant because they believe they will have to wait for a table for a long period of time.

Both of these disadvantages have to do with the attitude, convenience, and beliefs of the guests. Many guests do not want to wait for a table. They want to be assured that they will have a table when they arrive at a restaurant. If reservations are not taken, the guest may decide to go to another restaurant where accommodations can be secured without waiting for a table.

The second disadvantage occurs after the restaurant has been in business for some time. The restaurant is a success and it attracts a large volume of business. The wait for a table becomes longer than an hour. The word of mouth network that the public uses so well informs other potential guests of this fact. This works negatively for the restaurant. Many people will not want to wait that long, so they do not try to get into the restaurant. Eventually, because so many people decide to go to other restaurants, the amount of business decreases. However, the belief that the restaurant still has a long time for a wait persists in the community, even though it might not be true.

ADVANTAGES AND DISADVANTAGES FOR THE GUEST

In a no-reservation system, the disadvantages for the guest far outweigh the advantages. There are no outstanding advantages for the guest. It might be argued that everyone has the same opportunity of obtaining a table; however, it is a common practice in many no-reservation establishments to "push" regular customers to the top of the waiting list.

The disadvantages for the guest are many. Most of them have been stated already. Two more disadvantages:

1. The guests have to wait for a table; a large party may experience an extended wait if the restaurant does not take any reservations.
2. If the guests are planning some other event besides dinner (such as the theater), there is no guarantee that they will be seated in time to attend.

Regardless of whether the restaurant has a reservation or no-reservation policy, knowing how to reserve tables is an integral part of the host's job. This is because all restaurants should take reservations on holidays and for large parties (usually, six or more guests).

Reserving Tables, Blocking Reservations

The term **blocking** means to reserve a certain table at a certain time for a guest. Its purpose is to enable the host to avoid overbooking. As was previously stated, each restaurant must determine the residence time for each meal period. Once this is known, the dining room can be blocked correctly. The process of blocking begins with taking the reservation correctly. All reservations should be taken on some organized form like the one shown in Figure 8-2.

Successful blocking depends upon an organized system. There are a few common procedures involved in all systems. Regardless of the method that is used, all blocking is to be entered in one book or place, such as a three-ring binder. This is preferable to individual sheets of paper, which may get lost. The physical layout of the dining room (with tables and numbers) is designed and duplicated. Restaurants that have entered the computer age may block tables using a computer program. However, all methods use the same basic principle: A table can only have one party reserved to use the table at each time period.

BLOCKING IN A SMALL RESTAURANT

The simplest way of blocking tables occurs when a restaurant has set meal periods and a limited number of tables. In addition to the preprinted reservation pad, all that is needed is a chart. The chart should be designed as in Figure 8-3.

Across the top of the chart is the day of the week and date. Obviously, the restaurant would have a different chart for each day of the week and for each meal period. The next line of headings shows table number, number of seats at each table, and the times of the reservations. This restaurant is only accepting reservations at 5:30 P.M. and 8 P.M.

SUNDAY, APRIL 3, 19__			
Table Number	# seats	5:30	8:00
1	4	Smith (2)	Jones (4)
2	6	Strianese (6)	Larkin (5)
3	2	Philips (2)	Woodcock (2)
4	4	Gepfert (4)	
5	2		Geleso (2)
6	4		Malary (4)

FIGURE 8-3

A blocking form for a small restaurant

This is an easy chart for the host to use to avoid overbooking. Notice that table 3 seats two people. It is booked for the evening. If a guest requested table 3 for Sunday, April 3, the host would see that the table is booked. In this restaurant of six tables with twenty-two seats, there are only three unreserved tables. By using this form, the restaurant can avoid the problem of overbooking. All employees know exactly at all times how many tables can be reserved. When a guest desires a reservation, the host can turn to the date in the book to see if the party can be accommodated. Then all the information needed for a reservation can be obtained from the guest.

RESTAURANTS WITHOUT SET MEAL TIMES FOR RESERVATIONS

Some small restaurants will take reservations on a first-come, first-seated basis. They will take reservations at any time during their meal period. Basically, the blocking is accomplished in the same manner as in Figure 8-3, but with three differences. First, the restaurant must know the residence time of the guests. This residence time is then incorporated into the planning for reserving tables. Second, the times that the restaurant will take reservations are stated in time segments at the top of the chart. Third, the guests' names must be written on the chart and their residence time blocked out. Figure 8-4 illustrates how to block in this type of restaurant.

Notice that in Figure 8-4, table 5, the Zorn party, is booked from 6 P.M. to 8 P.M. The residence time for their party of three is two hours. The restaurant can take another reservation at 8 P.M. What problems do you envision using this type of system? Will the restaurant obtain maximum use of the tables? This is another example of a system that works well for a small restaurant. But how will a large restaurant avoid overbooking?

FIGURE 8-4

A blocking form for a restaurant that takes reservations with open seating

MONDAY, APRIL 4, 19__						
Table Number	# of guests	Time 5 5:30	Time 6 6:30	Time 7 7:30	Time 8 8:30	
1	4	Smith- - - - - - - - - - - - - - - - -				
2	2			Jones- - - - - - - - - - - - - -		
3	2		Malary- -		Strianese- - -	
4	6				Glock (5)- - -	
5	4		Zorn (3)- - - - - - - - - - - - - - - -			
6	2					
7	2					

BLOCKING IN A LARGE RESTAURANT

First, a decision must be made whether to accept reservations at any time the guest desires or only at specified times that the restaurant sets. The principle of blocking tables in a large restaurant is the same as for a small restaurant, but it is impossible to block out reservations using the same method because of the large number of tables involved. There would be too much paperwork at the host's desk. The system in a large restaurant relies on having a person responsible for the planning and blocking of all reservations. This person is also responsible for informing those who take reservations about the number of tables left for each meal period. A large restaurant may have a person whose sole job is to be the **reservation manager**.

BLOCKING WITH SET MEAL TIMES

This method of blocking tables requires four steps. It is referred to as the **checkoff** method. The first thing that the manager determines is the number of tables available to be reserved in the restaurant. For example, a restaurant has four tables that seat six or eight; twelve tables that seat two; and sixteen tables that seat up to four. A chart, shown in Figure 8-5, is made for the 2 P.M. seating and placed into the three-ring binder where the reservations are being recorded. Each seating has its own individual chart.

The person taking the reservations checks off the size of the table that has been reserved. When Mrs. Smith reserves a table for six at 2 P.M., the reserving and blocking would occur in the following manner: The person taking the reservation would look at the checkoff sheet for

Mother's Day at the 2 P.M. seating. Seeing that there is a table available, all information would be obtained on the preprinted reservation form. The first table under the 6-8 column would be crossed out and the name Smith would be placed next to it. The first line of the chart would appear as it does in Figure 8-6.

The chart would continue to be crossed off and filled out until all the tables are used. If a guest desired a reservation larger than six or eight, the reservation manager would have to establish a policy for accepting or rejecting the request. As large parties require combining existing tables, the reservation manager must carefully plan for the large parties, or overbooking will occur. Each restaurant should decide the maximum number of large parties that can be accepted. A set formula has to be determined for checking off tables so the restaurant will not overbook. For example, a reservation for twelve may include putting together four 4-tops and a deuce. When a reservation is made

FIGURE 8-5

A checkoff sheet. The checkoff sheet is used to assist the reservation manager in blocking.

SUNDAY, MAY 9, 19__ (MOTHER'S DAY)		
2 p.m. Seating		
2	**4**	**6-8**
12	16	4
11	15	3
10	14	2
9	13	1
8	12	
7	11	
6	10	
5	9	
4	8	
3	7	
2	6	
1	5	
	4	
	3	
	2	
	1	

FIGURE 8-6

The checkoff sheet after a reservation for Smith has been taken

SUNDAY, MAY 9, 19__ (MOTHER'S DAY)		
2 p.m. Seating		
2	**4**	**6-8**
12	16	4̶ (Smith) (6)

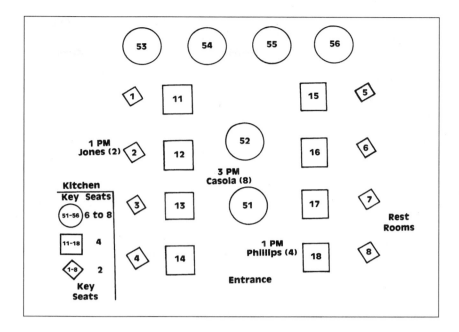

FIGURE 8-7

The dining room blocked with three reservations

for a party of twelve, four 4-tops and a table for two must be crossed off. The reservation manager, to assist in the planning of reservations, will have a printed diagram of the dining room and will block the guests' names and time next to the table that they have been assigned, as shown in Figure 8-7. The Jones, Casola, and Phillips reservations have been blocked off. As more reservations arrive, the remainder of the dining room can be blocked off. The key factor in making this system work is to have constant communication between the reservation manager and the people taking the reservations.

ACCEPTING RESERVATIONS AT ANY TIME

If the restaurant allows guests to reserve tables for any time (called **open seating**), then even more planning and organizing must be done to avoid overbooking. The checkoff sheet would be used, except that the sheet would have the guest's name and the time of the reservation. Figure 8-8 shows how the sheet would look after the restaurant had accepted the first reservation for the Jones party of two guests.

The time is placed next to the Jones name. This informs all people taking reservations that the reservation is for 1 P.M. As the people taking reservations know that the usual residence time for a guest table is two hours, they may accept another reservation at 3 P.M. for the table.

SUNDAY, MAY 9, 19__ (MOTHER'S DAY)		
Open Seating		
2	**4**	**6-8**
~~12~~ Jones (1 p.m.)	16	4

However, this system could become very confusing when multiple reservations are made and/or for guests who come late or early or overstay the residence time. Therefore, the reservation manager would be advised to block out tables daily on the master chart of the dining room, as you have seen in Figure 8-7. Each day, an updated sheet should be put in the three-ring binder showing the number of tables left to reserve. It is easy to understand why a computer software program that reserves seats would be ideal for a large restaurant.

BLOCKING EFFECTIVELY

The previous examples show how the blocking can be done in one step. For the small restaurant, blocking is a simple process. Large restaurants create more of a challenge. Blocking involves much planning and organization so that the guests will have their tables available when they arrive. In order to block effectively, the reservation manager needs three items: a diagram of the dining room, the reservations, and the checkoff sheet.

The diagram of the dining room must have the table number and the number of people that can be seated at each table. The reservations are the preprinted forms that the person taking the reservations has completed. And the checkoff sheet is the control sheet that was located where the reservations have been taken.

Blocking is accomplished by the way of an organized process. First, the reservation manager assigns the reservation to an appropriately-sized table. Then the guest's name and time is placed on the diagram at the table, as shown in Figure 8-7. Figure 8-8 shows the blocking sheet for open reservations. Finally, an alphabetized listing of the guests arriving is completed alongside their expected arrival time and their assigned table. An example of the list is shown in Figure 8-9. From the list and a copy of the blocking diagram, it is easy for the host to know what tables are blocked and what guests are to be seated at which table. Because the reservations are set up first by time and then alphabetized, the host's job becomes easier, as much planning has taken place before the guest has arrived.

FIGURE 8-9

The alphabetized reservation list. After the reservation manager has blocked the tables, the guests' names are organized on a reservation form.

RESERVATIONS FOR SUNDAY, APRIL 30, 19__		
Name	**Number in Party**	**Table Assigned**
1 p.m.		
Feldman	4	12
Jones	6	51
Strianese	2	4
1:30 p.m.		
Collins	4	16
Malary	6	55
Zorn	2	8

This system works well if planned and executed properly.

However, there are some problems that can be associated with this system. First, if the guests do not like the table they have been assigned, the host may have a problem with the guests. The host has a few options. For example, the guests' table could be switched to another comparable table (a 4-top for a 4-top). Or an apology could be offered and an explanation given why the guests cannot have the table they desire (e.g., all the other tables are reserved). If the host ever does switch a table for the guest, the master sheet also has to be updated.

Second, if the guests stay beyond the residence time, the next party will have to wait for their table. Another problem that can occur is to have a party appear for their reservation and state that they have a few more people to add to the party. This can create a real headache for the restaurant. The host must calmly talk to the person in charge of the reservation and assure him or her that the restaurant will accommodate the party as soon as it is possible. Next, the host should make whatever arrangements are necessary (add an extra seat to a table, put two tables together, etc.) to seat the guests. This is one of the situations in which the host has to use his or her good judgement, tact, and diplomacy to keep everyone happy: the guests, service staff, and other guests.

Does the System Work?

In a word, yes, if the host does not deviate from the system. A restaurant that only takes holiday reservations is an example.

On Easter Sunday, the restaurant accepted reservations and served over eight hundred guests. A month later on Mother's Day it served over twelve hundred. For both holidays, it used the open-seating policy on taking reservations. In addition to the regular dining room, it also used three banquet rooms for parties of six or more. The dining rooms at

Easter were running smoothly until 4 P.M. At that time, the staff began to get tired (both dining room and kitchen) and the residence time increased. Some guests had to wait for their assigned tables. As a solution, the hosts deviated from the plan, putting guests at tables that they were not assigned. From 4 P.M. to 6 P.M. the staff had a mess on their hands. Guests were being brought to tables that should have been vacant and were not. The hosts could not keep up with the changes that were being made. Confusion reigned for those two hours. Fortunately, they learned from their mistakes.

A few weeks later, Mother's Day was almost perfect. The restaurant's planning took into account the fatigue factor of the staff. It increased the residence time of the guests for later in the day and did not deviate from the plan. The result of the planning was that just one party of guests was not seated at its assigned time. When the guests arrived, an explanation was offered to them, admitting that it was the restaurant's problem, not theirs. To show its concern, the restaurant invited them to go to the bar and to have either complimentary drinks or complimentary Champagne with their meal. In addition, the host kept checking back with the guests to advise them how long it would be before their table was available.

The result was phenomenal: over twelve hundred guests served with only one problem!

Taking reservations and blocking requires a lot of organization and preplanning, but it allows the restaurant to have a table ready for the guest and to avoid overbooking. Some would say it is too much work to do all that preplanning. Some would say, "I'll take some shortcuts and not put the names next to the table." This can be done if the host is experienced and knows the room. But it comes only with time and experience. A person using this system initially should follow the steps stated above, and the problems of overbooking will be eliminated. Once again, the reader can see the importance of the five Ps of management: Prior Planning Prevents Poor Performance.

CALL-AHEAD OR PRIORITY SEATING

Many guests will not patronize a restaurant that does not take reservations. Long waits for a table prompt many complaints from guests. Restaurants have a relatively new technique called **call-ahead** or **priority seating**.

Guests call the restaurant and have their name added to the seating list. It holds a waiting spot for the guest for dinner that day. The guest's name is logged immediately onto the seating list so that when he or she arrives, the wait will not be as long. It does not guarantee the guest a table for a certain time, but a place in line. The guest is waiting some other place than in the restaurant; therefore, this system keeps the wait to a minimum. For example, a man calls the restaurant and states, he would like a table for four people at 6 P.M. His name is added to the list under the 4-tops, and when he arrives at 6 P.M., his party gets the next available table.

HOW TO ALLEVIATE NO-SHOWS

A major problem that restaurants have in taking reservations is with guests who do not show up for their reservations. Restaurants have been trying to solve the problem of **no-shows** for many years. There are some proven methods that work in reducing the number of no-shows.

The first step in preventing no-shows is to properly train the person who takes reservations. Proper training means informing the guest of all policies of the restaurant pertaining to the reservation. Also, when the guest makes a reservation, information has to be obtained correctly.

Some restaurants request the guest to call them back on the day of the reservation to confirm the reservation. However, many people object to this, because the restaurant is making the guest do the work.

A better method is to inform the guests that on the day of the reservation, the staff will contact them within a certain time frame—for example, between 12 P.M. and 3 P.M.—to confirm the reservation. The guests are told that if they are unable to be reached, their reservation will not be honored unless the guests themselves confirm the reservation.

Other restaurants have begun to employ the same methods as hotels do for lodging rooms: they take a deposit for the reservations. In towns where there is a large demand for tables on weekends, restaurants have asked for a guest's credit card number or for cash to hold the table.

Some owners use a personal computer to keep track of guests who are no-shows. Once the guest becomes a no-show, the name is put on an alphabetized list for the reservation taker. When a guest calls and asks for a reservation, the name is checked against the list. If the name is on the list, the employee informs the guest that there was a reservation scheduled for a certain date for which the guest did not show up. The policy is further explained to the guest that if he or she does not show up for the reservation or does not cancel, then the restaurant will no longer take any reservations under his or her name.

By using one or a combination of these methods, the number of no-shows in the restaurant will be greatly decreased.

Suing a No-Show

David Pelzman, owner of David's on Main in Columbus, Ohio, a 46-seat American bistro, sued customer Jeff Burrey who was a no-show on New Year's Eve.

Pelzman decided to sue Burrey after his party of four did not show up on New Year's Eve. The table was held and Pelzman calculated that he lost $240 in revenue ($60 per person). The $240 suit was dropped by Pelzman after Burrey's attorney presented the judge with a thank-you letter sent to Burrey for his donation to the Mid-Ohio Food Bank. Pelzman earlier had requested that Burrey make a donation for any amount to a food service charity in exchange for Pelzman's dropping the suit.

David's on Main now requires advance credit card payments for reservations on New Year's Eve.[1]

SUMMARY

1. Each establishment must decide its own policy on accepting or not accepting reservations.
2. Both policies have advantages and disadvantages for the establishment.
3. In taking reservations, it is important to follow established procedures to avoid the problem of overbooking.
4. Blocking tables in small restaurants differs from blocking tables in large restaurants.

REVIEW QUESTIONS

1. Your superior wants to have a no-reservation policy. The restaurant is located in a large metropolitan city. What reasons would you give to your superior either to have a no-reservation policy or to have the policy of accepting reservations?
2. Based on Figure 8-3, what type of cuisine would the restaurant that uses this type of blocking system have in order to make the system work? What will be the cost of the average meal: high, average, or low? In other words, what factors must exist for a restaurant to use this system?
3. What are walk-ins? How are they different from guests who have a reservation?
4. What are the benefits and disadvantages for the guest at a restaurant that takes reservations?

5. What are the benefits and disadvantages for a restaurant that takes reservations?
6. What are the benefits and disadvantages for the guest at a restaurant that does not take reservations?
7. What are the benefits and disadvantages for the restaurant that does not take reservations?
8. What information should be obtained from a guest when taking a reservation? Why is this information important?
9. Guests arrive at the restaurant where you are the host. They have a reservation for 7 P.M. It is 6:45, but they are not dressed according to the restaurant's dress code. What will you do?
10. Should restaurants overbook when they take reservations? Explain your answer.
11. Explain how reservations can be structured to avoid overbooking. Include in your answer reservation taking, blocking, and drawing up seating charts.

REFERENCE

1. "David's Settles No-Show Suit," *Nation's Restaurant* News, 21 November 1994, 11.

Managing the Dining Experience

OBJECTIVES

At the completion of this chapter, the reader will be able to:

1. Recite, recognize, and know how to correct or avoid the seven deadly sins of service, as stated in this chapter
2. Explain the method of handling complaints of guests who have a problem with reservations, the food, or any part of the dining experience
3. Use a turn sheet and know its purpose
4. Work the floor
5. Seat guests (those with reservations, as well as walk-ins) using the tools available to the host

The Operation of the Dining Room

A pleasurable dining experience will result in guests' returning to the restaurant for another meal. Return business is the key to making a restaurant profitable.

The restaurant business world would do well to adopt the model of service created by the Swedish businessman Jan Carlzon. In the early 1980s, he sought to make the financially troubled Scandinavian Air

System the best airline in Europe. He was able to change it from a losing business to a profitable one by using service as its main strategy. Carlzon keyed his system to "the moment of truth." A moment of truth occurs each time a customer (or guest) comes into direct contact with the restaurant's people or system. The model states that the service image of a business (restaurant) is the sum of all its moments of truth.

The host is a key player in a restaurant's moment of truth. Many times, the first employee of the restaurant who comes in contact with the guests is the host. The host may also be responsible for training and managing the service employees in the dining room. The service staff have many moments of truth with the guests. The author of the book *Service America*, Karl Albrecht, stated at a conference of chain restaurant executives in Orlando, Florida: "Your service image is not in the hands of your managers. Rather, it's won or lost by your service personnel."[1] It becomes the responsibility of the host to ensure that the staff excels in giving the guests positive moments of truth.

The Seven Deadly Sins of Service

Karl Albrecht also states that there are seven deadly sins concerning service. They are listed in Figure 9-1. Being aware of them and of how to prevent them is the obligation of both the host and the service staff. The seven deadly sins of service are: apathy, the brush-off, coldness, condescension, robotism, rule book excuses, and the runaround. Let's examine how each one of these sins relates to the job of the host.

APATHY

Apathy can be described as a lack of emotion or interest. An example of an apathetic host is found in the following example: The guest enters the restaurant and sees the host standing at the host's desk (the podium). The host does not acknowledge the guest's presence. Instead, the host appears to be interested in reading something that is much more important than greeting the guests. To avoid the sin of apathy, greet guests immediately when they enter the restaurant. Studies have shown that the *impression made in the first thirty seconds of contact between the guest and the restaurant* determines the feeling of the guest about the total dining experience. This is the first moment of truth for the restaurant. The host can create a positive one by greeting the guest within thirty seconds of arrival.

```
┌─────────────────────────────────────────────────┐
│ THE SEVEN DEADLY SINS OF SERVICE                  │
├─────────────────────────────────────────────────┤
│                    Apathy                         │
│                 The Brush-Off                     │
│                   Coldness                        │
│                Condescension                      │
│                   Robotism                        │
│               Rule Book Excuses                   │
│                 The Runaround                     │
└─────────────────────────────────────────────────┘
```

FIGURE 9-1

THE BRUSH-OFF

Brush-off is a slang term that means rebuff, according to *The Random House Dictionary*.[2] Relating it to the host's job, an example of brushing off the guest occurs in the following cases: The guest approaches the host and asks (usually in a timid manner), "When will my table be ready? You told me it would be ready now and it isn't." The host replies, "In a few minutes," and walks away from the guest without any explanation or comment. The second moment of truth has been negative for the restaurant. To prevent committing the second sin, the host should strive to give the guest undivided attention. To avoid brushing off the guest, the host could apologize to the guest and assure the guest that the party will be seated as soon as possible. The host will then seat that party when the next table is available. If the problem persists and a table is not ready, it becomes the responsibility of the host to tell the guest about the status of the seating. Eye contact should be made with the guests, so that they do not get the impression that the host is trying to brush them off.

COLDNESS

Have you even been to a restaurant where the food was excellent and the prices reasonable, but you still felt something was missing? That something was a problem that you could not identify. Most of the time, it was that the restaurant left you with a cold feeling toward it. The host who responds to the guest's question with one-phrase or one-word answers is guilty of committing the sin of coldness. For example, a guest might ask the host, "How long has the restaurant been in business?" The host answers, "Two years." The next question is also answered with a brisk reply. This is the one opportunity for the host to make the guest the restaurant's ally; instead, the host has turned off the guest. Answers are best if they are complete and friendly. This will benefit the restaurant in two ways. First, the guest will have questions answered, and second, it will create a warm feeling toward the restaurant by the guest.

TIP$

TO INSURE PROPER SERVICE

"Basic service is giving the customer what they want, when they want it, and at a price they are willing to pay," states Peter O'Connor, Executive Vice President and Managing Director of the Grand Wailea Resort Hotel & Spa in Wailea, Maui, Hawaii.[3]

CONDESCENSION

Condescension can be described as an air of superiority that an individual shows toward another person. A host who is guilty of the sin of condescension would give the guest the impression that he or she does not belong in the restaurant. Unfortunately, condescension is frequently directed at high school students. This most often occurs when they have a prom, and go to the dinner before the dance. The host's attitude conveys the impression to the staff that the high school students are not very good customers. Notice the word *customers* is used, not *guests*. That is an example of a condescending attitude. To correct this problem, the host should lead by setting an example, and should treat all the individuals who enter the restaurant as guests. All guests receiving positive treatment by all employees will increase repeat business for the establishment. The host or the staff should not be allowed to feel that they are better than any of the guests. By treating the high school student as guests, and by realizing that this is an important night for them, the host can make them feel important. Therefore, the host should greet them warmly and treat them like the valued, respectable guests they are.

ROBOTISM

Robots do not belong in the dining room of a restaurant. A robot can do many repetitive, boring tasks well. However, the job of the host is not repetitive or boring. An example of robotism is when the host seats guests. The host picks up the menus; says, "Follow me"; and sprints to the table. The host then places the menus at the place settings and says, "Have a good meal." The next group of people are treated to the same robotic antics. This method of dealing with guests is eventually transferred to the actions of the service staff. It becomes especially obvious when the service person is going through the "Hi, my name is…" canned speech. To alleviate the sin of robotism, the host should act natural, and should encourage the staff to act natural also. The host's movements should be energetic, and his or her speech should be cordial toward the guests. A robot would be great to do the dishes, but not to manage the dining room.

RULE BOOK EXCUSES

Rules are a necessary part of any business. However, when a host manages only by rules, and does not use common sense, the restaurant will suffer.

No Excuses, Please!

A couple decided to try a new restaurant that had windows overlooking a beautiful view. The tables directly in front of the windows were all booths for four people. When the hostess seated them at a deuce away from the windows, they asked for a window seat. The hostess said "I'm sorry but I have to save those seats for parties of four." They tried to buy the table by giving her a five-dollar bill. She still said that she could not give them the table. The time was 5 P.M., just when the restaurant opened and there were no other guests demanding to be seated. They could not understand why they could not have the table they desired. During their meal, they watched the table to see how many people she sat at the booths. When they left an hour and a half later, there still were no guests seated at the table they wanted. Of course, they never returned to the restaurant—and apparently not too many others did either, because the restaurant went out of business. This was another example of a host failing at the moment of truth.

The host must not fall victim of the sin of rule book excuses, and may bend the rules when it benefits the guests.

THE RUNAROUND

The final sin of service has been experienced by everyone at one time or another in life—the runaround. An example of this as it relates to the host often occurs when the guest is waiting for a table at a no-reservation restaurant. When the guest approaches the host and asks how long it will be before the party is seated, the host replies, "Just a short time." The guest waits for a table to be vacant, and after twenty minutes returns to the host and asks the same question. Again the host says it will be just a short while. When the guest demands a specific time, the host pretends to check the dining room and gets sidetracked. The definition of the runaround is to give vague answers or to refuse to answer the question by ignoring or changing the meaning of the question. The way to avoid the runaround is for the host to give definite answers. A definite time will satisfy the guest's question of "How long will it be before the table is ready? An appropriate answer would be fifteen to twenty minutes, not "In a short while."

Knowing and training the staff to recognize and avoid the seven deadly sins of service is important for the host. The restaurant business is filled with many moments of truth. The restaurant cannot afford to have sins committed at any moment of truth. The first moment of truth comes when the host greets guests into the restaurant. The last moment occurs when the guest leaves the establishment. Throughout their meal, they will experience a series of moments of truth. All of these moments of truth add up to the total service in the restaurant. If the staff fail in one of these moments of truths, then service will suffer.

The Greeting

The host is exactly that: a host. The greeting should be warm and cordial, just as it would be in the host's home. The first thirty seconds are critical for the guest. In those few seconds, the guest forms an opinion about the restaurant: it wants or does not want the guest's business. This is all determined from the greeting offered by the host.

The size and volume of the restaurant determine the number of hosts on duty and their responsibilities. Smaller restaurants usually have one host who has to perform all the jobs. At larger establishments there may be as many as four hosts. One remains at the podium to greet guests, take names, and assign tables. Another finds the guests in the waiting area or at the bar. The other two show the guests to their tables, each being responsible for one half of the dining room.

Other establishments use three hosts. One remains at the podium to greet guests, take names, and assign tables. Another gets the guests when their table is ready. The third seats people and does table checks.

Regardless of the size of the establishment or the number of hosts employed, one host is always responsible for greeting the guests. This individual is always in a position to see when a guest enters the restaurant.

Once the guest enters the restaurant, it becomes the host's responsibility to greet the guests immediately. If the host recognizes the guests, he or she will greet them by addressing them by name. If the guests are new to the restaurant, the greeting is cordial. When at the podium receiving guests, the host should not be leaning over the desk, chewing gum, smoking, or drinking. Instead, the guests receive the undivided attention of the host. If the restaurant takes reservations, the first question after the greeting will be, "Do you have a reservation?" If the guests do have a reservation, the host takes them to their table.

If the restaurant does not take reservations, or the guests do not have a reservation, an inquiry will be made about the size of the party. The host should be aware of obvious facts and avoid saying to a single person, "Table for one." Instead say, "I have a nice table for you, sir; would you please follow me?"

T I P $

TO INSURE PROPER SERVICE

"Always greet every guest with a smile, using the guest's name whenever possible," says Peter O'Connor.[4]

Assigning Tables

As with everything else in the restaurant business, there is a correct way to assign tables. There are also those hosts who take shortcuts and create problems for the guests, service staff, and the restaurant. Assigning tables correctly is another step to ensure that the restaurant obtains maximum income and the guests receive excellent service.

A good tactic used by many restaurants is to seat the guests who arrive when the restaurant opens at a table by the window. Studies have shown that people would rather dine in a busy restaurant than one that is not busy. If the host seats guests near a window, people walking or driving by will see the guests enjoying a meal, and it will create an impression in their minds that the restaurant is a good place to dine.

Rotation of the seating of the guests among the different stations is also advised. The wrong way to seat guests is for the host to seat the first twenty guests at one station, and then fill up the next section. Instead, the first party is seated at station one, the second at station two, and so on. Rotating the seating in this manner allows the service person to give the guests excellent service. If the service person's station were filled up all at once, the service person would have difficulty giving the guests good service because he or she would be overwhelmed (referred to as *swamped* or *in the weeds* in the business) with too many guests to serve at once. The rotation of assigning tables is also considered when stations are made and reservations are being blocked.

Occasionally a guest will request a special table or a different table from the one the host assigns. If the host can honor the request, it is good policy to do it. If there is a legitimate reason not to honor the request, it should be explained to the guest. For example, many times guests will request a 4-top for their party of two. If there is not too much business forecasted for the day, the host can give them the table they desire. If the host expects a heavy demand of business or has a reservation for the table they desire, the guests should be told the reason why they cannot have the table. Of course, if they are regular guests, the host should try to accommodate them and provide them the table. Always seat parties of two at 4-tops if those tables are not in demand.

When a large group of people request a table together, the host should inquire whether they are on a time schedule (sometimes guests are attending a conference and have only a limited time to eat). If they are, it would be wise for the host to explain that it would be faster service if the party broke up into groups of four. The host could then seat the guests at different stations in the dining room. In this way, they will have more service staff to wait on them, instead of just one service person.

Forms Needed to Seat Guests

In addition to the ability to think quickly, the host needs a few forms that will assist in doing the job correctly and efficiently. The forms needed are: a diagram of the tables in the restaurant, the reservation list, the turnsheet, a table check form, and a waitlist.

DIAGRAM OF THE TABLES IN THE RESTAURANT

At the host's desk, there should be a diagram of the floor plan of the restaurant. Many restaurants place this diagram under a glass top. The hosts are given a grease pencil so they can write on the glass to indicate the vacant or occupied status of the table. Using the grease pencil and glass top makes it easier for the host to keep track of the status of the tables. It is also easier to erase and neater than trying to keep track on individual paper diagrams.

THE LIST OF RESERVATIONS

Along with the diagram of the restaurant, the host should also have an alphabetized list of the names of the guests who have reserved a table. Included on the list should be the names of the guests, the number of guests, and the table number they have been assigned. The list should be set up in chronological order. This will allow the host to check off the names as the guests come in to the restaurant, and will make for a smoother operation. Figure 9-2 shows the reader how the reservation list should be set up.

The listing would continue throughout the entire day. By setting this up in an organized fashion, the host can spend time attending to the guests' needs. If the host did not write this seating out in advance, he or she would have to spend an enormous amount of time and effort correctly seating the guests with reservations.

THE TURNSHEET

The next form needed to seat guests effectively is called a **turnsheet**. Figure 9-3 illustrates how this form allows the host to keep track of how many guests have been seated at each station and what station should receive the next party.

Our turnsheet shows that we have five service staff. After each person's name there is a series of numbers. Find the 6/6 fraction after Tom's name. The top number of the fraction represents the number of guests in the party. The bottom number is the cumulative total of all guests seated on Tom's station during this meal period. From this example, Tom has only had 8 guests, while John and Jan have had 10 each, Jim 11, and Pam 13. The host will seat the next party at Tom's station.

FIGURE 9-2

A reservation list set up for the host

RESERVATIONS FOR SUNDAY, APRIL 30, 19__		
Name	**Number in Party**	**Table Assigned**
	1 P.M.	
Feldman	4	12
Jones	6	51
Strianese	2	4
	1:30 P.M.	
Collins	4	16
Malary	6	55
Zorn	2 8	

TURNSHEET			
Name			
Jan	3/3	3/6	4/10
Pam	2/2	4/6	7/13
Jim	1/1	2/3	8/11
John	4/4	4/8	2/10
Tom	6/6	2/8	

FIGURE 9-3

A turnsheet keeps track of how many guests have been seated at each station and what station should receive the next party.

Most hosts use the turnsheet to seat the guests equitably among the service staff. However, when the restaurant becomes busy, often the host has no choice but to seat the guests at the next available table. However, in order to avoid a controversy with the service staff, it is advisable for the host to keep track of the guests served by using the turnsheet.

How Not to Seat Guests

Restaurants that do not take reservations, or only reserve a small percentage of tables, need a method to seat the guests. When there are tables available, there are no problems; guests are seated at an available table. Problems arise when all tables are occupied.

No guest wants to be treated in the following manner. In this no-reservations policy restaurant, when guests approached the host and asked for a table, the host would seat them. However, if the dining room was full, the host would tell the guest to go to the bar and check back in a few moments. The guest would say, "Aren't you going to put my name down?" The host would reply, "No." The guest wanted to know how he would know when his table would be ready. "Just come back, and if there is a table you get it," said the host. The guest suggested that a better method would be to take his name down. The host replied, "What do you think I am, a secretary?" The host is no longer employed at this establishment.

TABLE CHECK

The **table check** (see Figure 9-4) is a tool that allows the host to know the point of the meal that each table has reached. This form is continuously updated throughout the meal. For instance, some restaurants will have it done every twenty minutes. The table check is completed by one of the hosts whose job it is to walk around the dining room and observe each table's progress. The host writes down the

FIGURE 9-4

A table check form allows the host to know at what point of the meal guests at each table are.

TABLE CHECK					
No. in party	JS	SS	Entree	Coff	Up
2	11	14	75	71	74
4	24	34	64	62	61
Big Table	17	18	19	20	
			8:20		

course each table is on under the appropriate column. For instance, if table 71 is having coffee, a 71 goes under the coffee column, as you will observe in Figure 9-4.

From Figure 9-4, the reader can see that table 74 is available for a party of two, and table 61 is available for a party of four. *Up* means the table is available; *JS* refers to just seated; *SS* means soup or salad; entree means the guests are eating their main course; and *coff* means the guests are having coffee. Using the table check, which was completed at 8:20, the host greeting guests at the podium knows the status of all tables at all times. When a party of two approaches the podium and requests a table for two the host can seat them immediately at table 74. The next party of two will have to wait until table 71 finishes their coffee. The host will know that it generally takes fifteen to twenty minutes before that table will be vacant. When all the tables are filled, the table check gives the host a guideline of how long it will be before the guests can be seated. The approximate waiting times would be as follows:

If the guests are on:	
Soup and salad	45-60 minutes
Entree	30-45 minutes
Coffee	15-20 minutes

Some restaurants do table checks every twenty minutes, while other hosts do table checks informally. The Perry Restaurant Group and Hooters use electronic devices to assist with the table check. The host remains at the desk greeting guests, while another employee roams throughout the dining room, communicating the availability of the tables directly to the host via a headset microphone. Once the host knows how long the wait will be, the proper method of informing the guest of the wait for the table can be used.

Informing the Guests about the Wait

When a guest arrives at a restaurant that does not take reservations and there is a long waiting time, the host has an obligation to tell the guests approximately how long they will have to wait for a table. Most guests do not mind waiting; however, some guests will object. The host should never state to a guest that it will just be a few minutes for a table. Instead, the host should give the guest an approximate time. This time has to be one that the host can honor. For example, if the host knows that a table will be vacant in fifteen minutes, the guest should be told that there is a wait of fifteen to twenty minutes. If the guest is seated before the fifteen minutes, that will be great for the guest. If the wait is more than twenty minutes, the restaurant has failed in this moment of truth.

When the host informs the guest of the length of the wait, the responsibility of staying or leaving rests upon the guest. Many restaurants have a friendly working relationship with their competitors. The host will phone the competitors and find out how long a wait there is at the competitor's restaurant, if any. The host can use this information in a variety of ways to assist the guests. First, if there is a long wait at the competitor's restaurant, this knowledge relayed to the guests may keep them at the host's restaurant. This is especially true after the guests have to factor in driving time to the competitor's restaurant. However, if the competitor has space available or a much shorter waiting list, this can be relayed to the guests.

The host should keep the guests informed whenever possible about problems that arise that may keep the table from being available when promised. If guests cannot be seated when promised, management policy may allow the host to give the guests some complimentary item to let them know that their business is appreciated. One restaurant takes this a step further. Any guests who are told the waiting time and decide that it is too long for them to stay, receive a card that can be redeemed for a complimentary drink on their next visit to the restaurant.

THE WAITLIST

All restaurants that take walk-ins must have a **waitlist**. This form allows the host to seat guests in an organized manner. The waitlist is used when all the tables are occupied in the restaurant and guests are waiting for a table. The waitlist is shown in Figure 9-5.

The waitlist is set up with the names of the guests who are waiting for a table. The next column is for guests who want a table for four or more guests. The number in parenthesis, 51, represents the table that the host plans to use for that party. *Est. wait time* refers to the amount of time the host has estimated that the guest will have to wait for a table. *Time in* refers to when the guest entered the restaurant. *Time seated* is when the guest has been seated at the table. The next column is for groups of two. Finally, the table number where the guest was actually seated is recorded. In our example in Figure 9-5, Mr. Smith entered the restaurant at 8:02 P.M. and wanted a table for two guests. From the

FIGURE 9-5

The waitlist form allows the host to seat walk-in guests in an organized manner.

THE WAITLIST						
Name	4 or 6 guests	Est. wait time	Time In	Time Seated	2	Table Number
Smith	(51)	30/45	8:02	8:32	2	51
Jones	4(62)	30/45	8:15			
Brown	6(22)	30/45	8:17			

host's table check chart, the host decides to seat Mr. Smith at table 51, because the guests at the table are on their entree. He informs the waiting guests that there will be a thirty to forty-five minute wait. Mr. Smith decides to stay and have dinner. The host gives Mr. Smith a card with his name on it, instructs him to give it to the host when his name is called, and keeps a duplicate copy for himself. This stops guests from trying to claim a table when it is not their reservation or name called.

INFORMING GUESTS THAT THEIR TABLE IS AVAILABLE

Different establishments have different methods for informing their guests when their tables are ready. Many have loudspeakers that announce their names. A more professional method is to have a system that instructs the bartenders and cocktail servers to ask the guests if they are having dinner. If the guests say they are, they ask them for their card. When their table is ready, the host calls the bar and informs the bartender that there is a table available for the Smith party of two. Another method is for the host to walk through the waiting area and announce the names of the guests that he or she is seeking.

The Dishonest Table Snatcher

At a twentieth-year high school reunion, a classmate boasted that he had never waited very long for a table at places that had a no-reservation policy. He and his date would go to restaurants that took the names of walk-in guests waiting for a table. Sometimes, they would go to the bar and have a drink; other times they would obtain their table immediately. This is how he did it: As soon as he heard the host calling the name and number of guests in the party, (for instance, the Smith party of two), he would go to the host and claim the table. Most of the time he was seated because the restaurant did not give out any cards to the guests.

Another method uses technology. Guests waiting for a table are given pagers and allowed to roam the vicinity. When their table is ready, they are beeped by the host. Of course, a few pagers may be lost by forgetful patrons.

Keeping the Waitlist Accurate

The host must keep an accurate waitlist to avoid problems in seating guests, and to aid in planning future business. The time that Mr. Smith is seated is noted under the time seated column, along with the actual table number that he has been assigned.

All restaurants have their own codes to assist them with the waitlist. At one restaurant, when a guest requests a table for six, the host places a big black mark around the guest's name. This is to signify that they have a large party waiting. As the number of tables that will accommodate six people are limited, the host does not want to make the guest's party wait longer than they are told. In addition, once the host sends for a party, he or she underlines the name with the black pen. When the person has been located, the host puts a double mark under the name. If a person is not found, he or she puts down the time the guest was called, gives them fifteen minutes to appear, and if they are not there in that time, puts in large letters *NS* (for No-Show) through their name.

The information gained from the waitlist can be valuable for the host. The host can see how many guests had to wait for a table, the time the first guest had to wait, the average waiting time, the longest waiting time, and other factors that will help the host staff and plan for the business. Above all, the waitlist will provide a fair and organized tool for the host to seat the guests.

TIP$

TO INSURE PROPER SERVICE

Never tell your guests that their table is not ready because you have a problem. They do not care: they just want their table.

Leading and Seating Guests

The guests now need to be shown to their assigned table. The host has to take into account the age and the physical condition of the guests. Once the host determines the condition of the guests, the host gauges the walk leading the guest to the table at a comfortable pace. It is not a good idea to sprint to the table if the guest is elderly, because the guest may not be able to keep up with the pace.

Once the host reaches the table, it is proper to pull out chairs for the guests (women first) and assist them with seating. If the table is against the wall, it has become traditional to offer the seat that faces into the dining room to the female, while the male is seated facing the wall. The napkins are removed from the table by the host, opened, and handed to the guests.

Menus should be distributed next, both food and wine, if appropriate. Women are given their menus first. It is advisable to open up the menus to the entree page. This accomplishes two things. First, the host can see if the menu is the correct menu; second, it is another small detail that the guest will not have to attend to. Next, the host has to communicate important information to the guests.

TIP$

To Insure Proper Service

Check to make sure that you give each guest a menu that is for that meal period (dinner menus for dinner, not lunch menus).

Communicating Information

This is an area where most hosts fall short. Many hosts bring the guest to the table, drop off the menus, and are never seen again. After the guests have been seated and handed menus, the host should inform the guests of any chef's creations (and their prices) that are not listed on the written menu. The restaurant should not have more than three chef's specials, because the guests may become confused. Many restaurants use an alternative method. The host gives a list of daily specials to the guests along with the regular menus. The host points out the list, which includes prices, to the guests as they are seated.

It is strongly suggested that the host use the guests' names as much as possible when they are known. Once the guests have been told the additions to the menu, the host may also ask them if they would like to order a beverage. This is a key moment of truth in the restaurant business. According to Professor Gary Brenensthul of Schenectady County Community College, this is transition time. It is the time when the host turns over the guests from his care to the care of the service person. When the guest must wait for the service person to approach the table and take the drink order, the wait can be an uncomfortable one. Professor Brenensthul says that "the guest should have the drink order taken immediately." By having the host take the drink order, the guest will have been served immediately. The restaurant is saying to the guest that we value your business and do not want you to wait for anything. In addition, there is the possibility of selling more drinks, whether they are alcoholic or nonalcoholic. This serving or taking of a drink order should be done with every meal period. At breakfast, the host would offer coffee to the guest immediately. The last thing the host should do as he leaves the table is to tell the guests the name of the service person. To be most effective, it should be done in an informal manner, such as, "Jan will be your service person, she will be right over with your drink order." As the host leaves the table, the drink order is given to the service person so it can be delivered as soon as possible. The host can now concentrate on working the floor.

Working the Floor

Working the floor is a phrase used in the restaurant business to mean that the host is circulating around the dining room talking to guests and assisting service staff. When the guest has been seated by the host, the host should not go back and stand at the podium waiting for the next guest to come into the restaurant. Instead, the host has to walk around the dining room and make certain that the guests are being served properly. One of the key factors in working the floor is to communicate with the guests. If the host notices that the guests are sitting at the table with their menus for a long period of time, he should approach the table and ask, "Has Jan been here to take your order yet?" Is she has not, the host should take the order or find Jan so that she can take the order. The host should not just walk around the dining room, but should stop at tables and talk to guests—by name, if possible.

Working the floor also involves "getting your hands dirty." This means that the host (and dining room manager, if they are not the same person) may bus tables, serve food, serve drinks, and reset tables if a service person needs assistance. The host should be not just a pretty face but a vital working member of the staff.

The final responsibility of the host is to make sure that the guests are completely satisfied with their dining experience. As the guests complete their meals, the host inquires about their dining experience and shows appreciation to the guests for patronizing the restaurant. This appreciation can be shown in the form of a "Thank you," buying the guest a free dessert or after-dinner drink, or some other gesture that makes the guests feel special. Other establishments empower the host and the waitstaff to give a card to their guests that offers them a free appetizer or dessert upon their next visit.

A Host Who Almost Got It Right

A couple were at a restaurant. They watched and listened as the host approached and spoke to a party of two after they had finished their meal. One guest had ordered swordfish that was served on a bed of pasta. The host inquired about the food, asking how they liked it. The guest said that the swordfish was great, but the pasta was not cooked enough. The host replied that all the pasta is cooked the same way, al dente. He further added: "If you want, you can take the pasta home with you and microwave it. It will taste really good that way. The next time you come in, make sure you ask for it (the pasta) cooked more than al dente." If you were the guest would you be pleased with this response? What do you think the host did correctly and incorrectly? What improvements could you suggest to make the guest feel satisfied?

Seating Guests with Disabilities

Title III of the Americans with Disabilities Act (ADA), which became effective in 1992, requires that any private place of business be accessible for guests. There are specific guidelines for both new and existing restaurants that must be followed. The dining room manager should be aware of this law and the guidelines that must be followed. If the restaurant is not accessible, a plan should to put into effect to make the restaurant accessible. As an example, it has been reported that Planet Hollywood in Washington, D.C., has agreed to install a ramp leading to the front entrance, place an accessible restroom on the first floor, lower counters in the bar and retail areas, build a ramp into the science fiction theme dining area and install signage required by the ADA. This occurred because of a complaint brought by wheelchair users Atsuko Kuwana and her husband, Michael Winter, after they had to enter through a locked side service door because the three steps leading to the front entrance allegedly were not ramped.

TIP$

To Insure Proper Service

Talk directly to guests with disabilities. One hospitality student (who is in a wheelchair) gets most annoyed when servers ask his wife questions and treat his as if he were not even there.

With restaurants becoming more accessible to guests with disabilities, the host has to be aware of what can be done to make their dining experience enjoyable. The type of disability guests have will dictate their special needs as well as the consideration that the host gives them. For instance, a visually impaired guest should be led to the table and have the location of the utensils explained by the host by imagining the table as the face of a clock (e.g., the coffee cup is at five o'clock). If the guest has a seeing-eye dog, the host leads the guest to a table where the dog can lie down without being in the traffic flow.

Title III requires that there be an accessible route of travel to get into the dining room. In addition, guests must be seated in the least restrictive environment. A host cannot give people with disabilities the poorest table in the restaurant. The host would seat guests in wheelchairs at a table that is out of the flow of traffic, but where the guest is comfortable.[5] The host may assist the guest in whatever way possible to make the person feel welcome. It may be necessary to move the table so the guest can position his or her wheelchair comfortably at the place setting. In some instances, it might be necessary to raise the table to a height that will accommodate wheelchairs.

TIP$

TO INSURE PROPER SERVICE

Talk directly to guests with disabilities. One hospitality student (who is in a wheelchair) gets most annoyed when servers ask his wife questions and treat him as if he were not there.

Regardless of the disability of the guest, the host has to remember, and impress upon the staff, that these individuals are as valuable to the restaurant as guests who are not disabled. The staff has to be taught to treat all guests with courtesy, and to put forth extra effort so that all can enjoy themselves and have a pleasant dining experience.

TIP$

TO INSURE PROPER SERVICE

Have Braille menus available for your guests.

The Problem Guest

Unfortunately, there will be times when a guest has a complaint about the wait for the table, the food, the services, or prices. The host must know how to handle complaints and be able to resolve the situation so the guest feels that the problem has been solved satisfactorily.

TIP$

TO INSURE PROPER SERVICE

Never interrupt a guest who is complaining.

STEPS TO HANDLE COMPLAINTS

1. Give undivided attention and listen carefully to the guest's complaint.

2. Clarify the complaint by repeating it back to the guest.

3. Agree with the guest on some point about the complaint.

4. Solve the guest's problem. Ask what he or she would like you to do, or explain why the complaint cannot be solved.

5. Check back throughout the meal to be certain the problem was solved.

FIGURE 9-6

Clarify the complaint by repeating it back to the guest. By now the guest should have calmed down. Make the person realize that you understand the complaint. Next, try to agree on some point about their complaint. Finally, solve the problem or offer the guest some possible solutions to the problem. Throughout the meal, return to the guest's table and check to ensure that the problem has been solved. Using this approach, the host can turn a bad situation into a good situation. This skill in handing complaints is another area that the host must excel in to create a positive moment of truth for the restaurant.

Reservation Not Honored

Unfortunately, one of the major problems that occurs in restaurants is that reservations are not honored. This happens for a number of reasons. Occasionally there will be a problem because reservations have been taken incorrectly. Other times, guests will stay longer than their residence time. Regardless of the problem or reason why the restaurant does not have a table for the guests, it is the fault of the restaurant, not the guests.

To solve the problem, the host must seat the guests as soon as a table becomes available. However, the host first should explain the problem to the guests and offer an apology for their inconvenience. It is recommended that the host make some positive gesture to the guests to soothe their feelings for their inconvenience. If it is legal in your state, buy them a bottle of wine with the meal; or have them go to the bar and buy them a drink. If they don't drink, offer them a free dessert.

In the meantime, the host also has to deal with guests who are staying past their residence time. The host should find out the reason for the delay. If it is a problem that can be solved quickly (the service person has not given the guests their check), the host can rectify it immediately. The table can now be set (called **turning tables**) for the next guest. If the guests are sitting with an extra cup of coffee, the host may not be able to do anything. Or an offer may be made to move the guests to another area (such as the bar or a sitting room), where they can continue their conversation. However, this is a very tricky situation, and the host may do more harm than good by asking the guests to move. This is a decision that the host would make after considering whether asking the guests to move would create negative feelings in the guests.

After the problems have been solved, the host must identify the reason why the reservations were not honored. Then, adjustments to the reservation policy must be made so the problem will not occur again. The host must be able to solve the problem of not honoring reservations, so the guest will want to return to the restaurant for another meal.

Final Jobs of the Host

The host's job is not complete until long after the guests leave the restaurant.

After the guests have received their entrees, the host works the floor and talks to the guests, inquiring about their meals. Before the guests leave the restaurant, the host should inquire about the dining experience and offer the guests something free. This could be an after-dinner drink, dessert, or complimentary coffee. The key is to let the guests know that their business is appreciated.

A Cold January Night

A couple ventured out Friday night to patronize a restaurant. With the temperature of -5 degrees Fahrenheit and the wind chill down around -35 degrees Fahrenheit, the restaurant owner, manager, and staff should have been thrilled to see them and have done everything possible to make their meal memorable.

They walked into the restaurant right at opening time and were shown a nice table for two by the window. It was a cozy seat next to the window so they could see the people rushing by in the cold. But they were nice and warm because of the baseboard heater right at their feet. They opened up their menus and the wife said, "What a strange menu, there are no appetizers." After comparing both of their menus, they discovered that she had duplicate pages of the entree menu and no appetizer menu. The waitress came over to their table and asked if they would like a drink. They told her they would be ordering wine; please give them a few minutes. She then proceeded to talk to them about the weather and how slow business was going to be that night. She is off to a good start, the couple thought. She came back to the table a couple of times to see if they had any questions about the menu. Finally, they ordered their wine and food. They were both served properly. (She even refilled their wine glasses!) The food was acceptable—not great, but nothing special. By now they had a bottle of wine and their two entrees. They were finished, and she came to the table and asked them if they cared to see a dessert menu and have coffee. They said, "Sure, but let us finish our wine before you bring us the decaf and regular coffee." She then proceeded to clear their plates, stacking the dirty dishes on top of one another. She brought the coffee and decaf, making sure she told them which one was decaf. They had their two desserts and coffee, which were quite good. Now came another moment of truth. She brought the check to the table and placed it down. She failed to ask if they wanted another cup of coffee! There was no excuse for this. She was not busy, the restaurant was not busy, and they would have had to ask for a second cup of coffee. By her lack of perception, she had ended the service negatively. No manager or host ever came to the table throughout the meal to inquire about the meal. The couple paid the check, and as they were going out, the husband recognized the owner. He was putting on his coat in a leisurely fashion. He never spoke to them or the other patrons leaving. As they left, no one, not him, the waitress, the manager, or the two hostesses said anything to them. This was an opportunity for the restaurant to show a positive sign of hospitality. Instead, the few guests patronizing the restaurant were penalized for the lack of business.

When the guests leave the restaurant, it is imperative that the host thank them for their business and invite them to return to the restaurant.

Some restaurants employ a person to call up guests on the following day to inquire about their dining experience. This gives the guest an opportunity to give the restaurant feedback without having to do it face to face. It gives the restaurant an opportunity to find out about its performance and if there were any problems. If the person calling is told of a problem, the restaurant can take steps to correct it.

TIP$

TO INSURE PROPER SERVICE

Remember the 80/20 rule. Eighty percent of your business comes from 20 percent of your customers, your repeat customers.

The Logbook

Each restaurant should have a book that includes a record of the important happenings of the day. Items such as the number of meals that were served, the waiting time of reservations, the time first seated, and other items that will assist in the forecasting of the business may be included in the logbook. In addition, there is usually an area where messages are left for the next shift. By having this special area in the logbook, no messages are lost and there is proof that information was passed to the next shift. This logbook will help the restaurant run smoothly and efficiently.

The information in this chapter gives the reader the knowledge to be the perfect host. Does one exist? Have you ever found one?

The Perfect Host

In a little community ten minutes from Schenectady, New York, is a restaurant called The Bears. The owners of the restaurant, Bob and Pat Payne, or Papa and Mama Bear, along with their son, operate an excellent restaurant. This restaurant has been in business for over twenty-five years.

Everything works. The food, the service, the cleanliness, and the price value. When guests arrive at The Bears, they are greeted by name and by the owners. The owners act as if they are greeting long-lost friends. The new guests are introduced to the owners by the regulars. Once that is completed, the owners return to the kitchen to prepare the meal.

Next, the service explains the menu thoroughly and knowledgeably. However, for most guests, it is not necessary. This is because The Bears is noted for its beef. When the guests make their reservations, the meals have been ordered in advance. Usually, it will be Chateaubriand or prime ribs.

Next comes the food. And the food is great. Their specialty, Chateaubriand, is so tender that it can be cut with a fork. All the other items are good, and all are presented attractively. The service is proper and the service staff make certain that they take care of the needs of all their guests.

When the meal is completed, Papa Bear makes it a point to visit each table and ask all the guests if they liked their meal. He then offers them more food if they are still hungry, which almost everyone refuses because there is enough food left over for another complete meal. That leftover food is quickly placed in a container by the service staff to be taken home by the guest.

Guests leave The Bears completely satisfied and their word-of-mouth promotion fills the restaurant completely, week after week.

Marketing Your Business

All businesses, regardless of type, need a marketing plan. The plan is a blueprint for the business. Because the only constant in the business world is change, the restaurant or banquet manager has to complete this blueprint to guide the business for the upcoming year.

A marketing plan lets management know where the business is at present. It outlines problems and opportunities by identifying the operation's strengths and weaknesses as well as its competitors. Goals are set and strategies are planned based upon an analysis of the strengths and weaknesses. The marketing document will state how the plan will be implemented and executed. Included will be a budget to help the operation reach its desired goals. Finally, the plan will have criteria built into it to allow management to determine if the plan has been successful.

But remember, the number one reason for trying a restaurant is word-of-mouth. Incorporate that fact into your plan.

SUMMARY

1. The seven deadly sins of service are apathy, the brush-off, coldness, condescension, robotism, rule book excuses, and the runaround.
2. The first thirty seconds after a guest enters the restaurant are critical to the guest's opinion of the establishment. In this regard, the host's greeting is all-important.
3. The essential tools for seating guests are the reservations list, the turnsheet, the table check, and the waitlist.
4. Among the host's chief responsibilities during the dining experience are working the floor, accommodating physically disabled guests, dealing with problem guests, and showing the establishment's appreciation for the guest's patronage at the end of the dining experience.
5. The restaurant's logbook is important as a record of the day's business, a tool for forecasting future business, and a vehicle for leaving messages for the following shift.

REVIEW QUESTIONS

1. Why should a restaurant owner or host send business to the competition?
2. List the seven deadly sins of service. Explain what they are and how they relate to the host's job.
3. Explain how you would handle the following problem. A party of four comes into your restaurant. The host tells them it will be a short wait for their table. They are asked if they want to go to the bar, which they do. The service person ignores them in the bar. When they finally are seated after their short wait (thirty minutes),

the service person takes and serves their appetizers almost immediately. One half hour goes by and then the service person returns to the table and says: "I made a terrible mistake, I forgot to put your order into the kitchen. I just did it now." The food comes out twenty minutes later. One of the steaks was ordered medium well and comes out rare. The guest is upset. She asks to see the manager. You come to the table and she shoves her plate at you, complaining about your restaurant. What do you do?

4. What is a turnsheet? What is its purpose and how is it set up?
5. How is a table check form set up? What is its purpose?
6. What should a host do when seating a guest? What are the steps needed to seat guests properly?
7. What is a waitlist, and what is its purpose?
8. What does the phrase "working the floor" mean?
9. What considerations should be given to physically disabled guests?

REFERENCES

1. Jack Hayes, "Albrecht Stresses Need to Service America," *Nation's Restaurant News,* 14 March 1988, 4.
2. *The Random House Dictionary,* s.v. "brush-off."
3. Peter O'Connor, letter to the author, 1996.
4. Ibid.
5. James R. Abbey, *Hospitality Sales and Advertising,* 2nd ed. (East Lansing, Michigan: The Educational Institute of the American Hotel and Motel Association, 1996).

Part Three

Banquet
Management

The Banquet Business and the Banquet Manager

OBJECTIVES

At the completion of this chapter, the reader will be able to:

1. Define the term *banquet*
2. Explain the importance of banquets as they relate to the profitability of any hospitality establishment
3. List and explain the advantages that the banquet business has over restaurants that serve a la carte meals
4. Define the difference between a caterer and a banquet manager
5. List the advantages and disadvantages of a career as a banquet manager
6. Name the types and styles of service available for banquets
7. Explain the qualifications for being a banquet manager
8. List the job knowledge that a banquet manager must possess in order to do the job effectively
9. Explain the banquet manager's main responsibility as it relates to the client requesting the banquet
10. Explain the key to being a successful banquet manager

What is a Banquet?

A **banquet** is a meal that has a menu that is preselected by the client for all of the guests attending the event. A banquet usually occurs in a separate location and the client generally requests special items (color of tablecloths, centerpieces, different menu, etc.). The number of guests at a banquet usually ranges from ten to ten thousand or higher. The only reason there will be a maximum number is because the banquet facility has a limited amount of space to accommodate guests. However, if the space is available—as it is with a domed stadium like the Houston Astrodome—a banquet can accommodate two thousand guests or more.

Any restaurant that can successfully serve a banquet of ten people can serve any size banquet. This is because the principle of serving a banquet to a large group is the same as serving it to a small group.

Clients' Reasons for Having a Banquet

There are many reasons why clients hold banquets. Some hold them for the purpose of personal entertaining, while others must conduct them for business; some clients hold banquets for other reasons. Regardless of the reason, the banquet serves one main purpose: it allows the client to invite a large group of people, without doing the planning, buying, cooking, and serving of food. Nor does the client have to clean up after the party is finished. Having a banquet allows the client to greet and make the guests feel at home rather than act as a service person.

TIP$

TO INSURE PROPER SERVICE

Read your local newspapers daily to find out what type of clients are holding banquets, meetings, and social events. This will give you an indication of the type of events that are being held in your area.

FIGURE 10-1

Reasons for holding a banquet

REASONS FOR HAVING BANQUETS		
Personal Entertaining	**Business**	**Other Organizations**
Religious Ceremonies	Meetings	Weekly Meetings
Celebrations	Conferences	Sports Banquets
Social	Celebrations	Award Banquets

PERSONAL ENTERTAINMENT

The first thought most people have about the reasons why banquets are held concern personal entertaining. These banquets are conducted because the client wants to entertain his or her friends. Personal entertainment banquets are usually a result of religious ceremonies, celebrations, or social affairs.

One of the largest markets in the personal entertaining banquet business comes from wedding receptions. However, there are many other religious ceremonies that add to the list. For example, baptisms, first communions, confirmations, and even funerals. In communities where there is a large Jewish population, bar and bat mitzvahs may make up a large portion of a banquet establishment's business.

Each one of these requires the banquet manager to understand and know the religious customs of each group. For instance, a banquet celebrating a Catholic confirmation would require a different set of rules from a Jewish bar/bat mitzvah ceremony. The banquet manager must know the protocol regarding who is to give the blessing and when and how it will be given. The client will often ask the banquet manager for guidance to perform it correctly.

TIP\$

To Insure Proper Service

Learn and understand a new religious custom weekly.

The twenty-fifth and fiftieth wedding anniversaries are the ones that are often most celebrated with banquets. However, birthday and graduation parties also contribute greatly to the social business.

Finally, there are parties for social entertaining. Guests are invited to a **banquet facility** or to a party catered at the client's house for the purpose of having a party. Many of them occur during the winter holiday season; but they are a viable business all year long.

The personal entertaining business is an excellent market for a banquet facility or a caterer. There will always be a demand for banquets.

BUSINESS ENTERTAINING

Entertaining for the purpose of doing business is another large source of income for the caterer or banquet facility. The individual at the business responsible for planning the function, is employed by that particular business. This type of entertaining differs from personal entertain-

FIGURE 10-2

Catering business functions can be a lucrative source of income for the banquet manager. Photograph by Randall Perry.

ing because the business, not the individual, pays for the banquet. One of the main purposes for business entertaining is to conduct conferences or meetings. Other reasons are for celebrating a special business occurrence (anniversary, grand opening) and throwing parties to honor employees.

Conferences and meetings are often held off premises of the business, at a hotel or restaurant. Some large companies employ a meeting planner to select the facility to hold these conferences. However, the vast majority of companies assign an employee to head the event who has little or no experience in planning and conducting a conference. This person utilizes the experience and organization of the banquet manager to have a successful conference. His or her success in "pulling off the event" depends greatly on the banquet manager, especially if he or she has had little experience in organizing these type of events. The employee relies on the banquet manager for the planning, name tags, pens; in short, everything. These conferences can last as short a time as one meal or as long as a week. They usually involve the renting of meeting rooms and provisions for food and liquor service.

A great source of income for the banquet manager or caterer are business anniversary parties. Along with these anniversary parties, businesses often have special parties for their employees. These consist of retirement, Christmas, and special recognition banquets. Also, many schools have a "welcome party" for their new employees at the beginning of the school year.

The business market is a valuable addition to the caterer's market, as the vast majority of functions are held Monday through Friday; but a certain percentage also are held on weekends.

OTHER ORGANIZATIONS

Other types of organizations that have banquets are groups of people who belong to organized clubs. Some examples would be service clubs, like the Rotary and Lions. Youth sport groups such as soccer, baseball, football, and basketball would also have a need to use your banquet facilities. Bowling leagues are another group that can be a large source of revenue for a banquet house. These organizations can bring an enormous amount of business to a banquet house or a caterer.

TIP$

TO INSURE PROPER SERVICE
Have your banquet facility sponsor a youth sporting event.

The Key to Successful Banquet Management

The reasons explained above are only a partial list of why people have banquets. The reader can add to the list many more groups of people who would need the service of a banquet manager. However, regardless of the reasons for holding banquets, there is one key to being a successful banquet manager. It is the statement highlighted in Figure 10-3.

Why Banquets?

More and more restaurants are getting into the banquet business for a very simple reason: A restaurant can make more money, with a lot less chance of failure, by holding banquets. Put simply, the profit potential is much greater for selling banquets than for a restaurant with an a la carte business only.

The reason this is true becomes evident when a comparison is made between the way the a la carte restaurant and the banquet house must conduct business.

At a banquet, the establishment knows in advance many more facts about the food it has to prepare than does an a la carte restaurant. First, the banquet manager knows what all the guests are going to eat at

THE KEY TO SUCCESSFUL BANQUET MANAGEMENT

The banquet manager must take the
RESPONSIBILITY
for the total event off the client's shoulders
and put it on his or her shoulders.

FIGURE 10-3

the banquet. Because the banquet has been prearranged, the banquet manager knows how many guests are going to attend the banquet and how much food has been ordered.

At the **a la carte restaurant**, the manager never knows what or when the guests will eat. Therefore, the a la carte restaurant has to have more inventory to satisfy the guest's requests, while the banquet house only has to buy the food that has been ordered for the banquet.

The banquet manager knows in advance exactly how many guests will attend the banquet; as a matter of fact, the client of the party must guarantee the number of guests that will attend. If that number does not show up, the client must still pay for the guaranteed number. On the other hand, the restaurant has to forecast the number of guests that will patronize its establishment. If there is bad weather or some other event is scheduled that the guests would rather attend, then the guests do not show up at the restaurant. In addition, the banquet manager may obtain an advance payment; most banquet houses obtain a deposit large enough to cover all their expenses. The restaurant has to wait until the guests consume their meals before getting any money.

Staffing is another advantage the banquet house has over the a la carte restaurant. Because the banquet manager knows the number of people attending, the menu and the time the food will be served, he or she can staff for the event without any wasted labor cost. On the other hand, the restaurant has to be prepared for a large group of guests, when in fact no one may show up. The a la carte restaurant may have many people scheduled to work, with little work to do. As the restaurant has to pay these employees, their labor cost rises and their profits decrease.

There is virtually no leftover food at a banquet. Everything is purchased in advance and cooked correctly; therefore, waste is kept to a minimum. At an a la carte restaurant, there may be an enormous amount of waste, since the restaurant manager does not know what the patrons will order. Thus, the restaurant may have too much of one item and not enough of another. In an a la carte restaurant, specific items are often sold out; at a banquet, this never happens.

Advertising and selling of banquets is easier than for an a la carte restaurant. For an a la carte restaurant to get two hundred guests to have dinner at the establishment, it has to convince a large group of guests to patronize it by using a variety of advertising methods—often at a cost of between 3 percent to 7 percent of its gross sales. On the other hand, a banquet facility in order to get two hundred guests has to convince one or two people (just the client or clients) to have the banquet at its establishment. In addition, because everything is known about the banquet before the guests arrive, the quality of food and service will most likely be higher than at the a la carte restaurant. The end result is that when the banquet house does a superb job on the party, the banquet manager has two hundred potential guests to book a banquet.

TO INSURE PROPER SERVICE

It is five times more expensive to acquire a new customer than it is to keep an old one.

Monaco's Palace: the Banquet Specialists

TIP$

There was a restaurant in Columbus, Ohio, called Monaco's Palace. The owner of the restaurant, Baldino Monaco, chose to change the business from a la carte and banquets to strictly banquets. The restaurant had a banquet room that seated four hundred. The room was booked a year in advance for banquets. Baldino had a very good a la carte weekend business; his restaurant would have an hour and a half wait on Saturday night and a short wait on Friday. But during the week, there was never a wait for a table. In fact, business was very slow. He found he was getting more requests for his banquet room and had to turn business away. So he did the logical thing: he eliminated the a la carte business and changed the name of the restaurant from Monaco's Palace to Monaco's Palace: the Banquet Specialists. As a result of the change he was able to reduce his full time staff to five from about twenty-eight. He also appreciates the banquet business because it is guaranteed, and it has been a lot less strain on him.

The main reason a restaurant would seek out the banquet business is because it is a profit maker. A restaurant that serves banquets knows a vast amount of information about the party before the guest arrives. The restaurant knows how many people will be attending, how much food to order, the time of the event, its food cost, and its labor cost for the banquet. Everything about the banquet is known before the guests arrive. With proper planning (the 5 Ps) costs can be kept to a minimum while profits are maximized.

Catering vs. Banquets

Many people do not understand the difference between a caterer and a banquet manager. In reality, there is very little difference. In some areas of the country there is no distinction whatsoever. Both serve the guests by providing them with food, service staff, and cleanup There is only one difference.

In some geographical areas a caterer performs the service away from his own establishment. In other words, the caterer brings the food and the service to the guests. This can occur at many different locations. This is also called off-premise catering. On the other hand, the banquet manager usually works at the establishment that has space to hold a banquet and has the guests come to the establishment to partake of the food and service.

Both the caterer and banquet manager basically conduct their business in the same manner. However, the caterer does a tremendous amount of preplanning and organizing in order to have a successful banquet. This is because all the equipment and food must be brought to the job.

TIP$

TO INSURE PROPER SERVICE
It is a military, logistical operation to move food somewhere.

The banquet manager has the luxury of working in a familiar facility. If the banquet manager forgets or runs out of some item like salt, it is much easier for him to replace it than for the caterer. The banquet manager will go to the storeroom and get more salt; the caterer will have to find a store that sells salt, which will involve wasted time and money on the caterer's part. The caterer will have to charge for travel time and for transportation costs; obviously, the banquet manager does not have these costs. Because the jobs of caterer and banquet manager are so similar, many people use the terms interchangeably. However, there is a difference between them.

Staffing a Banquet Facility

The person responsible for the success of the banquet is the **banquet manager**. In larger operations, the banquet facility may have a sales manager, a head banquet waiter, and banquet captains, as well as the banquet manager. But in a smaller operation, the banquet manager performs all of the duties.

FIGURE 10-4

The difference between catering and banquets. In some geographical areas, the terms are interchangeable, while other areas use this distinction.

DIFFERENCE BETWEEN CATERING AND BANQUETS	
Catering	**Banquets**
Takes place AWAY FROM the establishment	Takes place AT the establishment

The job of the sales manager is to book the banquets. Booking of banquets can be done by conducting outside sales or inside sales. The outside salesperson travels to the client's home or business to convince the client to have the banquet at the salesperson's facility. The inside salesperson works at the banquet facility. Clients come to the restaurant and book the party.

A **head banquet waiter** is generally employed at an establishment where there are many function rooms. In these large banquet establishments, many banquets occur simultaneously. The head banquet waiter is responsible for the success of the party in the room in which he is supervising.

Banquet captains are responsible for the service in a section of the banquet room. They would be used when the banquet is large, perhaps over two hundred guests. Both the head banquet waiter and the banquet captains are working supervisors. They work along with the employees, as well as supervise them.

The banquet manger is the person who has the final responsibility for the success of the banquet. The banquet manager must make sure that all the details of the party are completed. He or she must make certain that whatever the client requested and was promised is delivered. If there are any problems with the banquet, it is the banquet manager's duty to solve them. The key in being an excellent banquet manager is to concentrate on details.

TIP$

To Insure Proper Service

It is just as important to tell the client what you are not doing for the banquet. "The price quoted is for food, china, and staff. I am not furnishing flowers for the church, the entertainment, etc."

The banquet manager has one main purpose in doing his or her job. It is not to cook the food. It is not to serve the food. *It is to take the responsibility of the total event off the client's shoulders and put it onto his or her own shoulders.* The main responsibility of the banquet manager or caterer is to allow the host to have fun with the guests while the banquet manager or caterer takes care of all the details of the party.

Banquet Manager Qualifications

A banquet manager has to be truly unique individual. The job requires a person who can be referred to as a generalist, rather than a specialist. The banquet manager must have the ability to deal with all types of guests. These guests are on many different socioeconomic and psychological levels.

The qualifications for becoming a banquet manager include having a cheerful personality; being attentive to details; having a neat appearance; using tact and diplomacy; being creative during an emergency; having the ability not to become flustered when problems occur; and having the ability to work with many different groups of individuals at the same time. In addition, the banquet manager has to be able to express himself or herself orally and in writing. Above all, the banquet manager must be organized.

PERSONALITY

The banquet manager will have to deal with a never-ending group of clients that will test his or her limits of patience and endurance. Their personality must be cheerful, because the banquet manager is almost always dealing with clients who are in a stressful situation. They (the clients) want their party to be perfect. Even though the banquet manager may have conducted a thousand wedding receptions, the mother of the bride feels that this is the only one that the banquet manager has ever done. All clients, regardless of how rich or poor, no matter the type of education they possess, no matter their ethnic background, share the same trait when they are the host of a banquet. They are all placed in a stressful situation. Because of this stress, they exhibit behavior that will test the limits of the banquet manager's patience. Almost always, their personality changes; they change from a nice, friendly, relaxed individual to a stressed-out person, which demands that the banquet manager handle them in a firm, yet friendly manner. In short, they could be referred to as temporarily insane.

BANQUET MANAGER QUALIFICATIONS

To become a banquet manager you MUST

1. Have a cheerful personality
2. Be attentive to details
3. Have a neat appearance
4. Have tact and diplomacy
5. Be able to react quickly to change
6. Not become flustered
7. Have excellent oral communication skills
8. Have excellent written communication skills
9. Have the ability to work with many different types of people at once
10. Be creative during an emergency

FIGURE 10-5

The Bride's Parents

At a very extravagant wedding, both the wedding and reception took place in the same location. The wedding took place in a garden under a tent. When the ceremony was over, the guests were to proceed into one room for cocktails and hors d'oeuvres. After an hour and a half, they were to go into the dining room for the meal.

The parents of the bride had planned everything in a calm atmosphere. They, their daughter, and their future son-in-law were well educated and articulate. The numerous meetings conducted with them were cordial and relaxed. The caterer had explained all that would happen on the day of the wedding.

After the ceremony, the bride's mother came into the dining room and began to panic because none of the tables had been set. The caterer had to calmly escort her out of the room while explaining that the room would be set up in time for the meal. In the meantime, the father of the bride came into the room and his wife asked him to put some gifts into their car. They started an argument, not because the room was not set up, nor because he had locked the keys in the car, but because they were both so stressed out over the wedding. It was the caterer's job to calm them both down and decrease their level of stress by assuring them that everything would be all right with the wedding reception. When the room was set up, the bride was brought into the room to see it. She immediately broke down in tears because the florist had put the wrong type of flowers at the place setting. Because the florist did not have the type of flowers she requested (and had never told her), it was up to the caterer to solve the problem. All that could be done at this point (five minutes before the guests were to enter the room) was to give her a reassuring hug and again calmly tell her everything would be all right. She calmed down and enjoyed her wedding reception.

A banquet manager will encounter this type of behavior at every wedding and almost all parties that he or she conducts. The banquet manager must have the personality to deal with these stressed-out clientele.

ATTENTION TO DETAILS

This trait is considered the most important for the banquet manager to have. Being attentive to details makes the difference between a good and great banquet manager.

TIP$

TO INSURE PROPER SERVICE

So much attention to detail is needed in off-premise catering that you should always use two checklists by two different people.

Raspberries

A woman was giving a catered party for her husband's fiftieth birthday. The staff arrived at her house and set up for the party. Everything was progressing smoothly; the food was being unloaded and cooked; the dining room was being set up; the hostess was acting normal—crazy and stressed out. Then she asked the fatal question that sent her over the edge: "Where are the raspberries?" The response was that the caterer had not sent any raspberries; instead, she sent other fruits as a substitute (mangos and papayas). The hostess broke down and started to cry. She said that the party was ruined because raspberries were her husband's favorite dessert and she was promised them by the caterer. The caterer was immediately called and the hostess talked to her about the problem. The hostess was not at all pleased about the lack of raspberries. The caterer claimed that she had told the woman only that she might be able to get the fruit for the party. The woman heard what she wanted to hear—that the caterer would have raspberries for the party. All the guests at the party loved the birthday celebration. But the hostess was convinced the party was ruined.

It is worth repeating: Attention to details makes the difference between being good and being great.

NEAT APPEARANCE

A banquet manager should look neat and clean. His or her appearance has to be professional at all times, even after twelve hours and twelve functions.

TACT AND DIPLOMACY

The banquet manager must be able to react with tact and diplomacy at all times.

The banquet manager has to use these traits often in dealing with different groups of guests. Tact is the ability to say or do the correct thing without offending the guest. **Diplomacy** is the ability to act tactfully with the guest.

No Sugar, Thank You!

At one party, two of the honored guests were seated at the head table. Another guest wanted to buy them an alcoholic beverage. However, because other guests would have been offended if they had seen the two drinking alcohol, the drinks had to be served without calling attention to the fact. An experienced waiter said, "Leave it to me, I'll solve the problem." He went to the honored guests, obtained their order, and served them their drinks. No one knew that they were drinking alcoholic beverages. This waiter was a master in the art of tact and diplomacy. He had exercised tact by not turning down or insulting the guest who wanted to buy the honored guests a drink, and he did not offend any of the other guests by blatantly serving the alcoholic drinks in glasses. He showed his diplomacy in this situation by serving the drinks in coffee cups.

ABILITY TO REACT QUICKLY TO CHANGES

Another qualification needed by the banquet manager is the ability to think and react quickly when a change has to be made. For instance, there are many times when more guests show up for a party than had been planned. The banquet manager has to be able to accommodate the extra guests without the other guests' realizing there is a problem.

TENDENCY NOT TO BECOME FLUSTERED

In the same vein, when a problem occurs, the banquet manager must remain calm and solve the problem without becoming visibly annoyed with the guests. The banquet manager should give the impression that everything is OK, even if there is a catastrophe in the kitchen.

ABILITY TO WORK WITH MANY DIFFERENT PERSONALITIES AT ONCE

The banquet manager is a boss. He or she has to manage his or her staff, as well as interact with the guests. In the banquet room, there may be a guest who holds an important position in the country or community. In the kitchen there are dishwashers and potwashers. The banquet manager generally is responsible for the performance of the dishwashers and service people, as well as for the success of the banquet. This means that at one moment the banquet manager may be talking to the dishwasher, while a second later he or she has to return to the banquet room and discuss an item with the host of the party, who may be the Vice President of the United States. Most likely these two individuals come from different social and intellectual classes, but the banquet manager has to be able to converse and act appropriately with them both. The banquet manager has to know and understand psychology and how to use it to make the banquet a success.

ORAL COMMUNICATION SKILLS

The banquet manager needs to possess excellent oral communication skills. In addition to the obvious responsibilities of communicating with the guests, at times the banquet manager may have to act as a master of ceremonies for a party. This may involve speaking before a group of five hundred guests. The banquet manager also conducts meetings with staff and presents proposals to committees of clients wishing to hold a banquet at the banquet facility.

TIP$

To Insure Proper Service
Master the art of working with committees!

WRITTEN COMMUNICATION SKILLS

The ability to communicate clearly and concisely through the use of memos and forms to the staff is another qualification needed by the banquet manager. In addition, the banquet manager must be able to communicate effectively with the guests in letters and contracts.

ORGANIZATIONAL SKILLS

Along with taking care of the details, the banquet manager must possess organizational skills. They are critical for becoming a banquet manager. He or she must be organized to do the vast amount of planning that goes into a banquet. Food has to be ordered, cooking time and service have to be coordinated. Often, the banquet manager arranges for music, flowers, wedding cakes, audio equipment, photographers, and even entertainment for a banquet. This person has to know where to find all of these services and have an organized system to obtain them.

At times, most likely on weekends, a second banquet is scheduled within one hour of the first banquet in the same room. The banquet manager must be organized and have a plan so that the room can be reset and ready for the next party at its scheduled time. Regardless of the time factor, without organization, any banquet becomes a disaster.

The above list of qualifications is not all-encompassing. But it is a list of the most crucial skills that the banquet manager must have in order to perform the job successfully.

Banquet Manager Benefits

There are many benefits to a career in banquet management. Prestige, salary, gratuities, and perquisites (perks) are among the benefits a person can receive as a banquet manager.

PRESTIGE

Prestige comes naturally to the banquet manager. This is because the job puts the banquet manager in direct contact with the most important and influential people in the social and business community. A banquet manager who excels at the job soon receives the accolades of the community. In addition, the manager makes valuable contacts that may be used to further his or her career. Because the banquet manager is the most visible employee and the one who comes in contact most often with the guests, the manager *is* the establishment in the eyes of the guests.

PSYCHIC INCOME

Another important benefit in the prestige category is the factor called *psychic income*. This is not money that the banquet manager receives; rather it is the positive feeling that the manager obtains from doing a job well, or from serving important guests and sometimes becoming the confidant of those guests.

PAY

The banquet manager is generally paid an excellent salary. Since the banquet manager represents the establishment to the guests, they are loyal to the banquet manager rather than the establishment. If the banquet manager leaves the establishment and goes to work for a competitor, the guests generally follow the banquet manager. Therefore, the banquet facility does not want to lose good banquet managers. They pay them handsomely for their services and contracts. In addition, the managers may receive a percentage of the service charge as an extra incentive to remain at the banquet house.

The banquet manager deals closely with the hosts of the parties, and in doing so usually creates an excellent rapport. If the banquet manager is competent in performing the job, it appears to be done effortlessly. The client often asks the banquet manager to do jobs that are not normally associated with the position. At the end of the party, it is not unusual for a satisfied guest to give a monetary gratuity to the banquet manager for a job well done.

TIP$

To Insure Proper Service
Consider all your benefits as your pay, not just the salary.

PERQUISITES

Perquisites or "perks" are additional benefits given to the banquet manager in addition to the regular salary. There is usually an allowance for clothing, and the expense of cleaning the clothes is generally paid for. The banquet manager generally has an expense account for the purpose of entertaining potential or repeat clients. Sometimes lodging may be included as a benefit. The value of the banquet manager to the business will determine the amount of perquisites he or she is offered.

Drawbacks to Being a Banquet Manager

As in any good job, there are also detriments to the banquet manager's position. Long hours, stressful parties, and the availability of food and liquor are all negative factors in the banquet manager's job.

LONG HOURS

The job of banquet manager requires the banquet manager to work when everyone else is playing. Social events occur on weekends, evenings, and holidays. The banquet manager may have had twelve parties during the week, but to the client, their party is the only one that matters. The banquet manager is responsible for all the parties being conducted at the establishment. Many times, this means supervising all the parties. Larger banquet houses will have assistant banquet managers, but the vast majority of operations cannot afford an assistant. Therefore, the banquet manager has to attend all parties.

STRESS

The banquet manager is under a tremendous amount of stress to do an excellent job. Even though guests do not expect the same high quality as they do when they go to an a la carte dining establishment, the hosts of the party want a gourmet meal. They also want everything done one way—perfectly. The hosts have chosen the banquet facility with the expectation that the party will be perfect. They want to enjoy themselves. At times this creates an unbearable amount of stress on the banquet manager.

TIP$

To Insure Proper Service

People do not care how much you know, until they know how much you care.

AVAILABILITY OF FOOD AND LIQUOR

Often the banquet manager, as a response to the stress in the job, turns to "the bottle" to solve problems. Because of the perquisite and the stature in the establishment, the banquet manager can "drink" as part of his job. By the same token, many people in this profession have poor diets. They have so many different foods available, they reward themselves with a poor nutritional diet that is detrimental to their health.

ILLEGAL ACTIVITIES

In addition to the above problems, there is the temptation for the manager to engage in illegal activities, such as drug use and gambling. Because of the contact with people in all walks of life, the banquet manager is often exposed to these types of activities.

Job Knowledge Needed

The banquet manager must know how to sell, plan, organize, and conduct banquets so they are a success for the clients. There are many details that make the difference between a successful or unsuccessful banquet. The following chapters will go into more depth on these nuances. However, to begin with, the banquet manager must know the following to conduct business successfully:

1. The style of banquets
2. The size of each room in the operation and how to diagram rooms
3. How to book banquets
4. The difference between tentative and firm reservations, and how to make a tentative one firm
5. The variety or choices of menu items from which the client may choose
6. The importance of communication with the guest and the kitchen
7. How to construct a menu that will be eye appealing, nutritionally sound, and that the kitchen will be able to serve in addition to all other foods they have to produce
8. The timing of the party so that the food arrives when the client desires it and the guests are ready
9. The variety of ways in which banquets can be served to the guests

Styles of Banquets

There are two general styles of banquets. The first is a sit-down meal, the second is a buffet. Both refer to the type of service the service staff gives to the guests. The sit-down banquet refers to the fact that the guests are served their complete meal by the service staff. At a banquet, the guests either obtain a portion or all their food by serving themselves from buffet tables.

Type of Service for Banquets

There are two types of service for sit-down banquets. Restaurants either use American or Russian banquet service. For buffets, there are three types of buffet services: buffet, modified buffet, and deluxe buffet.

American banquet is the type of service that most restaurants use because it is simple. It is referred to as "On the plate, no wait" It is easy to learn and use.

Russian service requires more skill by the service staff. The staff must transfer food from platters to guest plates by using a fork and spoon. This type of service most often occurs at expensive banquets, usually in large metropolitan hotels or at an off-premise event.

The service that does not deserve to be called service is the simple buffet. In this option, the guests go through a line and pick up their

---

TYPES OF SERVICE AT BANQUETS

Sit Down Meals	Buffets
American	Simple Buffet
Russian	Modified Deluxe
	Deluxe

FIGURE 10-6

own food, utensils, and beverages. The only thing the service staff does is clean up the dirty tables.

A modified buffet service requires the service staff to serve beverages and, perhaps, the dessert courses, while the guests obtain their appetizers, salad, and main entree items from the buffet table.

The deluxe buffet provides the guests with the most service. All the courses except the main course are served to the guest.

SUMMARY

1. The three main types of banquets are: personal entertaining, business meetings, and social organizations.
2. The main difference between a banquet manager and a caterer is that the banquet manager hosts the guests in his own establishment, whereas the caterer brings the food and service to the guests.
3. The key to banquet management is for the banquet manager to move the responsibility for the banquet's success off the client's shoulders and onto his or her own.
4. The qualities that a successful banquet manager must possess are many; among the most important are: attention to details, tact, a neat appearance, the ability to react quickly to change, the ability to work with many different types of personalities, the ability to communicate well both orally and in writing, and a high degree of organizational skills.
5. The advantages to the banquet manager's position are good pay, prestige, "psychic income," and perquisites.
6. The disadvantages to the banquet manager's position are long hours, stress, the availability of food and liquor, and the opportunity to engage in illegal activities.
7. The two types of banquet are sit-down and buffet.
8. Sit-down banquets may be of American service or Russian service.
9. Buffets may be buffet service, modified buffet service, or deluxe buffet service.

REVIEW QUESTIONS

1. A party of 150 is served its meal. You, as the banquet manager, observe that the noise level in the room is very high. No one is eating the main beef course! It is obvious that there is a problem with the meal. How do you solve this problem?

2. Remember the story about raspberries? What should the caterer have done to avoid this problem? Explain why the caterer did not exhibit the trait of attending to details.

3. Define the term *banquet.*

4. Explain the importance of banquets as they relate to the profitability of a hospitality establishment.

5. List and explain the advantages that the banquet business has over restaurants that serve a la carte meals.

6. Define the difference between a caterer and a banquet manager.

7. What are the advantages and disadvantages of the banquet manager's job?

8. What are the types and styles of service available for banquets?

9. What are the qualifications needed to become a banquet manager?

10. What job knowledge should the banquet manager possess in order to do the job effectively?

11. What is the banquet manager's main responsibility as it relates to the host of the banquet?

How to Book Functions

OBJECTIVES

At the completion of this chapter, the reader will be able to:

1. Define the term *function*
2. Name the sizes of the standard banquet tables and their uses
3. Describe some of the different types of room setups available for functions
4. Draw a diagram of a function room in a simple and concise manner
5. Define the difference between tentative and firm bookings
6. Explain the importance of a function book or computer program, and how to book functions at the establishment
7. Explain the word *qualified* as it relates to booking business
8. Explain the word *guarantee* and its importance in the banquet business
9. Describe the difference in policies on room rentals
10. Explain the importance of setting up policies as they relate to payment of functions

What is a Function?

A function is any use of banquet facilities. The room may be rented by the client or the establishment may allow the client to use the room at no charge. Examples of functions are meetings, dinners, conferences, and cocktail parties. Clients deal directly with the banquet office for the purpose of conducting these functions. Depending upon the size of the banquet facility, the banquet manager may be the only management person that comes in contact with the client from the initial booking until the function is complete. In larger establishments, there may be a catering and sales manager, as well as a group sales office that has the responsibility of booking the function. Once the event is booked, the responsibility for the success of the event belongs to the banquet manager. Conducting stressful functions begins with proper booking of the event.

What Must be Known about Function Room Setups

Regardless of the type of function that will be booked, the person booking the function must know specific facts about the individual banquet facility. First, the booking person has to know the number of rooms available and each room's capacity for either meal or meeting functions. Second, the type of physical setups that will accommodate guests comfortably and efficiently in each room should be known. Third, the banquet manager has to know the equipment available to be used in the establishment; whether it has been assigned to another function at the same time, as well as how, where, and at what cost extra equipment can be obtained. Finally, the manager will have to be able to perform the job without having to ask any questions about the room layout.

TIP$

TO INSURE PROPER SERVICE

Work a day with banquet setup people to understand the problems they have in physically setting up rooms.

Room Availability and Capacity

Architects and banquet managers never see a room the same way. It has been well documented that most restaurant facilities (especially kitchens) are designed by people who do not or have never worked in a kitchen. The same is true of function rooms. Many times, the square footage available is calculated upon the general formula of eight to twelve square feet of space for each person at a sit-down meal function.

Often, even though the formula is mathematically accepted, the projected number of guests will not fit into the room. This is because each function is an individual party which may require different demands on the space, resulting in a different capacity for the room. The location of exits, the shape of the head table, the traffic flow, the dance floor, the audio-visual equipment, and the type of function must be taken into consideration before the realistic capacity of a room, for each function, can be determined. For instance, more people will be accommodated in a room when it is being used for a stand-up cocktail party rather than for a meeting. Therefore, the banquet manager should get the "feel of the room" by setting up tables and conducting a few sample functions in it. By doing this, the banquet manager will generally know the capacity of each room for most kinds of functions.

Another "moment of truth" occurs when guests sit down to have their meal. If there is enough room at the table, they are pleased. If the room is too crowded, the banquet facility has failed this "moment of truth." Therefore, each person booking functions has to be aware of the realistic capacity and use of every room for every type of function, not relying on the proposed capacity determined by the architect.

Types of Room Setups for Functions

Guests do not want to be too crowded into a room; nor do they want a room where there is so much extra space that it looks as if the party is a failure. It is the banquet manager's responsibility to know the different ways a room can be set up to create a successful social or business event. Banquet managers must know how to use room space effectively in order to maximize revenue. In addition, anyone booking parties has to know the definition of the standard types of functions. The following descriptions are of those functions most widely used, but the list is not all-inclusive.

TABLES

All guests are seated at tables and are waited on by a service person. For social events, such as weddings or dinners, round tables are ideal because they encourage conversation. For business meetings, a block table, a T-shaped table, or an E-shaped table is better because it eliminates unnecessary conversation. Figures 11-1 through 11-3 illustrate the different shaped tables.

The block table is made up of four rectangular tables put together to form a block. This is an ideal setup for a maximum of twenty guests at a small business meeting where all guests can communicate freely.

The T-shaped table is ideal to use in a long, narrow room. The illustration shows three rectangular tables; however, in actual practice, four or five tables would make up the base of the T.

The third, the E-shaped table is ideal where there is a large delegation of guests who must be seated at the head table.

FIGURE 11-1

An illustration of a block table. Four rectangular tables are put together to form a block.

FIGURE 11-2

A T-shaped table made up of three or more rectangular tables

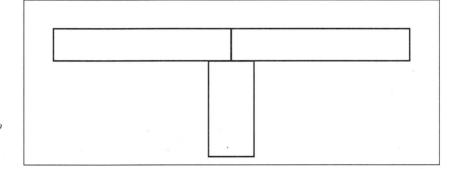

FIGURE 11-3

An E-shaped table made up of five or more rectangular tables

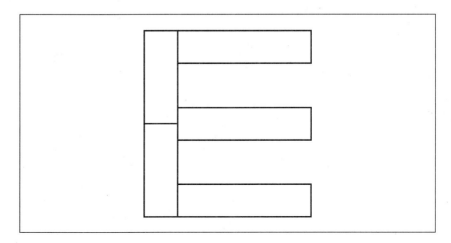

MEETING SETUPS

Usually there are two general types of setups for meetings. The easiest one to set up is referred to as theater style. The guests are provided only chairs, all facing in the same direction. This type of physical setup would be used when the guests are listening to a presentation.

The second type of meeting where all the guests have to face the front of the room is set up in a style called schoolroom or classroom. Figure 11-4 illustrates how all the guests are facing the front of the room while seated at the table for the purpose of writing notes. This setup would be used for a teaching seminar. Schoolroom style takes up the most amount of space, which results in a lessening of the amount of guests that may be accommodated in a room.

....

T I P $ **To Insure Proper Service**

To impress your clients, "skirt" all tables at meetings.

....

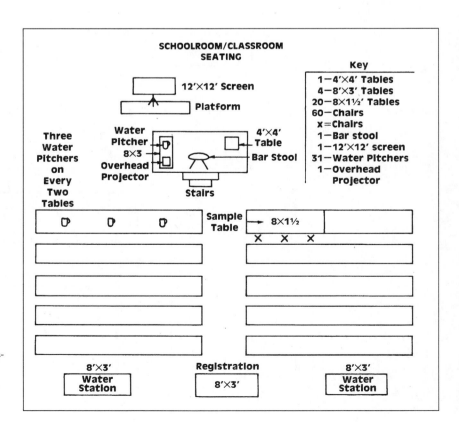

FIGURE 11-4

A classroom of schoolroom-style setup for a function. All seats are facing the front of the room.

HEAD TABLES

These tables are placed in front of the room, with the guests seated only on the side of the table from which they are facing the other members of the party. A new trend, at social events, is to have a round head table placed in the middle of the party. This eliminates the formality of the event and allows the guests at the head table to enjoy themselves more.

COCKTAIL PARTIES

The flow of guests is important for this type of function. The banquet manager can become creative and use all types of space for these parties. It can be the lobbies or pools of hotels, or it can be a function room. The position of both the bars and food stations becomes important for guest comfort and ease of service. Setting up a cocktail party is relatively easy because the banquet manager only has to use a few tables.

At a cocktail party, there should be fewer chairs than the number of guests that are expected. This forces the guests to socialize. Care must be used in locating food and drink stations away from one another to minimize traffic jams and facilitate mingling. A popular cocktail party concept that has caught on is to have stations where food is cooked and small portions are served to guests. For instance, there may be a fettuccine station, a chicken cordon bleu station, and a veal marsala station. More room must be allowed for this type of cocktail party than the traditional one in which food is precooked and put out for the guests in chafing dishes and on trays. At cocktail parties, during which guests typically stand, many more guests can be accommodated in the same space than at a sit-down dinner because not that many chairs are needed.

TIP$

To Insure Proper Service

Use any space that your facility has available to have a cocktail party: the pool area, a hallway, the lobby of your establishment. Be creative!

Once the banquet manager and the client have determined the number of guests expected to attend and the type of setup desired, the manager can decide which room can accommodate the group comfortably and efficiently. A diagram has to be drawn in order for the room to be set up correctly. But before this can be done, the banquet manager needs to know what equipment is available for setting up rooms.

Available Equipment

The manager knows the capacity of all the rooms and the types of functions that may be booked into each room. The next thing the banquet manger needs to know are the types and sizes of tables available, so the function can be planned with comfort for the guests and efficiency for the banquet establishment. Figure 11-5 illustrates the types of tables that are available for the banquet manager to use in setting up functions.

ROUND TABLES

Round tables are used to create a jovial atmosphere. They should always be used when the client wants a function where fun and enjoyment are among the key ingredients for the success of the party. Round tables are a must for wedding receptions to encourage conversation. Most banquet houses use one of two sizes of round tables. The standard round table is 60 inches in diameter. This will seat eight people comfortably at a meal. The other size is 72 inches, which seats ten. The main disadvantage of a banquet facility using round tables is that round tables take up more space than rectangular tables. Therefore, the banquet facility cannot seat as many people at a function using round tables as it could using rectangular tables.

TIP$

TO INSURE PROPER SERVICE

If you are planning to "make a name for yourself" in social catering, invest in round tables that seat eight to ten guests.

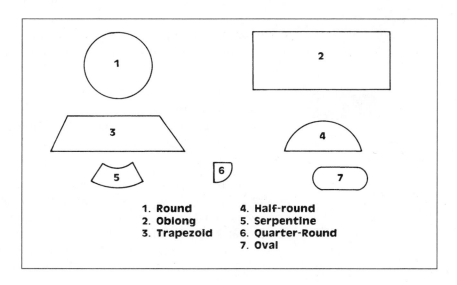

FIGURE 11-5

Shapes of tables available to use in setting up banquet functions

1. **Round**
2. **Oblong**
3. **Trapezoid**
4. **Half-round**
5. **Serpentine**
6. **Quarter-Round**
7. **Oval**

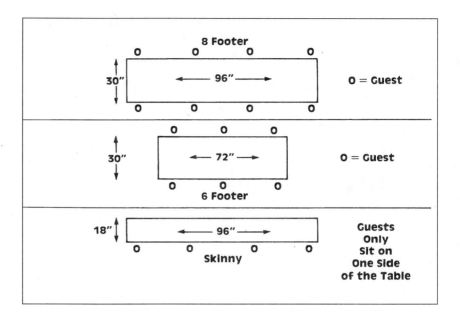

FIGURE 11-6

OBLONG OR RECTANGULAR TABLES

Figure 11-6 shows the three basic sizes of oblong or rectangular tables. They are 30 inches wide by 96 inches long (called an 8-foot table); 18 × 96 inches (8-foot by 1½-foot, or skinny); and 30 × 72 inches (6-foot). Each guest needs 24 inches of linear space to be comfortable. Therefore, an 8-footer will seat eight people (four on each side of the table). The 6-footer will accommodate six people, and the 8 × 1½-footer will only accommodate four people. The skinny table is used when guests have to sit on one side of the table (at a head table or for a schoolroom style setup). Eight foot by one-and-a-half foot tables can also be used for a block table. A block table is made by putting rectangular tables together to form a solid or hollow setup. This style of setup is used when all participants want to be able to see and communicate directly with each other. It is usually used at a meeting, but it can also be used for a small business dinner.

SPACE BETWEEN TABLES

When guests are seated back to back, which is the case when rectangular tables are used, it is recommended that 60 inches are allowed between tables. Using round tables, 54 inches of space is allowed. Both of the above guidelines take into account that chairs are placed in the 60 inches and 54 inches of space. However, this is another area in which the banquet manager should experiment by actually setting up the rooms to determine if there is enough space between tables for the guests to be comfortable and for the service personnel to do their job efficiently. When doing this experiment, the banquet manager should instruct the person setting up the chairs not to push them under the tables but to keep them pulled out as if a guest were sitting at the table. The banquet manager will soon discover the capacity of the function rooms in the establishment.

TIP$

To Insure Proper Service

Explain to your service staff the purpose of pulling the chairs out when the room is being set up by the banquet houseperson. The reason: to make sure the service staff has enough room to serve without creating a safety hazard.

SPECIAL-SHAPED TABLES

The trapezoid, serpentine, quarter-, and half-round tables are best used for setting up food or bar stations rather than for the guests' dining. A banquet manager and chef can create an interesting food setup using the different shaped tables.

LECTERNS

Lecterns are places in the center of the head table and take up 24 inches (the same amount of space that a guest requires). On the lectern there is a place for the notes of the guest speaker, a light, and a microphone.

PODIUM

A podium serves the same purpose as a lectern. The difference between the two is that a podium is freestanding, while the lectern sits on the table. It also takes up 24 inches of space.

MICROPHONES

Every banquet manager has to be aware of the types of microphones available for use in the function room. The banquet manager should know where the power source is for the microphone outlet, how to turn the system on, adjust the volume, and eliminate annoying feedback. One common mistake most people make when testing a microphone is not setting the volume loud enough. The microphone system should be tested before the guests arrive in the function room. Often, the person testing the system does not take into account that there will be many more people in the room when the system is in use. A room with four hundred guests will produce a higher decibel volume of miscellaneous sounds than one with no guests; so the microphone must sound loud when it is being tested.

TIP$

TO INSURE PROPER SERVICE

Work with the musicians or disc jockeys to keep the music at a comfortable level so the guests can talk.

AUDIOVISUAL EQUIPMENT

Most banquet facilities have movie screens, and some may have slide projectors. Other facilities have state-of-the-art rear projection systems. Regardless of the type of equipment the establishment owns, the banquet manager needs to know how to operate it. If a guest makes a request for equipment that the facility does not own, the banquet manager can rent it. Therefore, a knowledge of where to obtain the rental audiovisual equipment is needed, as must the amount of money to charge the guest for the rental.

Things to Keep in Mind

Every banquet manager must realize that planning the correct setup of a function room can be an integral part of the success or failure of a business meeting or party. There are a couple of facts that have to be stressed about equipment and use of function rooms.

Especially important is the fact that all equipment must be in the room and thoroughly tested before the guests arrive. For example, if the slide projector is rented, the banquet manager should have extra bulbs available, and know how to change bulbs if one burns out during a slide presentation. If the equipment is owned by the establishment, a regular maintenance schedule should be set up for changing bulbs so there will be no problem during the presentation. All equipment must be in working condition and ready to operate when the guests walk in.

The second fact that the banquet manager must consider has to do with the placement of different types of functions in the rooms. Many modern facilities have large function rooms that can be made into smaller rooms by the use of moveable walls. Many times these walls are not as soundproof as the manufacturer claims. A banquet manager would be wise not to place a business meeting in the same place as a wedding reception, with only the wall separating them.

The banquet manager can play an integral part in the success or failure of a party by the planning and use of equipment. Practice, common sense, and the banquet manager's experience will benefit all the guests. This will result in more repeat business for the establishment. However, sometimes the banquet manager will get some unusual requests for equipment.

A Quick Fix

A few days before a function was to take place, Governor Rockefeller's advance man made an appointment with the banquet manager to inspect the facilities for the Governor's speech. They entered the function room, the advance man checked where the windows were (to make sure the Governor would not be susceptible to a sniper's shot), told the banquet manager exactly what side the television cameras could be set up on (to present the best side of the Governor), and then asked to test out the lectern. The lectern was positioned on the head table as it would be for the Governor's speech. The advance man took out a tape measure and discovered that the place where "The Man's" (as he referred to him) notes would be placed were 43 inches from the floor. "This will never do," he said. "The notes must sit on a lectern or podium that is 44 inches from the floor." The question was asked, "Why?" "Because that is the perfect distance that allows the Man to read his notes without putting on his glasses," he replied. With that information, the problem was solved by getting the carpenter to cut a one-inch piece of wood to fit under the lectern. On the day of the speech, the wood was under the lectern, which elevated it to 44 inches from the floor, and the event was a success. From that day on, the wood was kept in the banquet manager's office and used every time the Governor was the guest speaker at functions at the hotel.

A Final Point about Room Setups

When scheduling a function the banquet manager should see to it that there is enough space to accommodate all the guests comfortably in the room. There is one exception to this rule. Often clients who plan this exception to the rule want to schedule space that is much too small for the number of people that is expected at the event. What type of event is it?

It is a press conference. This is done to make the event look like an overwhelming success. Think of a room that seats 100. If 100 people show up, the room is filled to capacity. Put the same press conference in a room that seats 500. Even if 200 people attend the event, it still appears that the event was a flop, because there are 300 empty seats.

Physically Setting up the Function Rooms

Once the banquet manager knows the proper manner for setting up and the use of the function rooms, the next step is to physically set up the rooms for the function. The banquet manager should not set up the rooms. However, he or she should know how to diagram the function so the setup people will be able to accomplish the task without asking any questions.

Most of the time, the people who have the responsibility of setting up the rooms are entry level workers. If they are trained properly (generally the banquet manager's job), they become excellent employees and are a valuable asset for the banquet manager. It is the banquet manager's responsibility to diagram all parties as requested by the client. This prepared diagram is then given to the setup people so they can physically set up the room.

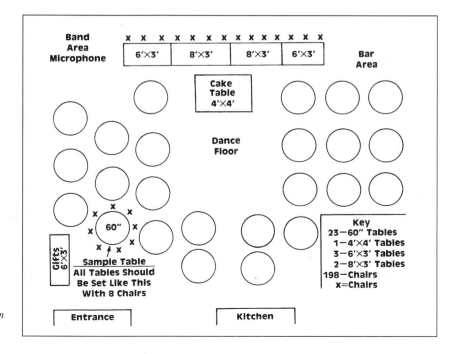

FIGURE 11-7

The correct way to diagram a wedding reception

Figure 11-7 shows the setup for a wedding reception for 198 guests. There is a key on the bottom of the diagram. All tables are clearly marked with their sizes, and there is a sample table for the setup person to follow. The head table has the exact specification of how many guests should be seated and where they should be seated. The key tells exactly how many tables, their sizes, and the number of chairs the setup people need to do their job. This diagram makes the setup of this party easy.

Every function should have a diagram such as that in Figure 11-7. Because most setups are done during the night when the banquet manager is not working, the diagrams should be as complete as possible. In the morning, the first thing the banquet manager will do is check the rooms to make sure they are set up correctly. If there is a problem, it can be corrected, and it can be determined whether the mistake was the setup person's or the banquet manager's. The banquet manager must know how to diagram function rooms simply and concisely.

Two Final Tips

All illustrations should be done on paper that is $8\frac{1}{2} \times 11$ inches (so the setup people can carry them around in their pockets). The diagrams do not have to be done to scale.

Finally, the banquet manager should try, whenever feasible, to suggest the same physical setup to the next client as was used for the previous function. This will cut down on the banquet facility's labor cost, as well as increase the morale of the setup crew.

Booking Functions

Once the banquet manager knows the capacity and use of the function rooms, the next task is to book functions. The booking of functions is done by a sales, catering, or banquet manager, or by a secretary. For the purpose of this chapter, the title banquet manager will encompass all of these job titles.

The banquet manager has to know exactly what types of meals, accommodations for meetings, and charges for these services the establishment can offer to the client. Usually this information is provided by the owners or the general manager of the establishment after the food has been costed out and the profit margin is added into the meal. Most banquet managers work from a set-price menu; caterers usually do not. Caterers set their prices based upon a variety of factors, such as what the client desires, the location of the party, day of the week, and how much demand there is for the caterer's services. Knowing all of this information, the booking process can begin.

How Would You Like to be in this Situation?

One Saturday morning a banquet establishment was setting up for their wedding of two hundred. As they had just about completed the setup, the waiter looked out and saw the wedding party arrive. He thought this was odd, as they were half an hour early. The banquet manager went out to greet the bride and groom; but to his surprise it was a different bride and groom who showed up. Another manager had booked another wedding on the same day, at the same time, with the same menu. In thirty minutes the other wedding party of two hundred showed up. And no, this is not made up. It really happened!

FUNCTION BOOK

To avoid the above situation, every facility must have an organized system to keep its bookings straight. In the past, the tool to use was a **function book**. Today, the function book is being replaced with computer software. However, whether a banquet establishment uses a function book or a computer, the basic principles are the same.

A function book is an organized piece of equipment that lists the rooms that the establishment has to rent on a daily basis. A typical page from a function book looks like the one in Figure 11-8.

In Figure 11-8, each meal period and each day of the year are in the book. In addition, every room would be listed in the book. The person doing the booking would open the page to the date and see if anything was booked into the room. If there was nothing entered, then the booking person could sell the space to the guest. In Figure 11-8, the booking person can see that the SeVille room is booked for Mr. Zorn. Furthermore, AJS booked the party and accepted the deposit on 3/21 and made the notation that the party was firm.

If another client wanted the SeVille room for lunch on September 12, the client would be told that the room had been previously booked. The banquet manager should then attempt to sell the client a different time, room, or a different date. If there are no open dates or if the client cannot change the requested date, the banquet manager may make suggestions or even assist the client in finding another banquet facility that is comparable in service and price. This practice is

MONDAY, SEPTEMBER 12, 19__   LUNCH

Room	Group	Estimated Number	Time
SeVille	Society of Wine Educators	250	11-1:30
	Ted Zorn		
	28 Oakbarrel Drive		
	Hammensport, NY		
	617-555-WINE (B)	Firm 3/21/19__	AJS
	315-555-6589 (H)	$300.00 Deposit	

FIGURE 11-8

A typical page from a function book. Its purpose is to avoid overbooking.

beneficial to the banquet manager in a couple of ways. First, the client will be impressed that the banquet manager is taking the time to assist in finding an alternative banquet establishment. Second, the competition will reciprocate when it is booked up.

The function book does not provide any information about the menu or the party; only who reserved the room, whether it is a firm or tentative booking, and the approximate time and number of guests that will attend the function. The main purpose of the system is to avoid overbooking, which is defined as having two parties in the same room at the same time.

CARE AND STORAGE OF THE BOOK

Because the function book is such an integral part of the banquet business, it should be kept in a permanent place. It should not be brought into another office or to a person's home when booking a party. When no one is in the office it should be kept in a locked area.

....

TIP$

TO INSURE PROPER SERVICE

Function books are gigantic. They cover all the rooms and all the meal periods. Some establishments have them for a year at a time; others only for three or six months. Devise a function book that works for your banquet facility.

....

The banquet facility must make certain that only authorized people are allowed to make entries into the book. All entries must be made in pencil, and the people who book the parties must identify themselves by putting their initials in the entry.

One advantage computer software has over the traditional function book is that backup copies of all bookings can be saved and/or printed.

There has always been a fear that if the book was stolen, lost, or damaged by fire, it would be difficult to reconfirm the bookings, and thus, overbooking would occur.

T I P $

To Insure Proper Service

Back up your computer software function book at least twice daily.

By taking the above steps, the establishment should almost eliminate the possibility of overbooking.

Qualifying Business

Each banquet establishment has to set up a policy to determine the amount of money that must be made when a room is booked. Once that determination and policy has been set, the banquet manager should attempt to book parties that will bring in the most revenue for the establishment. Some banquet establishments will accept any and all business while others attempt to specialize in certain market areas, such as the social business.

Qualifying a client means to determine how much money the client will be spending at the establishment. At some establishments there will be more demand for function space in particular months. "September is peak season for us as far as functions go," states the Sales and Catering Manager at The Desmond in Albany, New York. "It is primarily our large conference and convention season. There is minimal space available. If a room is available for fifty guests, we are going to try to find a client that has an open-bar, extensive hors d'oeuvres, high revenue dinner, and possibly wine sales, in comparison to a cash bar and a chicken dinner."

The second part of qualifying means to determine if the client can pay for the party. Some clients have booked parties with no intention of paying for them. Unfortunately, this is usually people running for political office. It is best to make candidates pay for their functions in advance. There are many documented stories about candidates who have both won and lost elections, and still owe for their parties. The accepted method of payment should be explained to the client when the party is booked. The establishment has to decide if it will accept personal checks and/or credit cards, and how much of a deposit to charge the client.

Once the business is qualified, the date can be entered into the function book as either a tentative or firm booking.

How Far in Advance May Banquets be Booked

Each banquet facility has to determine, based upon the demand for space, a policy concerning how far in advance banquets may be booked. The goal of the facility is to obtain the most revenue. For example, a new banquet business would probably book any business, while one that is established and more in demand may set a limit on advance bookings.

Guidelines are clearly outlined at The Desmond in Albany. They have specific booking policies. For instance, the group sales office can take bookings far in advance, as long as the business is qualified. On the other hand, the catering office can take social events only nine months in advance of the event. The exception is on holiday weekends. They can book as far in advance as requested on a weekend such as Labor Day. So if they had a request for a wedding, it cannot be booked a year in advance unless it was on a holiday weekend. Small business meetings of between fifteen or twenty-five people may only be booked three months in advance of the date. This is done in order to get events that will bring in the highest revenues.

Once the guidelines and policies are set, the banquet manager should "qualify the business" before booking the party.

The Difference between Tentative and Firm

Bookings can be called either *tentative* or *firm*. Firm bookings are the easiest to understand. A client gives the banquet manager a deposit for a party. Once the establishment receives the client's money and in some banquet establishments a signed contract for the event, the amount and date of the deposit, as well as the word *firm*, is entered into the function book.

Tentative policy usually means that the banquet manager will put the client's name into the function book, and the client will have first refusal if another person calls and wants the same room at the same time. Again, a policy is established by the banquet facility and tentative bookings. At many banquet establishments tentative can mean that the space is held tentatively without a deposit for one week. After the week, the person who booked the party will call the client and ask if he or she is still interested in the date. If the client is still interested, a deposit must be brought in. The person who books the function writes in the book the term Firm, with the date and the amount of the deposit received. If the client does not bring the deposit within one week, he or she is called and informed that the deposit must be brought in before the close of business that day or the function will be canceled.

PROBLEMS WITH TENTATIVE BOOKINGS

Banquet managers find that some dates are more particular than others. Often, the manager will have a tentative booking and then a client will come in a day later with a deposit for a firm booking. The banquet establishment needs a policy to determine which party to take and which party to refuse.

Deposits

A deposit is required for almost all banquet events. The deposit protects both parties. The banquet house will not sell the date that the client has reserved to another client; while the client will not cancel the event without losing the money that has been put down for the event.

Each banquet house should determine the amount of deposit that it will charge. It should be expensive enough to deter the client from canceling the party, while moderate enough not to deter the guest from booking the party with the banquet house. As an example, one banquet facility requires $200 deposit for social events that occur in any month except December. Deposits on Christmas parties vary from $500 to $1,000. Other establishments have a different policy. However, excellent repeat customers are often not charged a deposit.

Different operations have different policies on refunding the deposits. Some will never refund a deposit; other places will refund the deposit if the party is cancelled four months prior to the event; still other banquet houses will not give back the deposit unless another group rebooks the date. Of course there are always circumstances in which the manager will have to determine if giving back or keeping the deposit would be in the best interests of the business.

TIP$

To Insure Proper Service

All policies regarding your banquet facility must be in writing and distributed to your clients when the first contact is made.

Guarantees

When booking functions, clients should be informed of the policy on guarantees of the establishment. A **guarantee** is a promise made by the host of the party that a certain number of guests will show up for the party and that the client will pay for that number unless more guests attend.

When a client originally books an event, he or she gives an estimate of how many people will attend the party. Most banquet establishments require that the guarantee must be given three or four days prior to the event. Most establishments will take that number and set up 5 percent above that guaranteed number (one hundred guaranteed, 105 seats). The client pays for a minimum of one hundred people unless more guests show up.

TIP$

To Insure Proper Service

Use common sense in charging a client if the guaranteed number does not show up because of circumstances beyond the client's control. What long-term benefit does a banquet establishment obtain from charging a client for two hundred guests when a blizzard or hurricane prevented 175 guests from attending the reception?

Room Rentals

Clients will be using the function rooms for food and beverage functions or meetings. There are different ways to charge for room rentals.

If a client has a food and beverage function in a room, one for a meeting and one for a food and beverage function, the client may be charged the full price for the meeting room. Naturally, if a client uses just a meeting room, the full price for the meeting room is charged.

At times, meeting room charges can be waived if the client spends additional money at the facility. For instance, if a client has booked two hundred rooms at a hotel, the meeting room charge is waived.

SUMMARY

1. Knowledge of room availability and capacity are necessary when booking functions.
2. There are four types of setups for functions: meal functions, meetings, head-table functions, and cocktail parties.
3. Equipment available for the various functions include: round tables, oblong or rectangular tables, serpentine tables, quarter-round tables, half-round tables, lecterns, podiums, microphones, and audiovisual equipment.
4. A diagram should be drawn to guide the setup crew for each function.
5. A function book must be kept to avoid overbooking.

6. All business should be qualified as to the amount of revenue that a function will bring in, the guest's ability to pay for the function, how far in advance a booking may be taken, whether a booking is firm or tentative, and whether a deposit is required.

7. A guarantee is a client's promise to pay for a minimum number of guests at a booked function.

REVIEW QUESTIONS

1. You are the banquet manager of a brand new hotel. You plan to open in December of this year. It is November and there is a lot of demand for June weddings. You have been very successful in booking parties. The one and only room you have is in demand for weddings. In the afternoon, a bride and her mother come into the establishment. You show them around, and by the time they leave they have a tentative booking on the room for June 21. That evening you go out on a sales call with your food and beverage manager to book a wedding. He has tentatively reserved June 28 in the logbook. You do a great job of selling your services. The parents of the bride say, "Yes, we would like to firm up the date." You say, "Great, that will be June 28." They reply, "No, it is the 21st and we want that date!" What do you do?

2. Referring to the problem of the two simultaneous wedding receptions that were cited earlier in this chapter, how would you handle the situation?

3. A guest has booked a tentative party. Unfortunately, you did not qualify the business. It is the typical chicken dinner for fifty guests with a cash bar. One of your best customers comes into your office and says that his boss is retiring and he wants the same date as that booked for the tentative party. In addition to being a great customer, he informs you that they want a filet mignon party for two hundred guests with an open bar, wine, and a cocktail party. What party should you take, and how will you explain the rejection to the guest to whom you deny the date?

4. Would you give back a deposit if a couple broke up two weeks before their planned wedding? What if the prospective bride got killed in an accident?

5. What does the term *function* mean?

6. What are the sizes of the standard banquet tables, and what type of parties use them?

7. Explain the difference between a tentative and a firm booking.

The Banquet Function Sheet

OBJECTIVES   At the completion of this chapter, the reader will be able to:

1. Define a banquet function sheet and know its purpose
2. Obtain information from the client concerning the event
3. Suggest options to enhance the success of the event
4. Complete the information needed on the banquet function sheet
5. Explain the different meal options a client can have for a banquet
6. Define "details" as it pertains to the banquet business
7. Explain the importance of details in organizing and planning a banquet
8. Illustrate how to serve more than one main course item to guests at a banquet
9. Understand the importance of communication and cooperation with all the staff, especially the chef
10. Plan, staff, and organize a banquet to result in a perfect event
11. Explain the different alcoholic beverage choices to a client at a banquet
12. Set up seating arrangements for a party

Organization: The Key to a Successful Banquet

After booking function rooms, the next step in the banquet management process is to obtain all information concerning the event. Once the banquet manager has the information, it has to be transmitted to the staff in a clear, concise manner.

Different banquet managers use different techniques for accomplishing this task. However, they all have one thing in common: every successful banquet manager has an organized system. The banquet manager at the Astro Hall in Houston, Texas, uses informal lists to keep organized. The banquet manager is responsible for parties from ten to one thousand in the Astro Hall. Additional responsibilities include banquets at the Houston Astrodome. Parties are served that have as many as two thousand guests. These guests are served in the same physical area where baseball and football games are played. In such cases, the banquet manager becomes the off-premise caterer for the Astrodome.

Both facilities have a limited kitchen area and equipment to accommodate the large number of guests. The banquet manager must plan and organize the banquets, keeping in mind the limitations of both facilities. He or she also has the responsibility for obtaining all utensils and plates to feed the many guests. In addition, the banquet manager must obtain all the service staff to serve the guests.

Once a party is booked, the banquet manager should make lists of what they have to do for the event. By compiling these lists, he or she makes certain that nothing is forgotten for the event. Finally, the banquet manager must have everything the client has ordered and make sure it is served the way the client desires it. Another banquet facility, The Desmond in Albany, New York, uses a more sophisticated process in the planning and operation of functions. Each day, the sales and banquet staff receive a computerized print-out which consists of five parts: deposits due, banquet event order (beo) due, guarantee due, personal thank you, and signed beo received.

All tasks are assigned to the staff in the sales and catering office. They are to complete these tasks daily. Figure 12-1 illustrates page two of the Morning Report for Kimberly A. Spiak. This page is concerned with personal thank you notes and the signed beo. Once the task has been completed, Kim will check off the task.

Organization is one of the keys for a banquet manager to be successful in this business. Both of the above individuals have a system to help them do their job. Without organization, their jobs would be impossible to accomplish.

Obtaining Information about the Function

Once the client has reserved a date, the banquet manager must schedule an appointment to discuss all the particulars concerning the event. At this meeting the banquet manager will listen, then suggest and guide the client to make correct choices about the function. Included in the discussion will be the physical setup of the room, planning the program and time schedule, and selecting the food and beverage menu.

The banquet manager usually will offer suggestions to the client to make the party a success. Often, a client has a general idea of what he or she desires for the function. As banquet manager you must help with details of the event that the client did not think about. It is the job and the responsibility of the banquet manager to help plan the event so it will be precisely what the client desires within the limits of your operation.

In order to do the job effectively, the banquet manager has to rely on the sense of hearing more than any of the other senses. The banquet manager must listen carefully to the client. The banquet manager's mind cannot be thinking of next week's party; all attention must be given to the client. By listening to the client, the banquet manager can offer suggestions to make the party a success.

```
DELPHI -- Morning Report for Kimberly A. Spiak - KS
2

PERSONAL THANK YOU...........

Group Name                        (Account ID)    Arrival Date Trace Date Action
- - - - - - - - - - - - - - - -   - - - - - - -   - - - - - -  - - - - -  - - - - - - - - - - - - - - - -
Quench Beverage                   (Quench Bev)     7/ 5/88      7/ 9/88    __ Complete/New Trace: __/__/__
Scarlett County Farmers Assoc.    (Scarlett Farm)  7/ 6/88      7/10/88    __ Complete/New Trace: __/__/__
APEX Savings and Loan             (APEX S & L)     7/ 7/88      7/11/88    __ Complete/New Trace: __/__/__
Red Rupert Insurance              (Rupert Ins)     7/ 7/88      7/11/88    __ Complete/New Trace: __/__/__
Professional Paints               (Prof Paint)     7/ 7/88      7/11/88    __ Complete/New Trace: __/__/__

SIGNED BED RECEIVED?.........

Group Name                        (Account ID)    Arrival Date Trace Date Action
- - - - - - - - - - - - - - - -   - - - - - - -   - - - - - -  - - - - -  - - - - - - - - - - - - - - - -
Glucose Associates                (Glucose)        7/ 5/88      7/ 9/88    __ Complete/New Trace: __/__/__
Wildnut Spring Corp.              (Wild Spring)    7/ 6/88      7/10/88    __ Complete/New Trace: __/__/__
Ardor, Beetle and Beason, Inc.    (Ardor, Bee)     7/ 7/88      7/11/88    __ Complete/New Trace: __/__/__
Wearever Tires and Shocks         (Wearev Tires)   7/ 7/88      7/11/88    __ Complete/New Trace: __/__/__
People's Bank                     (People Bank)    7/ 7/88      7/11/88    __ Complete/New Trace: __/__/__
```

FIGURE 12-1

A morning report form for a banquet manager. This comes from a computer printout that is obtained daily. It assigns tasks to complete concerning past and future functions.

The Policy Sheet

Each banquet facility must have a printed sheet that lists specific policies concerning banquets. This **policy sheet** must be given to and reviewed with the client at the initial planning meeting. Items on the sheet should include: the length of time a room would be reserved; the cost of extra service staff and bartenders; how long in advance a function room will be set up; and the policy on deposits, guarantees, and contracts. The list can be as short as one page or, for conferences, can be several pages. With a printed policy statement, most questions are answered. This alleviates misunderstanding between the client and the banquet management. Figure 12-2 illustrates a portion of a banquet and meeting policy information form.

The Function Sheet

When the banquet manager and client decide what is desired for the function, it must be placed on an organized written document. The purpose of this document is to have the banquet house give the client exactly what has been requested, when it is requested. Everything that the client and the banquet manager have agreed upon appears on this document.

This document has many different names, depending on the banquet establishment. For the purpose of this book, it is called the **function sheet**. It is sometimes named the banquet event order or banquet stencil. Regardless of the name, the purpose is to list in detail everything that the client desires for the event. Every banquet establishment must have a function sheet in order to successfully serve banquets. Figure 12-3 illustrates a standard function sheet.

Function sheets are generally broken down into three main areas. The top third is information obtained at the time of the booking. Only the banquet and sales office employees need this information. Part 1

FIGURE 12-2

Part of a policy sheet. All banquet facilities need a sheet that lists the policies of the banquet establishment.

BANQUET AND MEETING POLICY INFORMATION

Thank you for your interest in our facilities
The following is an outline of our standard policies:

1. Rooms will be set one hour before an event is to begin. If the client desires to have the room set up earlier, he or she must pay the standard room rental fee for the time period.
2. One bartender is provided for every 50 guests. Additional bartenders may be requested at the current rate of pay.
3. The rest of the policies will be continued.

FUNCTION SHEET

Event Date _____ Payment Arrangement _____

Organization_____ Business Phone _____

Address _____ Home Phone _____

Person in Charge _____

Estimated Number _____ Guarantee _____ Set_____

Room _____ Time_____

Food   Program

Liquor

Price_____ Booked By _____

Guest Signature & Date _____

FIGURE 12-3

All banquet establishments need a form to transmit information from the client to the rest of the staff. This is accomplished through the use of a standard function sheet.

begins at the top of the sheet and includes the information through the estimated number of guests.

At large properties that have many banquet rooms, banquet managers, and assistants, Part 1 of the function sheet also includes the names of the staff people in the hotel who are responsible for the event. An example of a large facility is Marriott's Orlando World Center in Orlando, Florida. They have 143,000 square feet of public function space, which includes a 40,000-square-foot Crystal Ballroom and a 51,000-square-foot Palms Ballroom. In addition they have three boardrooms for high-level meetings and fourteen other meeting rooms. When conventions occur, job assignments are broken down into two areas: meeting requirements, which are handled by the Convention Services Department and Catered Foods and Entertainment. Regardless of how big or small the event, the Marriott must use a function sheet.

Part 3, from price to the date, is also information primarily needed by the banquet office. This part can only be completed after the client and banquet manager have agreed upon all items desired for the event. The banquet manager completes this area by filling in the price, signing, and dating it. Then it is sent to the client to be signed.

Part 2 of the function sheet is the key to the success of the event; that is where all of the information about the event is recorded. In effect, this part of the function sheet becomes a work order for the event.

PART 1 OF THE FUNCTION SHEET

Figure 12-4 illustrates Part 1 of the function sheet, as filled in for Mr. Lockwood's daughter's wedding.

Notice that the date includes the day of the week. This will avoid any confusion by you, the client, or the staff. People often get confused about what day of the week a date falls on. The banquet manager needs to put the day of the week on the function sheet to avoid any confusion.

Usually, there are so many departments involved with a large event such as the Lockwood wedding that everyone knows what day of the week August 1 falls on. However, mistakes are more likely to occur for small functions (groups of ten to twenty), because fewer employees are scheduled to work. A party of twenty may be served by the staff on duty rather than having a separate banquet staff.

Sorry, Chief!

Once a party was scheduled for twenty guests. The function sheet was completed and distributed. At noon, the guests arrived for the luncheon; no food was prepared, nor was the room set up. Both the waiter and the cook misread the date on the function sheet, which said July 1. Fortunately, it was the New York State Chiefs of Police Organization, regular guests of the hotel, who were most understanding of the problem. They conducted their meeting while the staff set up the room and prepared the food. But from that day on, the day of the week always went on function sheets.

FIGURE 12-4

Part 1 of the function sheet. This part covers information that is obtained at the time of the booking.

PART 1 OF THE FUNCTION SHEET

Event Date Saturday, August 1	Payment Arrangement Cash
Organization Lockwood-Jones Wedding	Business Phone 555-0978
Address 7 Lark Ave	Home Phone 555-0878
Cranston, RI	
Person in Charge Jim Lockwood	
Estimated Number 200	

The rest of Part 1 of the function sheet is straightforward information. The banquet manager should always obtain both the client's business and home phone in case a question occurs concerning the event. By having both phone numbers, the banquet manager can contact the client with relative ease. Information in Part 1 should be filled in completely, and be verified as correct.

TIP$

To Insure Proper Service

Always check on the client's ability to pay before providing services.

Right a Wrong

At one party, the host guaranteed one hundred people for breakfast for an organization whose goal was to legalize marijuana. Only twenty-five of the invited state legislators attended. At the end of the event, the head waiter gave the host the check for one hundred breakfasts. The guest signed it and was billed directly for the event. A few days later, the bill was returned with the words, "addressee unknown." A call was made to the one phone number listed in the function book and on the function sheet. It was the number of a pool hall in a large city. They had never heard of the guest. The phone number and the address were never checked. No money was ever received for the party. It ended up in the bad debt category.

The estimated number is the number of guests that the client expects to attend the event. It is usually the number of people that will be invited. This number is almost always larger than the guaranteed number. For instance, at wedding receptions, the banquet manager can calculate that 20 percent of the invited guests (which is usually the estimated number) will refuse the invitation because of traveling distance or other commitments. Of course, sometimes the guarantee will exceed the estimate. But this number is always a general figure; the client is never responsible for paying for the estimated number of guests. Guarantee and set will be covered later in this chapter.

PART 2 OF THE FUNCTION SHEET

This is the area of the function sheet that is of utmost importance to the employees. In reality, it is their work order. For example, it specifies the exact time that all events are scheduled. The service staff can obtain the information needed to lay the place setting and cover from the function sheet; the chef will be able to calculate how much food to order based upon the menu and estimated number of guests; the kitchen staff has an exact description of the food that must be cooked and served; and the bar knows what liquor the client has ordered and when to serve it. In short, everything about the function should be written on this sheet.

TIP$

TO INSURE PROPER SERVICE

Training your employees to fill out function sheets accurately and completely will avoid major problems and decrease the stress placed upon your staff.

However, before Part 2 can be completed, the banquet manager has to suggest and discuss different ideas with the client. Figure 12-5 is a blank Part 2 of the function sheet. The following sections illustrate the step-by-step process that the banquet manager goes through with the client in order to obtain all the information needed to fill in the sheet.

PART 3 OF THE FUNCTION SHEET

Figure 12-6 illustrates the last area of the function sheet. This area is completed after all the information about the event has been received from the client.

Notice that the price includes the gratuity and the sales tax. The price area should specify all the charges. Some banquet houses eliminate this section on the copy that goes to the staff.

FIGURE 12-5

Part 2 of the function sheet. This part becomes the work order for the employees after the banquet manager determines the client's needs.

PART 2 OF THE FUNCTION SHEET

Estimated Number 200   Guarantee   Set

Food   Program   Liquor

FIGURE 12-6

Part 3 of the function sheet. This part is filled in after all the plans have been made for the party.

PART 3 OF THE FUNCTION SHEET

Price $35.00 + 20% grat and Sales tax   Booked by AJS

Guest Signature & Date _____

The only thing left to be completed on the function sheet is for the client to read, sign, and date it. At some establishments a separate contract is sent with the function sheet. At other banquet facilities, the function sheet is used as the contract between the client and the banquet establishment.

Purpose of the Function

The first thing that the banquet manager must determine about the function is the purpose. It will either be for a social or a business event.

Most of the time the main purpose of an event is not to consume a gourmet meal. The food, even though it is an important part of the success of the event, is secondary to the purpose of the event. The banquet manager has to plan the meal to serve the guests quickly and efficiently so the client can begin the program.

When the client is having a social event, the purpose of the party is to honor someone or something. It could be celebrating a wedding or an anniversary. It may be a retirement party, or a company may have a banquet as a reward to honor its top sales producers.

Business meetings have many purposes. Some are held to introduce a new product. Others are held for the staff as a reward for a job well done. Other meetings serve as a sales meeting for the staff; while still others are actually used to sell a product to a potential customer.

Once the banquet manager determines the purpose of the event, the room and meal can be chosen.

Menu Planning

Choosing a meal is important for both the client and the banquet manager. A meal has to be chosen that can be served efficiently by the banquet establishment, taste good, and meet the needs of the client.

TIP$

TO INSURE PROPER SERVICE

At Marriott's Orlando World Center Resort and Convention Center, when the client has decided on specific food items, he or she is then invited to a tasting of the product. This is called the Taste Panel. Initiate a taste panel at your banquet facility.

For instance, one client wanted his party served quickly. He stated that his guests had been up since 6 A.M. and did not want to spend a lot of time over a meal. The banquet house suggested having the appetizer placed on the table before the guests arrived. It is standard practice to present the appetizer. However, the client wanted not only the appetizer but the salad and dessert on the table before the guests arrived. The only item that was served was the main course.

The banquet manager and client have to agree upon a meal that will meet the nutritional needs of the guests, as well as the financial needs of the client.

The meal should look appealing on the plate. A boneless breast of chicken, with a white sauce served on a bed of rice with mashed potatoes looks bland. It has no color, and having two starches (potatoes and rice) is not nutritionally sound.

Menu planning also takes into account whether the client desires a heavy or light meal for the guests. This is determined by the purpose of the event. A lunch followed by a meeting should be light, with a chicken or fish item. A dinner celebration may include hearty meats, wines, and even a decadent chocolate dessert buffet bar.

Other factors that determine the menu selection are the makeup of the guests who will be attending the event. For instance, at Italian weddings it is customary to serve a pasta course before the main course.

Once the menu has been set, the banquet manager and client can plan for the event.

Planning the Details of the Event

The main part of the function sheet is an open-ended area in which the banquet manager writes exactly what the client desires. All facets of the event must be included in this area: serving times for food and liquor; color of linen; a complete detailed menu specifying everything that was promised to the client; liquor service; and special instructions. All this information must be included on Part 2 of the function sheet. This is where the word *details* takes on utmost importance for the success of the event.

DETAILS

Details are defined in *The Random House Dictionary* as "attention to a subject's individual or minute parts."[1] That is how the banquet manager should approach running every event. The client wants the banquet manager to take care of all the little things (details) that will make the party a success. Again, the premise of this section on banquet management is that the main job of the banquet manager is to **take the responsibility of that party off of the client's shoulders and put it on his or her own shoulders**. Doing this will make the event a success and result in repeat business for the banquet establishment.

DISCUSSING THE DETAILS OF THE PARTY

The banquet manager needs to discuss every aspect regarding the event with the client. This is a must for obtaining all the information necessary for running the function. The banquet manager should always listen to what the client desires and then offer proper suggestions based upon the discussion. Once the client makes the decisions about the event, the function sheet can be completed.

Because no two functions are alike, the following text will include discussions concerning different options that the client can have at banquets.

Types of Meals

Banquet houses offer three types of meals: the cocktail reception, serving drinks and finger foods; the sit-down served meal; and the buffet meal.

The cocktail reception is beneficial for the client who wants the guests to mingle with each other. There is usually a variety of food and drinks for the guests, located at set places (called stations) in the room or passed by the service staff (called butler service).

Many times a cocktail reception precedes a sit-down dinner. As a general rule, guests should have approximately five hors d'oeuvres to eat per person if the cocktail reception precedes a sit-down meal. If the cocktail reception is the only meal, the amount of food must be doubled. However, one fear almost all clients have is that they will not have enough food to serve all of their guests. Therefore, the banquet manager should find out from the client the makeup of the group of people who will be attending the event. The time of day and the type of event also influence the amount of food that will be eaten. The banquet manager can then suggest the correct amount of food based upon the information provided by the client. For example, younger guests will eat more food than senior citizens.

The sit-down meal is the most popular type to be served at a banquet. At this type of banquet, all guests receive the same meal, chosen by the host of the party. Many times a client will ask if the banquet establishment can offer the guests a choice of more than one main course meal. This will depend strictly on the capability of the kitchen and the serving staff.

Because the purpose of a banquet is to serve the meal quickly, limiting the number of choices is a wise idea for the banquet establishment. If the client insists that the guest have a choice of food, offer a choice only for the main course and limit it to two selections. The number of guests ordering each choice has to be given when the guarantee is called into the establishment. The client will be responsible for identifying which guest gets which entree choice. The easiest way to do this is by having different colored tickets (red for beef, yellow for chicken) for the client to distribute.

Also, it is a poor idea to have the service staff take guest orders on how food (such as steaks) is to be cooked at a banquet. Taking individual orders takes too much time for the service person and too much time for the cook. Imagine serving steak for two hundred guests!

If the client wants the guests to have many food choices, then the best meal selection is the buffet. Buffets offer guests an enormous choice of foods and a variety of serving options. The kitchen staff enjoys preparing buffets because they have the opportunity to present foods artistically.

Clients have three service styles of buffets from which to choose. The first is referred to as the simple buffet style, where guests serve themselves. Service staff is only needed to clear dirty dishes. The guest obtains all food, drinks, and utensils.

The second, called the modified deluxe buffet, has waitstaff set up tables with utensils, clear each course, and serve guests beverages. The guests obtain all additional food.

The third, the deluxe buffet, combines excellent service with the opportunity for the guest to have a wide variety of foods. The guests are served their appetizer, salad, beverage, and dessert. They obtain their main course from the buffet.

A banquet manager can tailor a buffet type service to meet the needs of the client. The above three types of buffets are only a guideline to the style of services for the buffets. The banquet manager can be creative and mix up the styles of service to create a new style to meet the needs of the client.

FIGURE 12-7

A preprinted dinner menu for a sit-down dinner banquet. Photograph by Randall Perry.

Dinner Buffets

The Courtyard
(Minimum of 100 Guests)

Chef's Salad Bar

A Selection of Fresh Salad Greens
Accompanied by Julienne of Ham, Turkey,
Salami and Cheese,
Bacon Bits, Crumbled Bleu Cheese,
Chopped Egg
Croutons and Assorted Dressings

Almond Chicken Salad

Chilled Gulf Shrimp Salad

Chicken Stir-Fry

Seafood Pasta

Sauteed Shrimp, Scallops and Crabmeat
Served with a Lobster Sauce

Roast New York Sirloin Of Beef

Served with Bordelaise Sauce,
And Carved Buffetside

Roasted New Potatoes
Garden Vegetables
Fresh Rolls
Brewed Coffees and Tea

A Selection Of Pastries

The Patroon
(Minimum of 100 Guests)

Selection of Imported and Domestic Cheeses
An Array of Chilled Fresh Vegetables and
Assorted Dips

Salad Fare

Spinach Salad
Caesar Salad
Seafood Tortillini Salad

Chicken Tarragon

Served with a Mushroom Cream Sauce

Seafood Saint Jacques

Prime Rib of Beef

Carved Buffetside. Served with Creamed
Horseradish Sauce

Roasted New Potatoes
Selected Stir-Fried Vegetables
Rice Pilaf
Fresh Rolls and Butter
Brewed Coffees or Tea

Pastry Table

A Selection of Assorted Pastries and Sweets

Menu Builder

To **Enhance Your** Dinner Buffet, May We Suggest the Following at an Additional Charge

- *Ice Cream Sundae Buffet*

Vanilla and Chocolate Ice Cream with a Let-Yourself-Go Selection of Banana Nirvana, Hot Fudge,
Butterscotch, Marshmallow, Nuts, Cherries and Chocolate Sprinkles

- *Flambé*

Cherries Jubilee or Strawberries Chambord
Flambéed in your Dining Room

The Desmond
Albany, New York

FIGURE 12-8

A preprinted dinner menu for a sit-down dinner buffet

Once the client decides on the type of meal service desired for the guests, a menu may be chosen. Most banquet houses have preprinted menu selection choices. Figure 12-7 illustrates the dinner selection, while Figure 12-8 illustrates the buffet menu that the host may choose from. Banquet houses usually have separate menus for each meal period, as well as a separate price list that includes the cost of all meals. Using a separate price list, the hotel only has to reprint one sheet of paper, rather than print up an entire set of menus when prices change.

Alcoholic Beverage Service

Once the client has decided on what type of meal to have, the next item to discuss is alcoholic beverage service.

There are two basic styles of alcoholic **beverage service** that are used for functions. Guests can obtain their drinks from an **open bar**, where the client pays for all drinks consumed. The other option is for the client to have the banquet establishment set up a **cash bar**. At the cash bar, the guests have to pay individually for each drink that they consume. Of course, there are some functions where it will not be appropriate or practical to have a bar in the function room; so none is set up. At those functions, guests who desire an alcoholic beverage will purchase one from the bar open to the general public, in another part of the establishment.

Alcoholic Service Choices

Open bars have many different options for serving alcoholic beverages. Like the meal service, the banquet manager has to suggest the correct type of alcoholic service based upon the desires of the client. The banquet manager should be able to estimate how much liquor the guests will consume. This should be based upon previous experience with parties of similar groups. For instance, the average consumption at an event used to be two-and-a-half drinks per person per hour. However, this number goes down significantly after food has been consumed, because the guests are full. Another reason for lower alcohol consumption after a meal is the public's awareness concerning drinking and driving.

Because alcohol laws differ state by state, the banquet manager must check the liquor laws in the state where the banquet establishment is located. The choices of service listed below should only be used as a guideline. Each establishment must decide on its own policy of alcoholic beverage service based upon the laws of its state.

TIP$

ALCOHOL PLACED ON THE GUESTS' TABLE

In this type of service, each table is provided with some type of alcoholic beverage. It may be pitchers of beer or bottles of wine. It could be two bottles of liquor with the appropriate mixers (called set-ups). The client is charged for the number of bottles that are placed on the tables. The guests serve themselves.

OPEN BAR

In this service, guests order a beverage at the bar and are served by a bartender. They may have whatever type of liquor the client has ordered. Generally, one bartender is needed for fifty guests at a cocktail party, and one for one hundred guests after the meal has been served.

With this type of service, the client may be charged in a variety of methods. The first is that the client pays for all bottles of liquor that are opened. Another way is that the client is charged for only the amount of liquor that is used. Another method is to use the public bar and charge the client for the number of drinks that have been consumed. The method that most clients prefer is a per person charge. This way they know exactly how much money they will spend for the event. Another method involves providing the guests with tickets which are good for a drink.

A LA CARTE DRINKS

At some events, the client wants the service staff to take individual drink orders and serve them to the guests. This may be done at an additional cost to the client if the banquet manager has to employ more staff to take and serve drink orders. The main job of the banquet staff should be to serve the food for the banquet, not to serve drink orders.

CASH BARS

This arrangement may cost the client nothing. The guests purchase their own drinks. Cash bars bring in less revenue than open bars.

Therefore, most banquet houses have a minimum amount of liquor sales that must be attained. If the guests do not meet this minimum, the cost of the bartender has to be paid by the client.

The banquet manager should attempt to convince the client to have an open bar, if at all possible. First, the open bar increases the profits of the establishment. But more importantly, an open bar contributes to making the event a success. An open bar does not mean that all guests get drunk; but it does mean that the client is hospitable. Guests attending a wedding reception or any banquet are more likely to be in a positive state of mind when they are provided with drinks than when they have to purchase their own. This goes back to Maslow's theory, the love and belonging stage. The client has invited the guest to the banquet. Guests should be treated as if they were guests at the client's home.

T I P $

To Insure Proper Service

Have more than one kind of glassware to serve drinks. The glassware you select affects the perception of the quality of the drinks you serve.

Once the bar service has been decided, all the other details concerning the event must be determined. The guarantee and set are filled in on the function sheet in Figure 12-9.

Guarantee and Set

The guarantee and set pertain to the number of guests that will attend the event. Both of these numbers are written onto the function sheet only after the guarantee from the client has been given to the banquet establishment.

FIGURE 12-9

Part 2 of the function sheet. This part covers the set and guarantee for the banquet.

PART 2 OF THE FUNCTION SHEET

Estimated Number 200   Guarantee 198   Set 198

Food   Program   Liquor

GUARANTEE

The guarantee is the minimum number of guests that the client must pay for, even if fewer guests attend the event. Most banquet establishments demand the guaranteed number of guests 72 business hours in advance of the event.

Most often this system works well. However, some establishments have found that clients play a dangerous game by underestimating their guarantee. If they have 200 affirmative replies for the event, the client knows that the banquet facility will set up approximately 10 percent additional seats, so he or she only guarantees 180. This way, the client saves money if some guests do not attend. This creates a problem with seating arrangements (which is explained in the set information), because many times all 200 guests show up. Some establishments, to solve this problem, have allowed the guarantee to go 10 percent in either direction. Therefore, if the host guarantees 200, a minimum of 180 will be charged; but the room is set for 220. What do you think of this technique?

SET

Once the guarantee has been given, the banquet manager decides on how many extra seats to set in the banquet room. Oversetting generally ranges from 5 percent to 10 percent above the guarantee. As the party becomes larger, the percentage of extra seats must diminish; otherwise, a banquet manager would be setting up two hundred extra seats for banquets at the Astrodome. Therefore, many establishments state on their policy sheet the maximum number of seats that will be overset.

The reason for oversetting is that more guests may attend the banquet than had been guaranteed. Another, more common, reason is that often guests are in groups of two or more, and do not want to break up their group. Therefore, the banquet manager sets extra seats because it is easier to set them before the guests arrive. Banquets are staffed economically with service people. If a service person has to stop what he or she is doing and set up extra tables, chairs, and covers, it is detracting from the event and almost always makes the staff play a game of "catch up."

The only time the banquet room is not overset is when the client has seating arrangements. With seating arrangements every guest is assigned a seat.

Setting up the Time Schedule

Most clients want their guests to eat promptly and their program to start immediately. The banquet manager must be firm in allowing the service staff enough time to serve and clean up the meal. For American banquet service, it usually takes between one-and-a-half to two hours from the time that the guests are seated until the dessert and extra items are removed. For instance, if the party starts at 7 P.M., speeches should be scheduled for 9 P.M.

One of the most challenging events to plan for is the wedding reception. There may be a receiving line, pictures, blessing, toast, first dance, cake cutting, and bouquet and garter ceremonies. A wedding reception meal generally takes three hours from the time the guests sit down. Time must be planned for extra alcoholic beverage service if there are cocktails before the meal.

Once the client has decided on all the details of the event, this information must be placed onto the function sheet. The information should appear on the function sheet exactly as has been discussed with the client. There should be no surprises. Look at the completed Part 2 of the function sheet in Figure 12-10. This is a completed work order for the wedding that will take place in the SeVille Room from 7 P.M. to 1 A.M.

As you notice, the banquet manager has specified everything that the client desires on this function sheet. The reader can see exactly what time the cake is to be cut and what time each course is to be served. This function sheet is set up thoroughly, even to the pink fan-folded napkins. Each function should have this type of function sheet. By doing this, mistakes will be kept to a minimum.

Confirming the Arrangements

Once the function sheet is completed, the banquet manager must send a copy of the function sheet to the client of the party. Along with the sheet, a cover letter must be included. Figure 12-11 is a sample cover letter that the banquet manager will send out to the client.

Scheduling Parties

Many banquet operations have more than one banquet room. Therefore, they may have more than one party occurring during a meal period. The banquet manager should not schedule two events to take place at the same time. Instead, try to stagger the times at fifteen minute intervals.

It would be great for the banquet manager to sell the clients the same meal items. If it is impossible to sell them the same main course item, at least give them the same accompaniments. This is another way to improve relations with the kitchen, and also it will make the parties run smoother. Remember that the reasons American banquet style service is used are speed and profitability.

PART 2 OF THE FUNCTION SHEET

Room SeVille	**Time 7 P.M. - 1 A.M.**
Toast	
NV Moet Chandon	7:00 P.M.
Food	
1/2 Pineapple filled with fresh fruit in season (preset on table)	
Tossed Garden Fresh Salad, Italian Dressing	7:25 P.M.
Prime Ribs of Beef, au jus	7:40 P.M.
Baked Stuffed Potatoes	
Fresh Green Beans with Fresh Onions	
1961 Chateau Lafite Rothschild served with the meal	
Homemade Rolls and Butter served as soon as the guests are seated	
Coffee, Tea, and Decaffeinated Coffee served immediately after the Prime Ribs have been served	
Wedding Cake served with SuperFudge Ice Cream	8:45 P.M.

Liquor Service
Open Bar from 8 P.M. to 1 A.M.
Three bars, four bartenders. Bars will open at 8 P.M.
Seagrams VO; Dewars White Label; Smirnoff Vodka; Peach Schnapps;
Molson Golden; 1961 Chateau Yquem available for after dinner wine.
Fetzer Chardonnay & Chenin Blanc
Iron Horse Cabernet Sauvignon (at least 10 years of age)

Program
White tablecloths with pink napkins fan-folded
Head table skirted with candelabras and fern
Seating arrangements
Cocktails from 5:45 to 6:45 at Pool (see attached function sheet)
7:00 P.M..-Announcement of Bride & Groom
7:05 P.M.-Blessing by Father Fitzpatrick
7:06 P.M.-Toast by Best Man
7:10 P.M.-First Dance
8:40 P.M.-Wedding Cake Ceremony
Midnight-Bouquet & Garter

Band–Rhythm & Rain 877-3245 (obtained by the bride)
Cake–Chocolate with white frosting (we supply)

FIGURE 12-10

The completed Part 2 of the function sheet. This provides everyone with complete information of what will be occurring at the wedding.

SAMPLE COVER LETTER

Dear Mr. & Mrs. Lockwood,

We are pleased to enclose the function sheet for Jill's wedding that will be held in the SeVille Room on Saturday, August 1, of this year.

Please examine the function sheet carefully. If you are satisfied with the arrangements specified on the function sheet, please sign, date it, and return it in the enclosed stamped self-addressed envelope. If you desire to change any item, please call me at 555-6211.

Our staff is proud of the job we do for our wedding receptions. We are excited to be able to share in your family's special day. A few weeks before the wedding, I will call you to set up a meeting with Chef Brown, Head Waiter Larkin, and Bar Manager Verrigni to review all the details of the wedding.

August 1 will be an exciting day for Jill. I am looking forward to sharing in the happiness of the day!

Sincerely yours,

Mr. Toby
Banquet Manager

FIGURE 12-11

A sample cover letter sent to the client with the function sheet

Distribution of the Function Sheet

The banquet establishment should set up a policy of when to distribute the function sheet to the department heads. This should be determined based on the amount of time needed to order the food and schedule the staff. Many establishments find that two weeks in advance of a party is a good time to distribute the sheet. Each department should receive its own copy of the function sheet.

Meeting with the Staff

In order for functions to run smoothly, there should be weekly staff meetings for the purpose of discussing all events. All specifics about functions can be discussed. The banquet manager will be able to explain any special requests that clients want for their event. Discussions can take place on any problems that occurred at previous functions.

TIP$

To Insure Proper Service

At the Marriott Orlando World Center, the day before a function, representatives from all service areas involved must attend a production meeting. All details about the event are discussed.

Many establishments use this meeting to have a dress rehearsal of the meal for the upcoming event. At this dress rehearsal, the kitchen prepares the meal for the staff meeting in order to work out any problems. After the food is prepared and eaten, the staff discusses any potential problems that may occur with the meal.

These weekly meetings alleviate problems and misunderstandings between the members of the staff.

Working with the Kitchen

The banquet manager must learn how to work effectively with the kitchen staff, and especially the chef. The secret is to treat them with respect and make them your allies.

In order to make the chef your ally, always ask the chef if it is possible to comply with a client's special request about a meal item before you promise it to the client. Include the chef in the planning for special menus for parties. Ask for and use the chef's knowledge in planning events. Most importantly, introduce the chef to the client of the party.

The kitchen staff should always be told when the food is excellent, as well as when there is a problem. One of the most effective methods of encouraging the cooks to prepare excellent food is to bring the host of the party into the kitchen immediately after the meal. The cooks will look forward to this positive feedback. As a result, meals will always be prepared superbly.

Communication and respect will make it easy to work with the kitchen. If the banquet manager does not have an excellent working relationship with the kitchen, major problems will occur at functions.

Checking Details

The banquet manager should check with the client three or four days before the event. At this time, the guarantee must be obtained from the client. This is also the time that the banquet manager must verbally recheck every item step by step to make sure there will be no misunderstanding with the client. The banquet manager must do this even though the client has signed the function sheet; the client may not have read what he or she has signed.

If the client gives the banquet manager any changes, it must be communicated on all the function sheets. Whenever any written changes are made on the function sheet, they must be initialed by the person who made the change, and the department head must be told verbally of the change.

T I P $

To Insure Proper Service

Contact the client three weeks in advance of the function to make sure his or her plans are on track. This may help to avoid last minute surprises.

Seating Arrangements

The banquet manager is often asked to help plan seating arrangements for the party. The following is a step-by-step procedure for planning seating arrangements:

1. The estimated number is received from the client. Give the client a tentative floor plan. The circled number is the number of guests to be seated at the table; the other number is the table number.
2. As the client receives positive responses, guests are placed in groups that correspond to the circled numbers.
3. The client assigns groups to tables.
4. After all guests have been assigned a table number, the client makes an alphabetized listing of the guests' names and table numbers.

FIGURE 12-12

A tentative floor plan given to the client by the banquet manager to set up seating arrangements for a party. The number in the circle represents the number of guests that can be accommodated at that table. The other number is the number of the table.

5. The client makes out cards that read "Mr. Mars Jones you are seated at table 7." The client does all the planning and writing of the names.

6. The client brings the alphabetized cards and list to the banquet establishment on the day of the party.

7. On the day of the party, the staff put table numbers on each table that correspond to the floor plan that the banquet manager has given the client.

8. On a table at the entrance to the banquet room, the cards are placed in alphabetical order. The guests find their names, read the cards, and proceed to the tables with the numbers that correspond to their cards.

9. The banquet manager should have the alphabetized list as a double check in case there is a problem with the cards.

FIGURE 12-13

A daily function sheet. Each day, a sheet is distributed to all departments informing them of events taking place in the banquet establishment.

DAILY FUNCTION SHEET

Saturday, July 9

KILROY MANNERS SKILLS WORKSHOP
POD/Joan Starker/KS/525

7 A.M.	Regent Room	*ACCESS*, 3 6′ registration tables, 3 chairs, 2 wastepaper baskets, water/glasses, have 10-13 of their boxes under this table by 7AM
7 A.M.	5, 7, 9 Madison Room	*ACCESS*, Classroom f/300 No ashtrays/no smoking signs 8 × 12 stage 10′ away from wall 6′ table on left side of stage 4′ table on right side of stage Steps center of stage Barstool center stage Water station in back of room in addition to water on each table Light colored linen (if available) Flipchart w/ markers (at registration table) 8 × 8 screen (on stage) Lavalier mic w/ 45 ft. cord
8:30 A.M.	Regent Room	Registration begins
8:30 A.M.-5 P.M.	5, 7, 9 Madison Room	Meeting

DAILY FUNCTION SHEET (continued)

BILOXI/KING RECEPTION
POD/Kevin Biloxi/KS/

12 Noon-1 P.M.	Lancaster Gallery	Open bar f/75
		Hors d'oeuvres
1-5 P.M.	24, 25 High Cafe	Diner: set 75, GTD 71
		(*SEE DIAGRAM*)
		Headtable f/10 on risers
		Predesignated seating
		Placecard Table
		Gift Table
		Cake Table

JOHNSON/PEABODY RECEPTION
POD/Julea Johnson/KS/

1:30-2:30 P.M.	Lancaster Gallery	Open bar f/58
		Hors d'oeuvres
2:30-6 P.M.	6, 8 Lancaster	Dinner: set 58, GTD 55 (*SEE DIAGRAM)
		Headtable f/6 on risers
		Predesignated seating
		Placecard Table
		Gift Table
		Cake Table
		No ashtrays, even on request, send people into courtyard

FIGURE 12-13

(continued)

TIP$

TO INSURE PROPER SERVICE

To set a positive tone for guests, start seating arrangements for events with table 10 instead of table 1. Always avoid using table 13 because of guests' superstitions.

The banquet manager now has all the information for the event on the function sheet.

Weekly and Daily Function Sheet

In order to let all the staff in the establishment know what events are happening, the banquet office uses two forms. One of these forms is a weekly function sheet (distributed on the same day every week), which is given to all departments. In addition, an updated daily function sheet should be distributed. See Figure 12-13 for an example of a daily function sheet.

Both of these sheets should have all the events taking place in the establishment, not just the food functions. This allows all staff to be in the "knowledge loop."

The daily function sheet is simply an update of the weekly function sheet. The guarantee is on the sheet.

Once all this information has been gathered, the banquet manager can proceed to run the party.

SUMMARY

1. Organization is the key to a successful banquet.
2. The purpose of the function determines the planning of the menu.
3. There are three types of banquet function meals: cocktail reception, sit-down meal, and buffet meal.
4. Buffets can be simple buffet, modified deluxe buffet, or deluxe buffet.
5. Alcoholic beverage services are: alcohol placed on guests' tables, open bar, a la carte drinks, or cash bar.

REVIEW QUESTIONS

1. Three days before the function, you contact the client for the guarantee. When checking the details of the event, you discover that the host has told the guests that they are going to receive sirloin steak for their main course. The signed function sheet clearly states that the meal will be top sirloin of beef. Because this is a retirement party of 150, and the guests have purchased their own tickets, you know a problem will develop. What would you do? Take into consideration the potential for repeat business in your answer.
2. Should Part 3 of the function sheet be distributed to all employees? Or do you believe that Part 3 would be better left off the function sheet? Explain your answer.
3. What problems would occur by having the service staff take individual cooking orders for guests at a banquet? For instance, the staff is told to ask the guest how they would want their filet mignons cooked: rare, medium, or well.
4. What is a banquet function sheet, and what is its purpose?
5. What important function should the banquet manger obtain from the host of the party? Why is that information important?
6. What does the term *details* mean as it pertains to the banquet business? Why is it an important term?

7. How would a banquet manager serve more than one main course entree to the guests at a banquet? Explain the steps that a banquet manager would have to take to achieve this goal.
8. What is the difference between a cash bar and an open bar?
9. Explain the different options of open bars that a host can choose for the guests at a banquet.
10. Explain how seating arrangements are set up. Give a step by step explanation.

REFERENCE

1. *The Random House Dictionary*, s.v. "details."

Managing the Function

OBJECTIVES

At the completion of this chapter, the reader will be able to:

1. Diagram the setup of a place setting from information provided on the function sheet
2. Plan all equipment needed for the banquet service based upon information contained on the function sheet
3. List the three styles of service for serving a sit-down banquet
4. Illustrate the quickest way to serve food from the kitchen to the banquet room
5. Explain the methods for staffing and ending bar service correctly at a banquet
6. Describe the proper sequence for setting up and serving a banquet room
7. Explain the methods for staffing and ending bar service correctly at a banquet
8. Explain the methods for controlling the amount of canapés and hors d'oeuvres at a party
9. Illustrate the proper method for setting up a buffet and controlling traffic flow
10. Describe how to clean up a meeting room and how to provide the guests with water, paper, and pencils

Preparing for the Function

As was stated in the preceding chapter, three days before the event is to be held, the banquet manager obtains the guaranteed number of guests from the host. Now the banquet manager's most critical part of the job begins.

The banquet manager must plan and organize the minute details of the function to make it a success. The banquet manager takes the responsibility for the event off of the client's shoulders and puts it on his or her own shoulders. Great service will be made up of many moments of truth that the banquet manager must control. If the banquet manager successfully attends to the details of planning, organizing, and managing the function, the event will be successful.

The function sheet from the Lockwood wedding, Figure 13-1, will help illustrate the type of details that the banquet manager's job encompasses.

THE FUNCTION SHEET

The banquet manager must use the information on the function sheet to organize, plan, and manage the wedding. The function sheet has been distributed to the department heads. Using the function sheet, the department heads have scheduled employees and obtained the food and beverages needed for the event. The banquet manager will make any last minute changes on the function sheet and forward them to all the department heads, highlighting the changes. These were obtained when the guarantee was obtained from the client.

Staffing the Wedding

The first job the banquet manager has to perform after the guarantee is received is to make certain there are the proper number of employees to serve the party. The banquet manager should be concerned with the number needed not only of service staff, but also of the bar and kitchen staff. The banquet manager is the one ultimately responsible for the service of the banquet. Having too few bartenders or kitchen staff results in slow service for the guests. Once again a reminder: American banquet service must be fast.

SERVICE STAFF NEEDED

The amount of staff that is scheduled by banquet establishments varies depending upon the number of guests at a table, the competency

FUNCTION SHEET

Event Date Saturday, August 1   Payment Arrangement Cash

Organization Lockwood-Jones Wedding   Business Phone 555-0978

Address 7 Lark Avenue   Home Phone 555-0878

Cranston, RI

Person in Charge Jim Lockwood

Estimated Number 200   Guarantee 198   Set 198

Room Seville   Time 7 P.M.–1 A.M.

Toast
    NV Moet Chandon   7:00 P.M.

Food
    1/2 Pineapple filled with Fresh Fruit in season   Preset on Table
    Tossed Garden Fresh Salad, Italian Dressing   7:25 P.M.
    Prime Ribs of Beef, Au Jus   7:40 P.M.
    Baked Stuffed Potatoes
    Fresh Green Beans with Fresh Onions
    1961 Chateau Lafite Rothschild served with the meal
    Homemade Rolls and Butter served as soon as the
       guests are seated
    Coffee, Tea, and Decaffeinated Coffee served
       immediately after the Prime Ribs have been served
Wedding Cake served with SuperFudge Ice Cream   8:45 P.M.

Liquor Service
    Open Bar from 8 P.M. to 1 A.M.
    Three bars, four bartenders   Bars will open at: 8 P.M.
    Fetzer Chardonnay & Chenin Blanc
    Iron Horse Cabernet Sauvigon (at least 10 years old)

Program
    White tablecloths with pink napkins fan-folded
    Head table skirted, candelabras and fern
    Seating arrangements
    Cocktails from 5:45 to 6:45 at Pool (on attached function sheet)
    7:00 P.M.–Introduction of Wedding Party
    7:05 P.M.–Blessing by Father Fitzpatrick
    7:06 P.M.–Toast by Best Man
    7:15 P.M.–First Dance after first course has been eaten
    8:40 P.M.–Wedding Cake Ceremony
    Midnight–Bouquet & Garter
Band–Misty Rain 555-3425 (obtained by the bride)
Cake–Chocolate with white frosting (from L & G Goodies, we obtain)
Price $50.00 + 20% grat and Sales tax   Booked by AJS

Guest Signature & Date

FIGURE 13-1

The function sheet for the Lockwood-Jones wedding reception. The banquet manager uses the information on the function sheet to make the wedding a success.

of the staff, and whether the staff is covered by union representation (in the case of union representation, the amount of staff required is clearly stated in the contract). Figure 13-2 can be used as a guideline for staffing service personnel and bartenders. Generally, one service person can serve between sixteen and twenty-four guests efficiently. Using this figure, one service person should be scheduled to serve two or three tables, depending on how many guests are seated at each table. For a buffet or cocktail party with butler service, one service person is needed for thirty-five guests. At a cocktail party, without butler service, one server is needed for every fifty guests.

At the Lockwood wedding, ten service personnel should be scheduled. Each person will serve approximately twenty guests. Because the cocktail party is before the main meal, some of the same staff can be used to pass the food butler-style during the cocktail reception.

BAR STAFF NEEDED

Normally, at a cocktail reception, either before dinner or by itself, one bartender is needed for every fifty guests; after dinner, one is needed for one hundred. This applies to both cash and open bars.

Often extra bartenders are needed only for the cocktail reception. As they are only needed for a short period, it becomes expensive to employ them for the entire night or for the minimum required by some state laws. One way to alleviate this problem is to have service people act as bartenders. Another method is to schedule bartenders from a previous party to work one or two hours overtime. For instance, if a bartender is scheduled to work from 10 A.M. to 6 P.M., have the bartender stay for two hours of overtime. During that period from 6 P.M. to 8 P.M., the bartender can set up the bar and serve the guests at the cocktail party. When the cocktail party is finished, the bartender is done working.

FIGURE 13-2

A staffing table guideline for staffing banquets using American banquet service

STAFFING TABLE

Position	Meal	One Employee Can Usually Serve
Service person	Lunch or Dinner	16-24 guests
Service person	Breakfast	24 guests
Service person	Buffet	35 guests
Service person	Butler Service	35 guests
Service person	Cocktail Reception	50 guests
Bartender	Cocktail Reception	50 guests
Bartender	Bar after Meal	100 guests

At the Lockwood wedding there is a special request to have four bartenders throughout the evening. Because most guests remain at their table when the meal is being served, we will use three bartenders for opening and serving wine during the meal. The other one will get the bar prepared for service after dinner.

T I P $

....

To Insure Proper Service

"The customer and food are what we're here for. They're the most important part of any restaurant," says Anthony Bommarito, owner of Anthony's in St. Louis. "The service staff should be there when you need them and remain in the background when you don't."[1]

....

KITCHEN STAFF

The staffing of the kitchen is an area of the function to which most banquet managers do not give proper consideration. At a banquet it is extremely important to serve the food as quickly as possible from the kitchen to the guests. In order to do this, the kitchen must be organized. If this has been delegated to a proven knowledgeable chef, your worries are over. If you have not worked with each other, you ought to work together to get the food plated efficiently and quickly.

There are two methods for serving that work well. Both methods need teamwork to serve the meal quickly. Only one skilled culinary person is required to be at each serving line. The other employees put the food on the plate and have to be able to work quickly. Both systems work fastest when the meat has been sauced before being placed on the plate.

The first method, which was used at The DeWitt Clinton Hotel, is shown in Figure 13-3. This requires four people at each station to serve the food. Each person has a specific item to put on the plate. There are two piles of plates. Employee 2, the skilled employee, puts on the main course, while employees 3 and 4 put on the potato and vegetable. Very quickly, they develop a rhythm to avoid crashes. The plate never moves until employee 1 removes it and puts the sauce on the meat, if needed. The service person garnishes the plate, covers it, and takes it out of the kitchen.

The other method, just as effective, is shown in Figure 13-4. This method, used at the Hall of Springs in Saratoga, New York, is similar to the DeWitt Clinton method. Three piles of plates are set up on a rectangular table. Employee 1 puts the main course item on plates from any one of the three piles. Employees 2 and 3 put on the potato and vegetable.

FIGURE 13-3

The DeWitt Clinton method of serving a banquet. This requires four people at each station to serve the food. Each person has a specific item to put on the plate. There are two piles of plates. Employee 2, the skilled employee, serves the main course, while employees 3 and 4 serve the potato and vegetable.

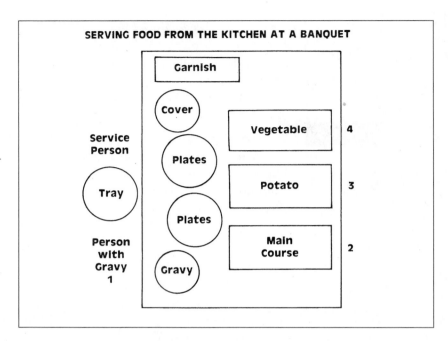

SERVING FOOD FROM THE KITCHEN AT A BANQUET

FIGURE 13-4

The Hall of Springs method of serving a banquet. Three piles of plates are set up on a rectangular table. Employee 1 serves the main course item on any one of the three piles of plates. Employees 2 and 3 serve the potato and vegetable. Both employees (2 with the left, 3 with the right hand) pull plates from the pile when the dish is complete. They place them on the table and a service person garnishes the plates, covers them, and brings them out into the dining room.

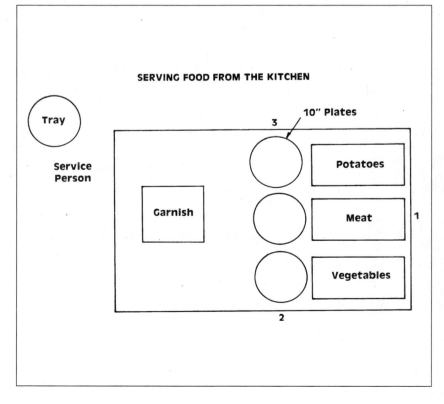

SERVING FOOD FROM THE KITCHEN

Both employees (2 with the left hand, 3 with the right hand) pull the plates from the pile when the dish is complete. They place them on the table, and a service person garnishes the plates, covers them, and brings them out into the dining room.

For the Lockwood wedding, there must be two serving stations for the 198 guests. A few days before the wedding, the banquet manager confers with the chef to develop a plan to serve the function. This plan has the names of the employees who will be serving the food; for example, Anne puts on the potatoes, John the prime ribs, and so on. In a non-union establishment, the extra bartenders, service people, or even dishwashers may help with the planning of the meal.

Both systems described above are workable. The key is to plate the food quickly. Plates should only be handled by one person when the food is being plated. Never allow the plates to be passed in an assembly line fashion. That slows up the service. Using either system, it should take between eight and twelve minutes to serve the main course to the guests. The time should always be the same, regardless of the size of the party, as the number of serving stations are increased proportionately.

With staffing planned, the banquet manager can now finalize the equipment that is needed for the event.

Planning for the Equipment

Information required for the planning of equipment that is needed for the function is obtained directly from the function sheet. The banquet manager determines exactly what plates and utensils are needed to consume the meal. Using the Lockwood wedding functions sheet, the banquet manager can plan the equipment that will be needed.

It is best to list the menu item along with the equipment that will be needed to eat the item.

ITEM	EQUIPMENT NEEDED
Toast	
NV Moet Chardon	Champagne Glass
Food	
1/2 Pineapple filled with Fresh fruit in season (preset on table)	Spoon, 7" Plate
Tossed Garden Fresh Salad, Italian Dressing	Fork, Salad Plate
Prime Ribs of Beef, au jus	Fork, Steak Knife, Dinner Plate

Baked Stuffed Potatoes ....Served on Dinner
Plate

Fresh Green Beans with Fresh Onions ....Served on Dinner
Plate

1961 Chateau Lafite Rothschild, ...Red Wine Glass
served with the meal

Homemade Rolls and Butter, served as soon as......Butter Knife, Bread
the guests are served   and Butter Plate

Coffee, Tea, and Decaffeinated Coffee, served ....Coffee Cup, Saucer,
immediately after the Prime Ribs   Coffee Spoon
have been served

Wedding Cake, served with ....Spoon, Fork, 7″ Plate
SuperFudge Ice Cream

From the above information, the banquet manager can now plan how much equipment is needed by multiplying the amount of each item by the set number (198) on the function sheet. For instance, 198 coffee cups and saucers are needed, while each guest requires three forks for a total of 594.

It is helpful to have a document such as the banquet checklist shown in Figure 13-5.

Using the banquet checklist, complete the planning of equipment for the Lockwood wedding.

Planning for the Needed Extra Equipment

In addition to figuring out how much equipment is needed for the guests, there are other items the banquet manager must make sure are available for the event. These include salt and pepper shakers, butter dishes, sugars, roll baskets, and cream containers. Figure 13-6 is a guideline for equipment that should be placed on the guest tables.

Having the correct amount of this equipment adds to the success of the event. The next time you attend a banquet, notice how many sets of salt and pepper shakers are on the tables. Most banquet houses provide one for a table of eight guests. Doesn't it make sense to have one set for every two people? When the main course is served, the guests do not have to wait for the salt and pepper to be used by the other seven people at the table. While they are waiting to use the shakers, their food gets cold. Remember, it is the job of the banquet house to make the guest have a pleasurable experience. Catering to that experience is having everything run so well that the guests never have to ask for any item.

BANQUET CHECKLIST FORM

Tables

_____ 6-Foot
_____ 8-Foot
_____ 72' Round
_____ 60" Round
_____ 8-Foot by 1½ feet

Linen

_____ 72 × 72
_____ Napkins
_____ 81 × 81
_____ 120 × 48

_____ 84 × 48

Flatware

_____ Teaspoons
_____ Soupspoons
_____ Cocktail Forks
_____ Dinner Forks
_____ Bread & Butter Knives
_____ Dinner Forks
_____ Steak Knives
_____ Ice Tea Spoons

Plates

_____ Bread and Butter
_____ Dinner
_____ Saucers
_____ Soup Cups
_____ Monkey Dish
_____ Coffee Cups

_____ Roll Basket
_____ Bread Board
_____ Ashtrays
_____ Sets of Salt and Pepper
_____ Sugar
_____ Cream Pitchers
_____ Salad Bowls

_____ Parfait
_____ Water
_____ Punch
_____ Water Pitchers
_____ Coffee Pots
_____ Tea Pots
_____ Ice Tea Glasses

_____ Table Number
_____ Candles
_____ Bud Vases

FIGURE 13-5

A banquet checklist helps the banquet manager organize the supplies needed for the banquet.

The guests should leave feeling great about the event, but without noticing how the banquet establishment accomplished it.

The same provisions should be made for the other items. All the items should be placed within easy reach of the guests. Try it yourself. Sit at a table like the one your guest will sit at and try to reach the items. This little experiment will give you a good idea of what your guests have to go through to obtain these items.

There should be one sugar and creamer for every four people. The rolls should be served hot, in a bread basket. The banquet manager should plan on having one and a half rolls for each guest.

In addition, the banquet manager has to order extra napkins for use as sidetowels and for use in the center of the banquet table. These napkins are usually a contrasting color from the tablecloth, but the

EQUIPMENT NEEDED FOR TABLE SERVICE

Item	Head	Round or Oblong
Whipped Butter	1 for 2	1 for 4 people
Butter Pats	2 pats on each Bread and Butter Dish	
Salt and Pepper Sets	1 set for every 2 people	
Sugar, Ashtrays	1 for 2	1 for 4
Cream	1 for 2	1 for 4
Amount of Cream	3 oz.	5 oz.
Roll Basket	1 for 3	1 for 4

Figure 1½ rolls per person. Rolls go on table with salad course. All sugar, cream, and butter are placed on underliners.

LINEN

Size	For What Table?
45 × 45	Deuces
54 × 54	4-tops
72 × 72	60-inch Rounds, Head, and Buffet
54 × 90	6-Foot by 3-Foot
54 × 108	8-Foot by 3-Foot

NOTE: Place a napkin in the center of the table, to place sugar, cream, etc. on. Only do this if the napkin is a different color from the tablecloth.

FIGURE 13-6

A guideline for equipment to be placed on guests' tables

same color as the guest napkins. On the napkin will be placed the ashtrays, rolls, salt and pepper shakers, and other items that the guest needs to enjoy the meal. Another item that has to be ordered is extra bread and butter plates to be used as coffee shields.

Once all this equipment has been calculated, the banquet checklist will be completed. The equipment can be obtained before the service staff arrives by a dishwasher or banquet steward. It should be ready for the service staff to set up the tables when they arrive. Obviously, if some equipment is not available, the banquet manager will know before the party is ready to be set up and can make adjustments.

A Little Tip for Planning for Equipment

Many times it becomes impractical to have all the plates and utensils that are needed to serve the party. The banquet establishment simply may not have a sufficient inventory to have three forks for each guest. If a caterer is renting the equipment, the cost may be prohibitive to rent an additional two hundred forks.

The banquet manager has a couple of choices. First, the guest can use the same fork for the salad and main course. The service staff are instructed to leave the fork at the place setting when picking up the salad course. This is not proper service, but it is done.

The best method is to determine what items can be washed and used for another course. For example, at the Lockwood wedding, the plate that is used for the pineapple can be washed, dried, and used for the cake course. The guests would have no idea that they are eating off the same plates that contained the pineapple. Can you discover any other multiple uses of equipment?

Organizing the Jobs for the Service Staff

When the service staff report to work, there should be a detailed work schedule for them. The banquet manager must plan these jobs before the employees report to work.

The banquet manger makes a job duty roster. It should be posted in the same location for each banquet. The service staff are usually scheduled to report to work two hours in advance of the function, or at a time determined by the banquet manager. Once the banquet manager masters this system, the amount of time needed to set up the function room is reduced. This is valuable if the establishment is paying the service staff by the hour. For instance, if a service person gets paid $10 per hour, eliminating one hour's work for ten staff members is a savings of $100. Over the course of a year, it would be a great savings.

When the service staff arrive for work, the roster will be posted on the wall. Figure 13-7 is the job duty roster for the Lockwood wedding. Notice that there are three columns. The first is the time by which the job must be completed; the second is who is responsible for doing the job; and the third is the specific job to be done. This duty roster should be completed for all banquets.

By having this duty roster, the banquet manager has an organized plan of attack. If the banquet manager has to leave the room, the staff know exactly what they need to do to set up the room. Notice also that the banquet room is set up on a team system, using an assembly-line method.

The first item on the duty roster is a meeting. Any special instructions about the event can be explained at this time. For instance, Steve and Sam will be told that their primary responsibility before the main meal is to take care of the food at the cocktail party.

By using a duty roster, the banquet manager can easily make changes and correct the situation if there is a problem.

THE FIRST JOB OF THE DAY

When the banquet manager arrives at the establishment, the banquet room is the first thing checked to see that is has been physically set

LOCKWOOD DUTY ROSTER

Time Completed By	Staff	Job
7P.M.	All	Room completely set up
	All	Champagne poured (head table poured last)
6:50	All	Assignments given out
6:40	Pam, Jane Beth, Sue	Water poured at tables
	Jim, John Tom, Gerri	Pineapple preset at tables
6:20	Pam, Jane Beth, Sue Tom, Gerri	Head Table skirted
	Jim, John	30 Butters on tables, 30 creamers in walk-in
6:00	Pam & Jane	Water glasses
	Beth, Sue	Wine glasses
	Tom, Gerri	Champagne glasses
	Jim, John	Salt & Peppers, Sugars on each table
	Steve, Sam	Cocktail Party room set up
5:45	Pam & Jane	Coffee cups & Saucers
	Beth, Sue	Bread & Butter Plates
	Tom	Dessert Fork
	Gerri	Dessert Spoon
	Jim & John	Bread & Butter Knives (follow Beth & Sue)
5:30	Steve, Sam	Chafing Dishes set up
	Pam & Jane	Knives
	Beth, Sue	Forks
	Tom, Gerri	Spoons
	Jim, John	Table Numbers & Napkins for center of table
	Jim, John	Tablecloths on tables
5:15	All staff	Meeting concerning function
5:00	All staff report	

FIGURE 13-7

A job duty roster for the Lockwood wedding. This form makes it easy for the staff and the banquet manager to have a successful banquet.

up. If it has not been, then it must be done. Yes, the banquet manger may have to move tables and chairs into their proper place.

Once it has been determined that the room has been set up properly, the banquet doors that the guests enter through are locked. This prevents guests from entering the room before it is set up.

One Great Tip for Wedding Receptions

According to Elsie Panza, whose family has operated banquet establishments on both the East and West Coasts of the United States, there is one piece of equipment a banquet manager should always have at hand to assist in the smooth operation of wedding receptions. It is a roll of Scotch tape. She uses it all the time to tape loose envelopes onto gifts, so the bride and groom know who gave them what gift. It is a small detail, but that is the key to the banquet business. No bride or groom ever has to wonder, "Who did this gift come from?"

PLANNING THE PLACE SETTING AND COVER

The banquet manager also plans the place setting and cover for the banquet. This information is also obtained from the notes the banquet manager made for the equipment that is needed. Figure 13-8 is the place setting for the Lockwood wedding. One setting is set on one table in the banquet room before the staff arrive. It is called the sample setting.

For the Lockwood wedding, the banquet manager has decided to use a variation of the Russian banquet setting. The dessert spoon and fork are placed above the starter plate. The coffee cup is already in place. All this is done to save time. If this were Russian banquet service, the coffee cup would be brought when the coffee was served. It would not be preset. In American banquet service, however, the coffee cup is preset. The napkin will be folded in the shape of a candle and placed in the red wine glass.

Setting up a sample place setting eliminates any questions the service staff may have.

DIRECTION OF SETTING UP THE ROOM

The proper way to set up a banquet room is to set the tables farthest from the kitchen first and work back toward the kitchen. If, for some reason, the tables are not completely set up when the guests arrive, the

FIGURE 13-8

A diagram of the place setting for the Lockwood wedding. The service staff will use this guide when setting up the dining room. A sample place setting is situated on one table to guide the service staff. A-bread and butter knife; B-bread and butter plate; C-salad fork; D-main course fork; E-plate for pineapple; F-serrated steak knife; G-fruit spoon; H-saucer and coffee cup (with handle at 5 o'clock); I-champagne glass; J-red wine glass; K-water glass; L-dessert fork; M-dessert spoon; N-napkin folded in candle fold, placed in wine glass; O-coffee spoon.

service staff do not have to carry items through the guests to the tables in the farthest part of the room. They can continue to work their way back toward the kitchen.

Serving the Party

Once the banquet manager has the event organized and the service staff are aware of their pre-party assignments, a decision will be made concerning the best method to serve the food to the guests.

There are three styles of service used in American banquet service to serve a party. The first is referred to as the *station method*; the second is the *follow-up method*; and the third is called the *combination method*.

THE STATION METHOD

In this method, each service person is assigned two tables of either eight or ten guests, for a total of between sixteen to twenty people. The service person is solely responsible for the service at those two tables. This system is best used when a large staff of temporary workers are hired to serve a large party. The advantage of this system is that the banquet manager knows who is responsible for service at all the tables.

This system has two main disadvantages. It is the slowest type of American banquet service. Also, guest tables usually will not be served in the proper order. For example, if Pam had tables 1 and 2, she would serve the guests at table 1 their food. Then she must return to the kitchen to obtain the food for table 2. In the meantime, the service person who has table 3 has already served that table. Table 3 is served before table 2, which is shown in Figure 13-9.

Another potential problem with using the station method is that service people will only set up their own tables. They will not assist in the setting up of the total banquet room. To avoid this problem, the banquet manager must not give out station assignments until the room is set up. Then the service people should be brought to the tables for which they are responsible, so there will be no mix-up concerning which table should be served by whom.

FIGURE 13-9

Service stations for an American-style banquet. This system is bad because the tables are not served in order. Table 18 will be served before Pam can serve table 2.

THE FOLLOW-UP METHOD

This is the most efficient method and quickest service if the staff can master the system. It takes planning, cooperation, and leadership by the banquet manager, the head service people, and the remaining service staff.

For the Lockwood wedding, the staff would be broken up into two teams of five. The responsibility of serving the food and removing the dirty dishes in the banquet room would be divided in half, as shown in Figure 13-10. Each group would have a head service person to supervise its side of the room. Three members of the team would carry the food into the banquet room. The other two (including the head service person) would serve the food to the guests. The head service person would instruct the other service person in the correct order of service. Each team would obtain its food from an assigned plating area in the kitchen.

When it is time to clear the dirty dishes, all five members of the team work together in removing the dishes. They work from the head table backwards toward the kitchen doors. The banquet manager should be in the banquet room making sure that all the guests get served and that the service is done correctly.

The advantages of this type of service are that it is fast and that all the guests are served in proper order. This is considered the best serving

FIGURE 13-10

The follow-up method for serving a banquet, the most efficient method and quickest service. The tables served first are closest to the head table.

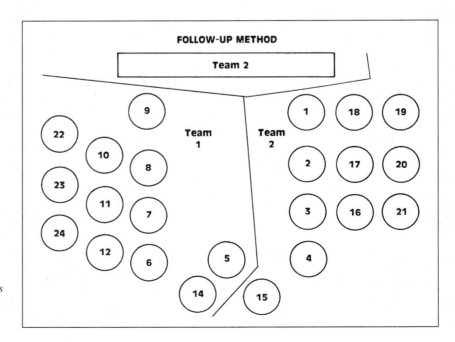

system from the kitchen's point of view, because the food is picked up quickly from the kitchen.

The main disadvantage is that it is difficult to teach temporary workers to use this system. They generally lack the organization and teamwork it requires.

THE COMBINATION METHOD

This system combines the best features of the follow-up and station methods. Serving the food is done by the team system. However, clearing dirty dishes and serving beverages is the responsibility of a service person who is assigned a station.

The advantage of this system is that it can be used with either permanent or temporary service staff. The only key people who must be employed are head service people. Another advantage is that tables are served in the proper order. Finally, confusion on the part of the service staff (Did we clear the dishes from table 14?) is eliminated.

The only disadvantage is that it is slower than the follow-up method.

The banquet manager should decide which of the above systems to use based on the capabilities of the staff and the organizational qualities of the manager. In addition to the above-mentioned styles of services, there are other variations of the three styles that banquet establishments use. For example, a variation of the station method is to have two service staff be responsible for four tables, but have them work as a team. One would carry the food from the kitchen, while the other would serve the food. Regardless of the system the banquet manager decides to use, the main factor in choosing one over the other must be guest satisfaction.

Whichever method is used, the banquet manager must be in the dining room at all times when the food is being served and the dirty dishes are being cleared. It is the manager's job to correct mistakes and oversee service.

Proper Order of Serving the Party

The banquet manager has to know the correct order in which to serve the guests at a banquet. The head table is always the first table served. Next served are the tables in front of the head table. The service of the rest of the dining room would follow in a logical manner, going from the head table to the back of the room.

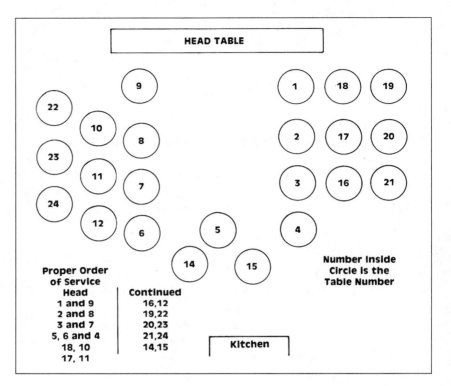

FIGURE 13-11

The proper sequence to serve the Lockwood wedding. The head table is served first, followed by tables 1 and 9, 2 and 8, 3 and 7, 5, 6, and 4, 18, 10, 17, 11, 16, 12, 19, 22, 20, 23, 21, 24, 14, and 15.

Figure 13-11 illustrates the floor plan for the Lockwood wedding. This is the way the guests should be served. The head table is served first, then the order is tables 1 and 9, 2 and 8, 3 and 7, 5, 6, and 4; 18, 10, 17, 11, 16, 12, 19, 22, 20, 23, 21, 24, 14, and 15.

Often guests farthest from the head table receive their food before guests nearest the head table at a banquet. This should never happen.

The banquet manager has to inform the service of proper serving order. This information may be put on the duty roster; however, it works better when the banquet manager verbally communicates the correct order to the key staff.

Serving Cocktail Parties

Many times the guest obtains the first impression of service at the banquet establishment during the cocktail reception or party. For this reason, both liquor and food service must be accomplished professionally and with dignity.

The bar manager is responsible for the performance of the bartenders, as the chef is for the cooks. A duty roster sheet, which the bar manager completes, should also be provided for the bar staff.

When the client arrives, the banquet manager should introduce the client to the bar manager. It is also an excellent idea to introduce the client to the bartenders. This is done to eliminate potential problems during the reception. For instance, if a guest desires a brand of liquor or drink different from those that have been ordered, the bartenders know who has the authority to approve changes.

The food being served at the cocktail party should be ample to provide the guests with the appetizers before the meal, but not so abundant as to spoil their appetite for the main meal. It should be presented attractively.

When the client requests service staff to pass hors d'oeuvres and drinks, it is called **butler style**. The staff passes the food carried on trays. They will have with them cocktail napkins, which are offered to the guests when an hors d'oeuvre is taken. The staff have to be knowledgeable about all items on their trays and be able to explain these items to the guests. Throughout the cocktail party, the staff are circulating throughout the room picking up dirty glasses and plates, changing ashtrays, and replenishing the food.

TIPS ABOUT COCKTAIL PARTIES

Always position bars away from entrances to the room and away from food tables.

Plan on staggering the service of hors d'oeuvres. For example, at a cocktail hour, do not serve them all within the first fifteen minutes of the event. Plan to serve the food on small trays staggering the amount of food throughout the cocktail hour. Butler style service, combined with hot and cold food displays, is always the most elegant type of service. This type of service keeps the food looking attractive and stops the guests from crowding around food displays.

The more food that is put out during the cocktail hour, the more food the guests will eat. Guests very seldom will take the last hors d'oeuvre. Instead they will wait until more food is brought out. Therefore, if you have to make food last, don't be too quick to bring out more food.

Plan on about five pieces of food per person at a cocktail party before a meal. Supplement the food with a bread and cheese table.

Tip Cups

One repeatedly controversial issue is tip cups for bartenders. Tip cups are placed on the bars to allow the guests to give extra money (to insure prompt service) to the bartenders.

Ending the Cocktail Reception

The banquet manager needs to have a method to end the cocktail party. It must be done without offending the guests or the host. This involves tact and diplomacy.

About ten minutes before the cocktail party is scheduled to end, the banquet manager locates the client and informs him or her of the exact time that the cocktail party will end. If a dinner follows the reception, it is critical that the party be ended on time; otherwise the food may be ruined. If no other meal is planned, the client can either end the party or extend it, depending on the policies of the establishment (which were set forth in the policy sheet).

If a meal follows the reception, the banquet manager would then circulate around the room informing the guests that dinner will be served shortly. The guests are asked to proceed to the dining room. Often this information is conveyed by making an announcement via a microphone.

Once the host agrees to end the party, the bars have to be shut down quickly. This is a critical moment in a party. The best way of closing bars is to have a prearranged sign with the bartenders. When the sign is given, the bartender should finish serving the drink they are serving, inform the guests that the bar is closed, and walk away from the bar.

Running the Banquet Party

When the doors to the banquet room are unlocked to allow guests in, the room has to be completely set to receive guests. All food that is supposed to be present should be in place, and the service staff should be ready to serve the party.

The main responsibility of the banquet manager now is to get all the guests seated and the meal served. If the client has arranged seating for the guests, everyone will have a seat and the meal can commence. However, if there are no seating arrangements, the banquet manager must see that every guest has a seat. This may involve breaking up groups of four or six people and having them sit with guests they do not know.

There is a way to avoid having this problem. When the party does not have seating arrangements, select the table that is the worst location (farthest from the head table, next to the kitchen) and place a reserved sign on it. That way no guests will sit at that table. The establishment should most likely have the extra table because the banquet establishment usually oversets by 10 percent. Guests coming in early will generally fill up all the other seats. When the latecomers arrive, there is a table left for them. If they don't show up, there is one less table to serve. It works every time!

SERVING AND CLEARING THE MEAL

Once all the guests have been seated and the introductions, blessings, or toasts have been given, the service staff can serve the meal.

It is the responsibility of the banquet manager to inform the service staff, as well as the kitchen staff, when to serve the meal. No one should serve any food, beverages, or rolls without being told by the banquet manager.

The same is true of clearing the dirty dishes. No service person should clean any dirty dishes without authorization from the banquet manager.

The objective in having the banquet manager tell the service staff when to serve and clear is to ensure that all the guests are served approximately at the same time.

GIVING THE NUMBER TO THE CHEF

One of the ways the banquet manager ensures a good working relationship with the kitchen is to keep the chef informed about the progress of the party. In order to have a successful banquet, the banquet manager and head service people should count the number of guests that are seated. Once the number of guests has been verified, the banquet manager should give that number to the chef. If there are more or less than the chef planned, adjustments can be made at that time. When late guests arrive, the chef should be informed immediately.

OBTAINING GUEST PREFERENCE FROM THE MAIN COURSE CHOICES OFFERED

More and more banquet facilities are allowing the client to offer more than one main course choice to the guests attending the event. Some banquet establishments allow as many as three choices.

To facilitate the serving of the main course items to the guests, the banquet manger should request that the guests place a colored ticket at their place setting. Each colored ticket represents a particular entree choice. The service people collect the tickets and record which and how many guests are having each item.

When the service people go into the kitchen to pick up the meals, they obtain the correct number of each item for each table. When a follow-up system is used, this requires much more organization from the staff. Again a reminder: All guests at the table should be served at approximately the same time. A banquet house should not serve all the chicken meals and then serve all the beef meals; but each table should receive the correct number of beef and chicken meals simultaneously.

The Improper Way vs. The Proper Way of Serving

At the Golden Anniversary of a large corporation, there was a choice of fish, chicken, or beef. Approximately eighty guests were in attendance. This was a great lesson in how not to serve a banquet. The guests made their choice of what they desired to eat when they RSVPed. However, the service staff did not ask who gets what entree. There were no colored tickets. They simply brought out the main courses. They were short one meal. The president of the corporation finally got his meal after everyone else had almost finished theirs!

On the other hand, at a wedding reception for three hundred guests, there were two options: either beef or chicken. The waitstaff asked each guest at each table what they had ordered. They took the orders and served everyone at once.

The difference between the parties: a supervisor was in the room at all times during the wedding reception.

Controlling the Function

Some clients will only pay their bill based upon the number of meal tickets that are collected. Under these conditions, the banquet manager should have a person in the kitchen collecting tickets from the service people. For example, when the service person picks up ten meals, that person should give ten tickets to the collector. At a buffet, a service person is stationed at the beginning of the buffet line to collect tickets.

The service person should be taught that if a guest does not have a ticket, the banquet manager is to be summoned immediately. The banquet manager then checks with the client of the party to determine if the person is really a guest or a crasher of the party (which happens often at conventions and weddings).

As soon as the meal has been served, the banquet manager informs the client of the number of guests that the banquet house has served. If there is a discrepancy, the client and the banquet manager can count the number of guests and solve the problem.

Buffets

When the client chooses the option of having a buffet, the banquet manager is responsible for having the buffet set up and ready for the guests at the scheduled time.

All buffets have a few basic principles. It goes without saying that all hot food must be served hot and all cold food must be served cold. Buffet lines are arranged so guests will not have to stand in a long line waiting for food. The buffet has to look neat and the food must be appetizing.

USE OF BUFFETS

Buffets are great for clients who want their guests to have a choice of meal items. Buffets are also great for serving a meal in a room that is located a distance from the kitchen. For instance, using a buffet at a

FIGURE 13-12

An attractive, tropical buffet. Photograph by Randall Perry.

pool is an ideal way to increase the use of the area around the pool, and in turn the revenue of an establishment.

Buffets are a lifesaver when the establishment has a limited amount of function rooms. As an example, a group would like to have an all-day meeting with lunch. The banquet house has only one room that will accommodate the guests. The solution is to have the meeting set up using tables. The client and banquet manager schedule a 30- to 45-minute break before lunch is served. By using a buffet, the establishment can serve the guests lunch. The service persons will not have to set up their utensils and food from the buffet. As with all banquet functions, this service option requires much organization by the banquet manager to make it a success.

FLOW AND LAYOUT OF THE BUFFET

If at all possible it is best to have separate islands for the different parts of the meal. There can be a separate table for beverages, one for appetizers and salads, one for main courses, and another for dessert.

One buffet line is needed to serve every one hundred guests. The establishment can use ice carvings to keep food cold and chafing dishes or heating units to keep food warm. Food can be displayed on mirrors, in ice carvings, or in edible bread items.

All condiments are to be placed in front of or next to the food they accompany. For example, next to the ham would be mustard. It is recommended that the condiments be placed in monkey dishes (small cuplike dishes), which should have underliners beneath them. The proper utensils to use for the condiments should be placed on the underliner.

THE SETUP OF THE BUFFET

Figures 13-13 and 13-14 illustrate the setup of a buffet. The first item at the beginning of the buffet line should be clean plates. The banquet manager instructs the service people to check not only the top of the plates but also the bottoms for cleanliness.

The buffet is usually arranged in the same manner as a meal would be served. Appetizers are placed first on the buffet line, followed by salads. Then the main course items, along with the starches and vegetables.

The rolls, butter, utensils, and beverages generally are the last items on the buffet line. Ideally, they should be on a separate table. By placing them at the end of the buffet line, it becomes easier for the guests to select the food and carry their plates without having to balance their utensils with their food. Of course, if the banquet establishment wants

BUFFET SETUP

Guests obtain their food								this direction
P	A	S	Main	S	V	R	S	B
L	P	A		T	E	O	I	E
A	P	L	Course	A	G	L	L	V
T	E	A		R	E	L	V	E
E	T	D	Items	C	T	S	E	R
S	I	S		H	A	&	R	A
	Z			E	B		W	G
	E			S	L	B	A	E
	R				E	U	R	S
	S				S	T	E	
						T		
						E		
						R		

FIGURE 13-13

The buffet is usually arranged in the same manner as a meal would be served. Appetizers are placed first on the buffet line, followed by salads, and then the main course items, along with the starches and vegetables.

the guests to take less of the main course items, they will position the rolls and butter, along with the utensils, immediately after the plates.

SERVICE STAFF JOBS AT A BUFFET

The amount of service assistance is limited by the service staff at a buffet. The service depends on the style of buffet that is chosen by the client. There are some jobs that have to be performed at a buffet that are not performed at a sit-down meal.

Service persons will be positioned behind the buffet line to assist the guests with their food. The service persons will portion out the food for the guests. They will also answer questions about the food, clean up any food spills, keep the buffet line moving, and replenish the food. Their job is to keep the buffet line looking neat and clean, and the food appetizing.

One of the problems the banquet manager wants to avoid is having the guests wait for food. Service persons are instructed to replenish food when there is between one-third and one-fourth remaining on the tray or in the pan. The banquet manager assigns an employee to act as a runner. It is the job of the runner to obtain food from the kitchen and bring it back to the buffet line when told to do so by the service person. More food is obtained from the kitchen in a clean tray or pan called an insert. The runner brings the new tray of food; the food is not transferred from one tray to another. The remaining food is brought back into the kitchen. There the tray is replenished and garnished to be used again.

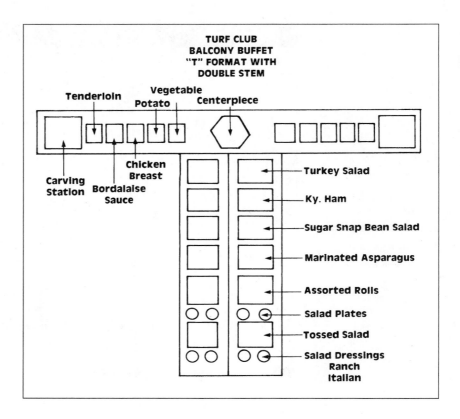

FIGURE 13-14

A planned buffet setup using a "T" format with a double stem. The chef has planned where each item on the buffet table will be placed.

Some establishments place signs near the food, which explain the item. This is recommended; however, it is more effective to have knowledgeable service staff explaining the food items. If the signs have only the name of the item, the guests may have to ask questions about the food.

CONTROLLING THE TRAFFIC FLOW

Another problem that has to be avoided is having all the guests rush up to the buffet table at once to obtain their food. The banquet manager has the responsibility of having the guests proceed to the buffet table in an organized fashion. This is how it is done.

When it is time to serve, the banquet manager announces that the guests may proceed to the buffet when their table is called. Informing the guests that they will be called to the buffet alleviates their fears about the establishment running out of food, even if they are the last table to be called. This system allows for a more controlled and civilized manner of serving a buffet.

T I P $

The first person who has the honor to see and choose the food at the buffet is the client. The banquet manager invites the host's table up to preview the buffet before anyone takes food. After the client's table guests take their food, the banquet manager invites other tables up to obtain their food from the buffet. To keep everyone calm, the banquet manager circulates among the guests telling them when it will be their turn. The next table is invited to proceed to the buffet when there are three or four people waiting in line to obtain their plates. This method eliminates many problems associated with buffets.

If during the preplanning for the event, the client informs you that the buffet must be served quickly, more buffet lines should be set up. Arranging buffet tables so guests may go on both sides of the table works extremely well.

CHAFING DISHES

Chafing dishes are used to keep food hot on a buffet. All employees need to know how they work and how to set them up.

The chafing dish consists of a frame, two pans, and a top, The top pan fits into the bottom pan, leaving two to three inches of space between the two pans. The bottom pan should be filled with about one inch of hot water.

Underneath the bottom pan, there are one or two containers that hold a can of jellied liquid that will burn for about an hour. This is referred to as canned heat. Sometimes, through careless handling and misuse, the container that holds the canned heat is lost. To solve the problem, an inverted bread and butter dish can be used as a substitute for the container. One problem to avoid is that of placing the canned heat too close to the bottom of the pan. When that occurs the flame from the canned heat will be smothered and it will go out, resulting in cold food. Also, avoid placing the canned heat directly on table surfaces. The can will get very hot and can harm the table.

Approximately ten minutes before the function starts, the service person should light the canned heat. The flame will heat up the water. When the water is heated, the top pan of food may be put into the chafing dish. Cover the food in the pan using the chafing dish top to keep the food hot. The chafing dish will act like a steam table. The heated water creates steam; the top pan does not let the steam out of the chafing dish, and the food stays hot. During the buffet, the service staff check to make sure that the canned heat does not go out. If it does, it is replaced with another can of heat. The service staff have to be careful to avoid being burned when taking off the covers or replacing a pan of food in the chafing dish.

TIP$

To Insure Proper Service

On a buffet line, keep all hot foods hot—above 165 degrees Fahrenheit. Keep all cold foods cold—below 45 degrees Fahrenheit.

Final Tip on Buffet Setups

The buffet should look as appetizing as possible. Many times even though the food is spectacular, the buffet looks boring. This is because the food is not displayed with any imagination.

Platters of food can be raised by using an inverted bread dish. Additionally, height may be created on the buffet table by using crates or boxes covered with linen. Flowers or food items are placed on these covered crates. Dishes with pedestals also add interest and height to a table.

Finally, stand back and look at the buffet. Then make adjustments to the items on the buffet table. These adjustments should be made based on the texture of the dishes, the color of the food, and the position of the items. The banquet manager may position an item away from its normal place to make the buffet more appealing.

KEEPING FOOD HOT

Besides using chafing dishes to keep food hot on a buffet, the banquet manager must know how to serve food hot at a sit-down meal. When the banquet manager has to serve a banquet in a room that is adjacent to the kitchen, a detailed plan (as you read about earlier in this chapter) has to be set up with the chef. In addition, all plates should be heated before the food is placed on them. Some establishments have special heating cabinets, others put the plates in the oven. If the food is placed on a cold plate, it will get cold.

When the banquet is served at a room distant from the kitchen, the food is generally transported in hot carts. Some are electrically heated while others use a form of canned heat to keep the food warm. Again, the key to keeping food hot is to preheat the cart. Once the food arrives at the location, a cook assists in taking the food out of the carts. This cook is responsible for the appearance and quality of the plates. Often, if the menu item requires a sauce, the cook puts it on at this area, which is called the staging area.

Timing is critical in making sure the food is available to be served to the guests when it is scheduled. If the party is to be served at noon, the banquet manager has to plan how long it will take to plate the food in the kitchen, transport it, and serve it, so the guests will obtain their meal at noon.

The Sequence of Service for a Sit-Down Meal

Using the Lockwood wedding as the guide, the sequence of service will be explained. The first three steps contain a reminder of proper service using American banquet service.

1. The appetizer course is served (from the guest's left side by the service persons left hand). It may be set as a part of the guest's place setting (as was the pineapple).
2. Two roll baskets are served. They are placed in the center of the table by the service person (using the left hand). The rolls should be put in a location that is easy for all the guests to reach. (A small tip: rolls and coffee are a lifesaver when the food is not ready to be served on time. Have the service person serve them to the guests and keep replenishing them. It gives the guests something to eat and drink, but more important it shows them that everything is under control. If the guests were not being served some item, they would be wondering when the food will arrive.)
3. The plate, spoon, and pineapple are removed by the service person (using the right hand, from the guest's right side).
4. The salad is served. At times, the salad can be preset on the table. It should be placed to the left of the salad fork.
5. The salad plate and fork are removed. The champagne glass should also be removed. If the guests have not finished their champagne or salad, instruct the service person to ask if they may be taken away. If

the answer is negative, the service person should move the salad out of the center of the place setting and put it to the left of the guest's setting. The service person should also check to see if water glasses and roll baskets need refilling. If they do, the service person should take the roll baskets back to the kitchen and bring them out with the next course. If he or she has time, the service person can refill the water glasses from water pitchers. Ashtrays should be changed, if needed. (Water pitchers, ashtrays, extra utensils, and napkins should be set up at strategically located service stations in advance of the banquet, so service staff do not have to waste time obtaining these items.)

6. The main course is served. Meat is positioned in front of the guests so the first cut made by the guest is into the tenderest part of the meal. (Remember: serve all the guests at one table, before serving another table. If the banquet establishment is using a station service setup and the service person cannot carry out ten dinners on the tray, have another service person carry out the remaining dinners so all the guests at the table are served at approximately the same time.)

7. Red wine should be poured by the bartenders. When the service person places a prime rib meal, the bartender should follow by pouring red wine to the guest.

8. The coffee course is served. The service person must use a coffee shield. Tea should be placed in an individual pot above the coffee cup. A wedge of lemon should be served with the tea. At times, the banquet manager can have the service staff put a whole pot of coffee on each table. The guests can pour the beverage themselves. This method is used especially for breakfast meals or when the client is on a limited time schedule.

9. The main course dishes are removed, along with utensils, red wine glasses, bread and butter plates, salt and pepper shakers, and rolls and butter. The only items left on the table are the utensils for dessert, cream, sugar, water glasses, and ashtrays.

10. Dessert is served, along with more coffee.

11. Dessert dishes, water glasses, utensils, and all items with which the guests have finished are removed. The banquet manager should also have an organized system for putting away items when they are returned to the kitchen. For example, the salt and pepper shakers should always be placed in the same location when they are cleared from the tables.

The banquet manager must be flexible when serving a meal. There are many parts to the meal. Some things may happen that the banquet manager has no control over. The ability to be flexible and to think quickly enough to use whatever items are necessary to keep the guests pleased is critical for the banquet manager. The above is simply a suggested serving sequence. Adjustments may have to be made in the sequence to satisfy the needs of the guests.

The Problem with Latecomers and Early-leavers

At many parties, guests will arrive after a few courses have been served. When this occurs, the banquet manager approaches the table and asks the guests if they would like to eat. If the answer is affirmative, the guests are served as quickly as possible whatever courses they desire. It may involve bringing out the pineapple course and salad course together.

You may also encounter guests who must leave in a hurry, before the meal will be served completely. Try to accommodate this type of guest also. This can be done by serving the guest the main course before or while other guests are eating their salad.

Both of these types of guests create a problem for the banquet manager. Using tact and diplomacy, the banquet manager can please the client and the guest by accommodating these individuals.

Banquet Checkbacks

To be a truly effective banquet manager, it is imperative to check the satisfaction of all the guest tables after the main course has been served to see if the meal and service were satisfactory.

An experienced banquet manger will know if the food has been satisfactory by observing the guest's plates. This is the ubiquitous quality needed by the banquet manager. The type of inquiry the banquet manager makes will be determined by the situation that is observed. For instance, if guests have not eaten their meal, inquire if they would like another choice (if it is possible). A fact to remember is the following: influencing one guest at a banquet has the potential to sell an additional banquet for many guests. It is easier to obtain business from people who have experienced your operation than to create a whole new market.

When the opportunity arises that the banquet manager can be introduced to the guests, take advantage of this situation. It will be beneficial for future business.

Throughout the event, the banquet manager should be constantly communicating with the client. The client has to be informed of what will happen next (such as the cake cutting ceremony). The banquet manager continues to inquire whether everything meets the client's satisfaction.

Keep in mind that musicians and photographers love to work at an establishment where the banquet manager informs them of the time and location of events at the function. If the banquet manager makes it easy for these individuals to do their job, it will benefit the establishment, because they will recommend the establishment to potential clients.

Managing the Meeting Room Business

Another type of business that the banquet manager may have concerns meeting rooms. Knowing the correct way to set up the rooms is important, but just as important is knowing how to manage the meeting room business.

Coffee breaks are often scheduled in the meeting rooms that the banquet establishment has to set up. As in other types of banquet management, the key to having repeat conference business is to make sure all items are in place and the room is correctly set up for the guests before they arrive.

Items such as water, glasses, pads, pencils, and ashtrays, if they are desired, should be on the tables. One water pitcher should be available for four guests. When the coffee break is scheduled for a specific time, make certain that the coffee and food arrive on time.

The timing is critical, but just as important is what happens while the guests are having their coffee break. During the break, the banquet manager should have a member of the staff in the meeting room, replenishing the water, cleaning ashtrays, and freshening up the room for the remainder of the meeting.

Again, organization is the key to successful meeting room business. All the equipment needed to freshen up the room should be set up outside the room in advance of the coffee break. At break time, the staff simply enter the room and replace, for example, the empty water pitchers with full ones.

Presenting the Bill to the Host and Rebooking the Party

The banquet manager's last job on the day of the function should be to present and explain the bill to the client. Payment should be obtained and the client should be thanked for holding the function at the establishment.

Finally, if the function is an annual event, ask the client if it may be rebooked for the following year. If the function was a wedding reception, ask the client to recommend your establishment to any future bride and groom.

And once again, thank the client for the opportunity to serve him or her! Of course, in a few days, you will send the client a hand-written thank you note.

Breakdown of the Function

When it is time for the party to end, inform the client. As the guests and client are leaving the banquet, assist the client with presents, the top of the wedding cake, or any other items with which he or she needs assistance.

Once the guests have departed, there is still work to be done. The banquet manager should have a system for cleaning up the dining room. The dirty dishes and equipment must be brought into the kitchen in an organized fashion. For instance, the staff should go into the dining room with big pots and glass racks. Glasses on the tables should have their contents dumped into the pots. The glasses can then be put into the racks, ready to be washed. Using a system like this eliminates confusion and breakage in the kitchen.

Finally, when the banquet room and kitchen are cleaned up to your satisfaction, the employees should be thanked and dismissed. And you, the banquet manager, should feel proud that you have just completed another great function!

Lawsuits and the Restaurant/ Banquet Manager

The food service industry has been sued increasingly by guests who claim they fell at the restaurant or received chipped teeth or caused their bridgework to fail. These are among the most common complaints that spark threats of legal action against food service establishments.

No case has received as much publicity as the one that resulted in a $2.9 million New Mexico jury verdict against McDonald's Corporation. This resulted from the spilling of a 49-cent cup of coffee onto an elderly woman. The jury ruled in favor of the woman, because they learned that McDonald's had settled more than 700 hot-beverage injury claims for more than half a million dollars over the previous ten years. Yet, the company had never considered lowering its standard coffee-holding temperature of 180 degrees, which is known to cause third-degree burns. Because coffee is not drinkable at 180 degrees, jury members said it constituted a defective product under state law.

Running a food service operation leaves a business open to some strange legal cases. Managers should be aware of the types of cases that have been filed and what advice experts have given on how to avoid these lawsuits.

Some cases include:

Sizzler International has been sued by the mother of an employee who cut himself with a knife in a California-based unit. The suit contended that the knife should have carried some type of warning.

The Rainbow Room in New York was hit with a lawsuit a couple of weeks after a honeymooning couple spent an evening dining and dancing. They left without mentioning any problems. However, they sued the restaurant for $1 million claiming the lingering cigarette and cigar smoke, "upset their right to conjugal happiness." The case never went to court.

A Muslim family in Houston sued On the Border Cafes for $600,000 after learning from a cook that the beef tacos they had eaten contained pork, a food strictly forbidden by Muslim dietary laws.

The Los Angeles City Attorney on behalf of only two complaining customers sued Gladstone's 4 Fish. The reason: Gladstone's ran out of $9.95-a-pound Maine lobsters in a promotion that fed 8,000 customers. The settlement: Gladstone's had to pay fines and fees totaling $30,000 and repeat the dinner offer for four weeks at the promotion price.

Foodmaker Inc. had to pay the families of children resulting from wrongful-death lawsuits from their $100 million liability. This was caused after four children on the West Coast died from eating bacteria-laden, undercooked Jack in the Box hamburgers. In addition, Foodmaker lost over $137 million in lost business from the resulting negative publicity.

Johnson & Wales University paid $434,000 to the family of former student James Brown, Jr., 27, of Williston, South Carolina. Brown died in 1992, after having an allergic reaction to shrimp that he had been served at a school dining hall.

Finally, the Americans with Disabilities Act passed in the 1990s provides that guests be served with reasonable accommodations.

A deaf woman from Santa Monica, California, sued Burger King after her hand-written drive-thru order was rejected by a worker. The settlement: Burger King agreed to revamp training policies, test visual electronic ordering devices, and offer order forms for speech- and hearing-impaired customers.

The manager is the person who can stop many of these lawsuits from getting beyond a complaint. Many, if not most, lawsuits can be prevented through management practices. Additional benefits are lower insurance rates, increased productivity, and enhanced loyalty from guests and employees.

Attorneys and food service professionals indicate that detailed hiring and firing guidelines are a must. Preemployment screening is needed to eliminate potentially violent or otherwise undesirable job candidates. Regularly updated and widely posted written policies against discrimination or harassment of any kind are also recommended. Managers must be aware of and adhere to prevailing wage and hour laws. The maintenance of safe work and public areas is required. Finally, ongoing worker education related to safely preparing and handling food is recommended.

Robert Spivk, president and chief executive of Grill Concepts Inc. in Los Angeles, advises just be humble. Give away lots of free meals and be sympathetic to appease disgruntled patrons and discourage lawsuits.

"Make sure that the guest knows that you care," said Spivk. His restaurants always send follow-up phone calls and letters to assure guests of management's concern for their problems. He always insists that his managers avoid arguing with lawsuit-minded guests. He estimates that the costs for the free food run "one-tenth of 1 percent" of the legal bills that could result from adversarial responses to patrons' gripes. Grill Concepts also increased its training of risk-reduction efforts such as safety education of employees.

All establishments should have a lawyer available to handle their legal problems. This part of the chapter only illustrates possibilities and should serve as a guideline for managers.[2-7]

A Final Tip

Throughout this book there have been a series of To Insure Proper Service tips for the reader. The last one has to do with the practice of tipping. The practice of tipping in use in a la carte restaurants will very likely exist in the twenty-first century. There are many reasons for this.

At the DeWitt Clinton Hotel, in Albany, New York, one could witness the end of the tipping at banquets. In 1968, the guests still tipped the waitstaff by passing the basket after a meal. Today, no banquet facility has "a pass the basket tip system." All banquets have a set fee added to the price of the meal. In some places, it is called a gratuity, but in New York state recent rulings have stated that a gratuity must go to the waitstaff serving the party. Therefore, banquet operators in New York state have changed the fee to a "service charge." This allows them to use the monies collected for any expense in the business. More and more banquet facilities are now paying their service staff a flat fee—$75.00 per function, $10.00 per hour, etc.—for working.

The a la carte tipping in restaurants will soon follow this type of payment. Service staff will no longer be compensated by tipping as we know it today: servers will be paid by the hour. Already some resorts (The Sagamore in New York, some Walt Disney World packages, The Grand Hotel at Mackinac Island, Michigan) have a service charge automatically added onto the guests' a la carte bills. Many restaurant menus state, "Parties of six or more will have a 15 percent service charge added to the final bill." The Perry Restaurant Group of Vermont has a tip pool policy that affects the front of the house staff. All tips are pooled. The tips are then distributed as wages based on a half tip or full tip criteria.

The final reason is the Internal Revenue Service. In 1995, the IRS started the Tip Reporting Alternative Commitment or TRAC. This program offers food service employers protection from IRS audits in exchange for their help in the tip tax education of employees and the collection of tip taxes.

Employees and employers in tipped industries have been required by law to pay FICA tip taxes on all tips since 1988. The IRS estimates that between $1.3 billion and $3 billion dollars in tip taxes go unpaid annually.

TRAC requires employers to take an active role in educating their employees about tip taxes as well as keeping track and reminding employees at least once a month of the charged tips they have accumulated. The idea is that employees will be well aware of their tax obligations under the law and will be forced to report a more accurate tip amount with a changed amount already on record.

In recognition of the wide variety of restaurants nationwide, the 11-page TRAC does not mandate what sort of educational and monitoring systems employers must create. Instead, employers have six months to establish systems suitable to their operations before the IRS evaluates them.[1]

Therefore, with all the pressure on the restaurant owner to keep track of the employees' tips, along with the changing attitudes toward service charges by guests, tipping as we know it will soon be replaced by the service charge.

SUMMARY

1. Based on information from the function sheet, the banquet manager must determine the amount of service staff, bar staff, and kitchen staff needed.

2. The three styles of service used in American banquet service are: the station method, the follow-up method, and the combination method.

3. Managers must be flexible enough to deal with such unexpected occurrences as equipment shortages, latecomers, and early-leavers.

REVIEW QUESTIONS

1. You have a doubleheader booked (two parties, one after another) in the same room. The first one is for 300, followed by a party for 150 guests. You only have an hour between the two parties. At the end of the first wedding reception, the father of the bride sees that everyone is having a good time. He tells the band to play an extra hour. What problems do you anticipate, and how could this situation have been avoided?

2. Using the banquet function sheet, complete the banquet checklist form by filling in how much equipment would be needed to serve the Lockwood wedding.

3. Using the banquet function sheet, state what utensils can be used over again and how you would accomplish it if you were a banquet manager.

4. Do you think that tip cups should be allowed at the Lockwood wedding? Should they be allowed at other events?

5. A group of eight guests were drinking and talking at the cocktail party and have just arrived in the room. All the other guests have been seated. There are enough seats to accommodate the eight guests; however, they must split their group up. Two people have to sit at one table, four at another, and two at a third table. They refuse, and want to sit together. What do you do to solve their problem?

6. The client has a party of four hundred, which must be served within fifteen minutes. Your room can physically hold only enough tables for two buffet lines. How would you solve this problem?

7. What is a chafing dish? How is it set up, and what is its purpose?

8. When should a buffet be used for a party? What are the advantages and disadvantages to a host in using a buffet?

9. What is the first and the last thing a banquet manager has to do on the day of a function? Why are both of these jobs important?

10. What is a duty roster? Why is it important and how does it help the banquet manger?

REFERENCES

1. *Nation's Restaurant News*, 4 May 1987, F4.
2. Robin Lee Allen, "IRS Unfurls New Tip-Tax Program," *Nation's Restaurant News* 29, no. 25 (19 June 1995): 1, 123.
3. "Food Court Litigation & Food Service," *Nation's Restaurant News* 28, no. 39 (9 October 1995): 101-150.
4. Alan Liddle, "Lawsuit Prevention: Strategies Focus on Safety, Education, Compliance with Laws and Regulations," *Nation's Restaurant News* 28, no. 39 (9 October 1995): 146-150.
5. Richard Martin, "Consumer Lawsuits: Wary Restauranteurs Seek Relief from Litigious Patrons' Reprisals," *Nation's Restaurant News*, 28 no. 39 (9 October 1995): 104, 108.
6. "Holding Down the Tort: Reform Bills Spell Relief for Operators," *Nation's Restaurant News* 29, no. 14 (a April 1995): 51.
7. "J&W to Pay $434K to Student's Family," *Nation's Restaurant News* 29, no. 25 (19 June 1995): 87.

Appendix

Eight Napkin Folds

THE TENT

1. Lay the napkin out flat in front of you.
2. Fold the napkin in half.
3. Fold the napkin in quarters.
4. Fold the napkin into a triangle.
5. Fold the napkin into a triangle again.
6. Place the open end of the triangle facing the guest's seat.

FIGURE A–1

The Tent Fan Fold.
An easy fold to learn.

THE CUFFED ROLL

1. Lay the napkin out flat in front of you.
2. Fold the napkin in half.
3. Fold the base of the napkin up approximately by 3 inches.
4. Turn the napkin over.
5. Going from left to right, make three even folds.
6. Place the silverware in the pocket.

FIGURE A–2

The Cuffed Roll. An ideal fold for buffet service.

THE CANDLE

1. Lay the napkin out flat in front of you in a diamond shape.
2. As if the napkin were a clock, fold the 6 o'clock point up to the 12 o'clock point to form a triangle.
3. Fold the base of the triangle up 2 inches so that it looks like a pirate's hat.
4. Turn the napkin over to hide the fold. The shape should still be a triangle.
5. Roll the napkin evenly from right to left, forming a candle.
6. Tuck the tail into the cuff formed by the fold.
7. Stand the candle in a wine glass at the place setting.

FIGURE A–3

The Candle. A great fold to give the impression of height.

THE LILLY

1. Lay the napkin out flat in front of you.
2. Fold the napkin in quarters.
3. Fold the napkin into a triangle, so that the solid base in front of you.
4. Make sure there are five ends at the top of the triangle.
5. Starting with the left base, accordion pleat the napkin from left to right.
6. Place in a wine glass at the place setting.
7. Separate out the five ends.

A–4 THE LILLY.

This fold can either be placed at the cover or in a wine glass.

THE CROWN

1. Lay the napkin out flat in front of you in a diamond shape.
2. Fold the napkin into a triangle, with the points at the top and the base facing you.
3. Take the 3 o'clock and 9 o'clock points and fold them up to the 12 o'clock point.
5. Crease the base of the napkin.
6. Still holding onto the 6 o'clock point, fold the point down to base.
7. Turn napkin over.
8. Place three or four fingers at the base of the napkin in the center of the napkin.
9. Wrap the right side around your fingers and tuck it under them.
10. Take the left side and fold it so that you can tuck the left side into the pocket made by the first fold.
11. Stand the napkin up and face it toward you.
12. Peel the two outside "wings" of the napkin down.

A–5 THE CROWN.

An excellent fold to use either at the cover or on a cover plate.

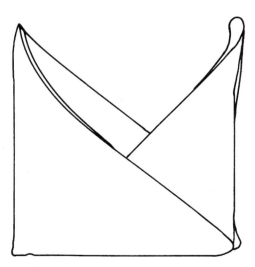

THE EASY CONE

1. Lay the napkin out flat in front of you in a diamond shape.
2. Fold the napkin into a triangle, with the points at the top and the base facing you.
3. Take the 3 o'clock and 9 o'clock points and fold them up the the 12 o'clock point.
4. Turn the napkin over.
5. Take the 6 o'clock point and fold it up one-quarter of the way toward the 12 o'clock point.
6. Turn the napkin over.
7. Place three fingers at the base of the napkin in the center of the napkin.
8. Wrap the right side around your fingers and tuck it under them.
9. Take the left side and fold it so that you can tuck the left side into the pocket made by the first fold.
10. Turn the napkin over and place it in the center of the place setting.

A–6

The Easy Cone. As its name implies, an easy fold for the service staff to accomplish.

THE COCK'S COMB

1. Lay the napkin out flat in front of you.
2. Fold the napkin in quarters.
3. Fold the napkin into a triangle so that the base is in front of you and the points of the napkin are at 12 o'clock.
4. Make sure that the five ends are in the 12 o'clock position.
5. Take the 3 o'clock and 9 o'clock points and fold them so that the sides of the triangle meet in a parallel line leaving a cone-shaped triangle.
6. Take the bottom of the cone (3 o'clock and 9 o'clock points) and fold under the base of the napkin to form a triangle.
7. Crease the napkin with your right hand while holding it in your left hand. The napkin is not lengthwise.
8. Place the napkin lengthwise and separate the top four ends.

A–7

The Cock's Comb. A fold that adds intrigue to the place setting.

THE FAN

1. Fold the napkin in half.
2. Arrange the napkin so that it is lengthwise in front of you.
3. Working up from the bottom, accordion pleat the napkin three-quarters of the way to the top.
4. Holding the pleated end in your right hand, fold the napkin in half so that the pleats are on the outside of the fold.
5. The pleated part is now at the right-hand side of the napkin.
6. Take the bottom of the unpleated part with your left hand and fold it into a triangle so that the triangle forms a base for the fan. Tuck the triangle into the pleats.
7. At this point, a rubber band can be placed on the napkin and the napkins can be used when needed. (This is an optional step.)
8. Stand the napkin up on the triangle base. The napkin will fan out.

A–8 THE FAN.

A favorite of many banquet houses, as fan-folded napkins can be done in advance.

Glossary

Aid: The member of the team (in the team system of service) who acts as a busperson, picks up dinners from the kitchen, and serves them to the guests.

a la carte restaurant: A business that serves guests individual meals on demand.

American banquet service: Service in which the guest's food is all placed on one plate. Often known as "on the plate, no wait."

American service: Service in which the food and beverage is served to the guest by either an individual service person or a team method. The food is plated in the kitchen. Also referred to as "plate" or "German" service.

back of the house: A term referring to employees who do not come into contact with the guest in their normal line of duty.

banquet: A meal with a menu that was preselected by the host for all of the guests attending the event.

banquet captain: The person responsible for service in a section of the banquet room.

banquet facility: A business that serves groups of guests the same meal, at the same time.

banquet manager: The individual responsible for planning, organizing, and running banquets.

beverage service: The type of alcoholic or nonalcoholic drinks requested by the host at a banquet function.

blocking: Reserving a certain table at a certain time for a guest.

buffet: A banquet meal at which guests obtain a portion of all of their food by serving themselves from buffet tables.

busperson: A restaurant employee who is responsible for assisting the service person.

butler style: A type of service used in cocktail parties, in which the staff circulate among the guests serving food (usually hors d'oeuvres) on trays.

call-ahead seating: Also called priority seating. A system used in restaurants that do not accept reservations, in which patrons can call ahead to be placed on a waitlist.

captain: A restaurant employee who is responsible for an area of the dining room.

cash bar: At a banquet, an arrangement by which guests are required to buy their own drinks, both alcoholic and nonalcoholic.

checkoff method: A method of blocking reservations used in a large restaurant.

chef de rang: An individual in French service who finishes off the food tableside.

commis de rang: An individual in French service who assists the chef de rang in the service of the meal.

competency: Serving food and drinks in the correct manner to the guest.

consumer orientation: The act of viewing your business from the perspective of your guests.

cover: The area or space for all utensils (including salt, pepper, and ashtrays) needed for each guest.

deluxe buffet: The most elegant kind of buffet service, in which guests obtain only their main course from a buffet, and are served everything else.

dependent needs: A part of Maslow's Hierarchy. They are needs that can only be met by someone else, not oneself. The first four needs of the hierarchy are dependent.

deuces: Tables that seat two guests.

diplomacy: The ability to act tactfully with the guest.

dupes: Stands for duplicate guest check. A copy of the original guest check turned into the kitchen or bar to obtain orders.

esteem needs: The fourth in Maslow's Hierarchy of needs. Esteem is the way in which people perceive the individual, which in turn affects the individual's ego.

flambé: Food served flaming in ignited liquor, usually prepared at the guest's table by the chef de rang in French service.

Follow-up: The member of the team (in the team system of service) who makes sure guests are satisfied, solves any problems, clears dishes, suggests and sells dessert, presents the check, and collects the money.

forecasting: Planning for anticipated business based upon previous history of the restaurant, reservations, and events that are planned for the community which will affect the business.

four-top: Also 4-top. A table that seats four.

French service: A style of service in which final preparation of food is done at the guest's table with flourish and fanfare.

friendliness: A way in which individuals make their guests feel important by talking to them, and by using Maslow's theory to make them feel comfortable in the restaurant.

front of the house: A term referring to employees who work in direct contact with guests.

function: Any use of banquet facilities.

function book: A constantly updated list of the rooms that the establishment has to rent on a daily basis, and the functions booked into those rooms.

function sheet: A form, prepared by the banquet office, which lists in detail everything that the host desires for the event.

guarantee: The minimum number of guests that the host will have to pay for at a banquet.

gueridon: A cart used in French service.

head banquet waiter: A person responsible for the success of the party in the room in which he or she is supervising.

health department: An agency that issues permits for operation of food service establishments and monitors the cleanliness of the establishments.

host: The person who greets guests in a dining room, seats them, and handles any problems that might arise during the course of their dinner.

"in the weeds":   A slang term used to describe an employee who has too many people to serve at once.

Lead: The member of the team (in the team system of service) who greets guests, takes dinner orders, sells and serves drink and wine, turns dinner orders into the kitchen and times the dinners, and sets the pace for the team.

logbook: A document kept at the establishment's host desk. Information included in the book concerns the number of meals served, the weather for the day, any special events, the money generated per hour, and the money per meal period. A section is reserved for messages between the day and night hosts.

love and belonging needs: The third in Maslow's Hierarchy of needs. This need deals with the fact that individuals must belong or be accepted by their peers.

Maslow's Hierarchy: A series of five needs that humans must satisfy. Before moving to a higher need, the lower need must be satisfied.

MBWA: Managing by wandering around.

modified deluxe buffet: A kind of buffet service in which tables are set and guests are served coffee and perhaps dessert at their tables, but obtain the rest of their food from a buffet.

no-shows: Guests who do not show up for their reservations.

occupancy rate: A figure used in a lodging establishment to anticipate the number of guests who will be staying in the establishment on a certain night.

open bar: At a banquet, an arrangement by which the host pays for all drinks consumed by the guests.

open seating: The practice of allowing guests to reserve tables for any time that the restaurant is open.

overbooking: The practice of taking more reservations than the restaurant can accommodate.

physiological need: The first in Maslow's Hierarchy of needs. Physiological needs deal with food, water, sex, and sleep.

place setting: All the utensils, linens, plates, and glasses needed by one guest to consume the meal, arranged in the proper sequence.

policy sheet: A sheet printed by banquet facilities that lists their specific policies on costs, deposits, guarantees, and contracts, among other things.

QSC: An acronym for the standards of business at McDonald's. Q stands for quality; S for service; and C for cleanliness.

rechaud: A small heating utensil used in French service.

reservation: A promise for a table in a restaurant.

reservation manager: A person whose sole job is to plan and organize reservations for the restaurant.

residence time: The time it takes a party of guests to eat its meal and pay its bill.

Russian banquet service: A style of service in which the service staff work as a team. All food is placed in silver trays in the kitchen, and the service staff work in teams of two.

Russian service: A style of service in which food is placed on silver trays in the kitchen and then transferred from the tray to the guest's plate by the service staff in the dining room.

sanitation: The process of keeping the restaurant clean of filth- and food-borne diseases.

seating: The tables in a restaurant used for one specific meal period.

self-actualization: The fifth of Maslow's Hierarchy of needs. Self-actualization comes from the individual, after the dependent needs have been met.

service: Competency and friendliness combined.

service person: The individual who has the responsibility of serving the guests their meals. Often this person is called a waiter or waitress.

shadowing: A method in which a new employee follows a trainer around and observes how to do the job.

sidework: Tasks other than waiting on guests which the service staff have to complete, such as filling salt and pepper shakers and folding napkins.

silver service: Another term for Russian service, so called because food is served on silver trays.

six-top: Also 6-top. A table that seats six.

station: An area of the dining room, which usually consists of from fourteen to eighteen seats.

sub rosa: A term from Roman times, meaning confidentiality.

table check: A form used to keep track of what point each table has reached in the course of its meal, enabling the host to know where and when he or she will be able to seat arriving guests.

table d'hôte: A complete meal served to all guests at a fixed price.

tact: The ability to say or do the correct thing so as not to offend the guest.

team system: A way of organizing a dining room for service, in which three people together serve a station of between forty and forty-five seats.

turning tables: Resetting the guest table for another party. The phrase is often used in conjunction with how many times a table is reset during the meal period. For example, "the tables were turned over three times" means that each table was used for three parties.

turnsheet: A form used to keep track of the number of guests that have been seated at a service person's station for a particular meal period.

ubiquitous: The ability to be everywhere at the same time.

underliner: A plate that goes beneath another plate to make it easier to serve food. For example, a saucer placed under a soup cup would be an underliner.

utensils: This refers to all forks, knives, and spoons used by the guests to eat their food.

waitlist: A form used by hosts that allows walk-ins to be seated in an organized manner.

walk-ins: These are guests who patronize the restaurant without making a reservation; in effect, they walk in the door expecting to obtain a table.

wine steward: The employee of the restaurant responsible for suggesting and selling wines to guests for their meals.

word of mouth: The most potent form of publicity; this occurs when people tell other people about their experiences (whether good or bad) with the business.

working the floor: Said of a host, it means circulating around the dining room talking to guests and assisting the service staff.

Bibliography

1. "David's settles no-show suit." *Nation's Restaurant News* (21 November 1994): 11.
2. Hayes, Jack. "The wait is over—or at least shorter—with call-ahead seating." *Nation's Restaurant News*, 11 March 1991, 25.
3. Knapp, Malcolm M., and Sue O. Knapp. "The Evolution of Union Square Care in New York City." *Nation's Restaurant News*, 24 September 1990, 88, 121.
4. Martin, Richard. "MUFSO Mandate: Move Forward!" *Nation's Restaurant News*, 21 October 1991, 7.
5. Migliore, Fran editor. *Walt Disney World Eyes & Ears* 24, no. 11 (16 March 1995): 3.
6. Nickolas, Nick. "Fine Dining Founded on Commitment to Service, Food." *Nation's Restaurant News*, 23 April 1990, 24.
7. "Red Lobster Debuts Call-Ahead Seating." *Restaurants & Institutions*, 22 August 1990, 112.

Index

place settings, 51, 70, 303
purpose of, 66
reasons for, 225–228
running, 310–312
selling, 229–230
serving order for, 85
service types, 241–242
setup, 302–304
staffing, 229
stewards, 300
styles of, 241
tablecloths, 61
types of, 225–228
typical menu, 67
why restaurants offer, 228–230
word origin, 66
Banquet event order. *See* function sheet
Banquet managers, 3, 5, 7, 15, 227, 230–231
    banquet room maintenance and, 36
    benefits, 238–239
    drawbacks to being, 239–240
    functions and, 245, 246, 253–254, 256, 266
    job knowledge needed, 240–241
    lawsuits and, 323–325
    physical condition of, 18
    qualifications of, 17–19, 232–238
    religious customs and, 226
    responsibilities of, 8–9, 25, 231, 232, 310
    table setting and, 49–50
    training by, 18, 73, 83
    ubiquitous, 16, 321
Banquet rooms
    appearance of, 36–37
    cleanliness of, 37
Banquet service
    guidelines, 84–95
    types of, 17, 67, 69–70
    utensils for, 67
Banquet stencil. *See* function sheet
Baptisms, 226
Bar manager, 308, 309
Bar mitzvahs, 226
Barnsider Restaurant, 104, 128
Bars
    cash, 17, 278, 279–280
    open, 17, 278, 279
Bat mitzvahs, 226
Bears, The, 219
Bechamel, 48
Bernstein, Benjamin, 28
Bernstein, Charles, 11–12
Bertucci's Inc., 134
Best of Gottlieb's Bottom Line, The (Gottlieb), 30

Beverage service, 17
    guidelines, 84, 88–91
    merchandising, 189–142
    tasting, 138
Bistro 100, 4, 101
Blackboards, 175
Blauberg, Erik, 7, 8
Blocking, 187–194
    charts, 187–188, 189, 190
    definition of, 187
    effectively, 192–194
    large restaurants and, 189
    problems with, 193
    small restaurants and, 193
Bodmer, R. J., 46
Body odor, 31, 86
Bommarito, Anthony, 295
Bonus fee, 109
Booking
    advance, 260
    computerized, 258
    firm, 260
    functions, 245, 256
    policies, 260
    rebooking, 322–323
    tentative, 260, 261
Braille, 215
Brenensthul, Gary, 212
Brinker International, Inc., 154
Brown, James Jr., 324
Brush-off, 200
Bubonia, Sam, 76
Buffet(s), 135, 274
    flow of, 314, 316–317
    layout, 314
    lines, 314
    look of, 318
    service staff jobs for, 315–316
    setup, 314–315, 318–319
    types of, 69, 241–242, 275
    use of, 313–314
Buffet service, 45, 47–48, 66, 69–70
    place settings, 70
    types of, 46, 69–70
Burger King, 324
Burrey, Jeff, 196
Busperson, 100, 101, 104, 113, 115, 117
    duties of, 102–103
Butler
    professional, 46
    service, 274
    style, 309